Build Your Own Server

Build Your Own Server

Tony C. Caputo

McGraw-Hill/Osborne

New York   Chicago   San Francisco   Lisbon   London   Madrid   Mexico City
Milan   New Delhi   San Juan   Seoul   Singapore   Sydney   Toronto

The McGraw·Hill Companies

McGraw-Hill/Osborne
2600 Tenth Street
Berkeley, California 94710
U.S.A.

To arrange bulk purchase discounts for sales promotions, premiums, or fund-raisers, please contact **McGraw-Hill**/Osborne at the above address. For information on translations or book distributors outside the U.S.A., please see the International Contact Information page immediately following the index of this book.

Build Your Own Server

1234567890 QPD QPD 019876543

ISBN 0-07222728-1

Publisher	**Proofreader**
Brandon A. Nordin	*Linda Medoff*
Vice President & Associate Publisher	**Indexer**
Scott Rogers	*Claire Splan*
Acquisitions Editor	**Computer Designers**
Franny Kelly	*George Toma Charbak, Tara Davis*
Project Editor	**Illustrators**
Jennifer Malnick	*Melinda Lytle, Michael Mueller, Lyssa Wald*
Technical Editor	**Series Design**
Rob Shimonski	*Jean Butterfield*
Copy Editor	**Cover Series Design**
Bill McManus	*Ted Holladay*

This book was composed with Corel VENTURA™ Publisher.

I dedicate this book to my wife,
Lisa, and my children,
Zachary, Gabriella, and Paul.
May your lives be as blessed
as you have blessed mine.
—Tony

About the Technical Editor

Robert J. Shimonski (TruSecure TICSA, Cisco CCDP, CCNP, Nortel NNCSS, Microsoft MCSE, MCP+I, Novell Master CNE, CIP, CIBS, IWA CWP, DCSE, Prosoft MCIW, SANS GSEC, GCIH, CompTIA HTI+, Security+, Server+, Network+, Inet+, A+, e-Biz+, Symantec SPS and NAI Sniffer SCP) is a lead network and security engineer for a leading manufacturing company. Robert's specialties include network infrastructure design, management and troubleshooting, and network security design and management on a wide range of vendor products including Cisco, Nortel, Microsoft, Novell, Citrix, Checkpoint, and many others. Robert is the author of many network- and security-related magazine articles and has published books, certification testing software, and certification study guides ranging all topics from application development and web design to security, server management, and network troubleshooting. You can contact Robert at rshimonski@rsnetworks.net.

About the Author

Tony C. Caputo is a Microsoft Certified Professional (MCP) and certified for e-Business with both IBM and the University of Chicago. He's a business system analyst and strategist with over 20 years of experience in multimedia, and over eight years of experience using technology to improve how companies do business. Tony has consulted for Walt Disney Company, American Licorice Company, City Video Productions, BMG Interactive, Warner Bros, GFI Genfare, Wako, USA (to name a few), and is currently a senior manager and consultant for Intellisys Technology, LLC (www.intellisystechnology.com), an international Information Technology consulting firm with offices in the U.S., Australia, Singapore, and India. He's planning to become a Microsoft Certified Engineer (MSCE) in 2003.

Tony is an author of books on a wide range of topics including the bestseller *Visual Storytelling, The Art & Technique* (www.visualstorytelling.com), and has written regular articles for TechRepublic.com, ChicagoTribune.com, ePrairie.com, StickyMinds.com, and Windows2000 Advantage.com.

You can reach him at tcaputo@intellisystechnology.com and at www.tonycaputo.com.

Contents at a Glance

Part III   Network Operating System Installation, Configuration, and Troubleshooting

Contents

Part III
Network Operating System Installation, Configuration, and Troubleshooting

Acknowledgments

I'd like to thank the great people at McGraw-Hill/Osborne: Francis Kelly, Jennifer Malnick, Bill McManus, and Rob Shimonski for helping me create this book. There's a special thanks to Liz Clinkenbeard at Lewis Public Relations and Bettina Faltermeier at McGraw-Hill public relations for doing what they do best.

I'd also like to thank Intellisys Technology, LLC, for creating a pleasant working environment, helping me get some components; and Ramesh and Sabeena for keeping me on my toes.

There's more *Build Your Own Server* online at www.buildyourownserver.com.

Introduction

The idea of building my own servers came to me initially out of economic necessity: I needed a server that gave me expandability, connectivity to both wired and wireless networks, a Zip drive and CD-RW, printer and fax, and plenty of hard drive space to hold data in various forms. It got to the point that one regular desktop PC couldn't handle everything I wanted without crashing or causing conflicts. I pushed it to its limit and it pushed back.

My next strategy was to split the load between my laptop and two desktops, but every time I needed, say, my scanner, I would have to boot that one computer for that single reason, and workstations seemed extreme. My writing files and folders went from about 20MB for an article with some images to 5–10GB per book. I needed more space, not only for the initial workups and final files, but also for a backup. Hundreds of files measuring 10GB were far too much work to lose; and if I did, it would be nothing less than a catastrophe.

Meanwhile, my consulting needs also exploded—with 20GB video capture files, audio files, thousands of high-resolution images, and those multimedia workups, experiments, and rejects. Even if I were open to purchasing a server, the cost of a machine that would meet my requirements would raise more than an eyebrow in accounting. I had to figure out something, and it came to me while I was hunting for an upgrade for my son's PC game machine and a few workstations for Intellisys Technology (my day job). I discovered that computer components were inexpensive, giving me more spending dollars for an operating system like Windows 2000 Server or Windows Server 2003, or my copy of Red Hat Linux, which I downloaded for free. Suddenly, buying a server seemed possible; I just had to build it. The most immediate need was a fileserver for backups and file sharing, which could also double as a web server for a local Intranet.

Thus, the server has become the catalyst for the preferred method of communications in the twenty-first century. Thanks, in part, to the Internet, with asynchronous communication (e-mail, chat, message boards, voice mail, and text messaging), you need not even be present to build a relationship (either personal or professional). We no longer need to be synchronized, yet still are able to build a connection between one another, without ever being physically in real-time. However, something needs to be there to "take the call."

That something is a server. I will teach you how to build one.

Who Can Benefit From This Book

There are a number of uses for a server, but the most advantageous is for that of a small-to-midsize growing business. As the administrator, building your own server gives you the flexibility to grow with your business. The components you'd use are mostly the same that you'd find in a $2,500 server but with the flexibility to upgrade far more easily and economically.

What You'll Learn From This Book

Build Your Own Server is divided into three sections, covering everything from picking the components and where you can find them to setting up a secured web server using Windows 2000 Server or Windows Server 2003. It covers the details of building your machine from scratch—with tips, hints, and troubleshooting steps.

Part I: Preparing to Build Your Own Server

Part I details the major components you need and a wide variety of places you can buy those components, new or used. Some are hard-to-find places I've uncovered in my own hunting adventures, and I'm sure you'll be amazed at some of the great deals that are out there for building your server, or even upgrading an existing system!

The part is wrapped up with a brief introduction to the network operating system, which can turn a computer serving the one into a machine that serves the many.

Part II: Step-By-Step Building Instructions

Here I detail the systematic blueprint for your server, with suggestions and detailed instructions on putting together each component. I begin with the heart of the machine, the motherboard and CPU. From there, I move into memory and video adapters, with some basic concepts and architecture so that you may optimize your system accordingly.

I then provide an evaluation of drives, from the floppy diskette drive to the hard drive and the DVD-ROM drive. I hope that my insight will explain how each one serves a purpose, and will help you with whatever configuration you choose.

In Chapter 7, I detail some of the more overlooked safeguards and suggested requirements for building a better server. Part II wraps up with the installation of the network adapters and an overview of the power of the network.

Part III: The Network Operating System

If you were to chisel down the one core element that makes a server a server, it would have to be its brain: the network operating system, or NOS. This component provides all the necessary applications for serving the many rather than the one, as with a workstation. There are various flavors of network operating systems, including Linux, UNIX, Novell, and Windows 2000 Server, as well as the newer Windows Server 2003. Although my instructions detail the configuration of a Windows 2000 Server and/or Windows Server 2003, this doesn't necessarily need to be your choice. There is valuable information within these pages of instruction that can benefit anyone using any NOS.

How to Read This Book

This book can be read cover to cover for those looking to start from scratch and build a server with expandability, reliability, and performance. You can also skim through it, digesting small tidbits that will no doubt save you time and money with any system you're maintaining, upgrading, or researching to buy.

Build Your Own Server will open your eyes to the power of the network and how you can unleash that power at a nominal cost.

Part I

Preparing to Build Your Own Server

Chapter 1

The Anatomy of a Server

This book offers you step-by-step instructions on how to take advantage of a server-based environment while still keeping your costs low. I'll show you the what, why, and how of building a network server designed for a small to midsize company, and how to extend your data for better decisions, security, and profits. We'll hunt for compatible components, and find those exceptional bargains and deals. I'll show you how to assemble those parts as if you were putting together a bicycle. Once we have our computer up and running, we'll turn it into a server. The transformation from a simple computer to a server requires add-on components and installation of a network operating system (NOS), giving you the power to share your printer, files, and the Internet; protect your data as a firewall; create remote connectivity to access your workstation at the office from home; and even turn it into an access point for secure wireless networking.

The following are highlights of what you'll find within the pages of this book:

❏ Instructions on how to install and configure Windows 2000 Server or Server 2003

❏ Instructions on how to set up a workgroup, domain (Active Directory), and using Windows 2000 Server or Server 2003

❏ Instructions on how to install and configure the remote administration capabilities of Terminal Server

❏ Tips on hardware component–level troubleshooting

❏ Real-world Windows 2000 or Server 2003 frequently asked questions (FAQ) and troubleshooting

What's a Server?

The *server* is the nucleus of the internetworking computer system. Smaller companies may have one or two servers, while Fortune 500 companies may use hundreds of servers to handle the ever-growing digital workload. These machines are used to handle a plethora of applications and systems that are designed to make business run better, faster, and cheaper. Servers handle the same functions for the Internet as a whole, which is made up of thousands of servers, and even for multiplayer networks, where PC gamers from all over the world congregate to simulate a virtual reality on their desktop.

A server is a hub in a wheel, connecting the spokes to a tire that makes it turn. A server is a heart of knowledge, bringing cohesiveness to the chaos of independent thinking. It's the one place that's always open and ready to serve you.

Although many people call the actual computer hardware the "server," it's the software (including NOS) on that computer that "serves" the others in the network. The term "server" originates from its position in the client/server architecture, in which a server is the program (or bundle of programs) that stands idle until called upon to fulfill requests from client machines, or *nodes*. Various types of servers exist, including database servers, file servers, web servers, and application servers, just to name a few. In a multilayered architecture, demanding applications, such as database, authentication, and firewall applications, may be distributed onto separate server machines for purposes of load balancing and added security.

The *client*, a typical workstation, runs any operating system desired, but can still access specific data and resources from the centralized server. A client can be defined as anybody using a computer to log into somewhere for something. Whether it's to access the Internet, to access a corporate database, or to grab your e-mail off the AOL mail server; the server serves the client's request.

Why Do You Need a Server?

A server may be needed for many reasons, and most larger organizations already recognize those benefits within an enterprise-size environment. However, I believe a server is especially important (and I'll provide some examples) for small to midsize companies. Microsoft's Windows 2000 Server or Server 2003 is an affordable server OS that comes with a suite of solutions. You can also use one of the many flavors of Linux, which is free, or the network-centric Novell solution. Any one of these solutions offers smaller companies the same cost efficiencies and improved processes that large-scale enterprises enjoy.

I'll show you how to build your own customized machine for about $400, enabling you to save thousands of dollars and stay up and running at 99.999 percent uptime. This can be done by focusing on your specific business needs and building a box around that, without the inflated cost of a pre-built, preinstalled server.

You can provide your customers with information 24 hours a day, 7 days a week (24/7), by setting up a web server for an intranet (a closed, corporate web site portal), effectively giving individuals secured access to unique data from their own web browser. Windows 2000 Server also has extended built-in functionalities, including the Dynamic Host Configuration Protocol (DHCP), a service that automatically provides a requesting workstation a new IP address, relieving the local administrator from having to manually configure a remote user's laptop or PC. This is one of the functionalities you can provide your business with the use of a server.

The following are some of the other functionalities you can provide with a server:

❑ Create a Value Added Network VAN, a secure tunnel through the Internet, between your server and your customer's server.

❑ Implement Terminal Services to gain administrative access from a remote location.

❑ Assign and maintain disk quotas easily.

❑ Restrict access to unwanted online content by blocking specific IP addresses.

❑ Set up automated nightly backups.

❑ Print a document at the office from home via Internet printing.

One of the greatest benefits of a server is that you can share resources within any office environment (commercial building or at home). If you're sharing a color inkjet printer, CD writer, DVD-ROM, Zip drive, or even hard drive space with "Bob's" computer in Accounting (because they get all the good stuff), you're limited to Bob's schedule. By moving all those goodies to a server, they always are open and ready to "serve" from anywhere.

How Can You Afford a Server?

The prices for computer-related components have plummeted and continue to drop. I've picked up new memory for $8.00 and refurbished 4.5GB hard drives for $5.00. It's all about being at the right place at the right time, and recognizing the right components to use from your computer graveyard.

Using New vs. Used Parts

Chances are you have some older computers collecting dust in storage somewhere, so you may have a few parts you can use for your server. However, only a handful of used components have limited enough risk that I would dare to use them in a mission-critical machine. Failure of those few components would have little impact on your uptime, and would require minimal maintenance, if required. Components such as floppy or CD-ROM drives, a system fan, and the computer chassis have limited risk. If your floppy drive fails, you'll discover it either when you use it next or when you reboot, in which case you'll get a "floppy failure" message. Other components are more critical and must have a dependable history.

A *known good* (and compatible) power supply, CPU, and memory have capabilities for reuse. Used components such as memory, motherboards, and expansion cards are too delicate and sensitive, with many potential compatibility problems, to depend on 100 percent, unless you're planning on using a reliable combination of motherboard/CPU/memory from another system. Overall, it's important to be confident that those used parts have a *known good history* and are not throwaways. I do not recommend, under any circumstances, building the center of your entire business system on a mishmash of old parts you salvaged out of junk.

If you don't have any reliable components to scavenge, you can still build your own server for about $400, plus the license for the operating system. The overall cost of building the machine will drop if you have any of those known good components from older computers, but, depending on their age, there could also be serious compatibility issues. If you've chosen to use Microsoft's Windows 2000/.NET Server as your OS, then you can check the Microsoft Hardware Compatibility List (HCL) at www.microsoft.com, or you can download the latest list from ftp://ftp.microsoft.com/services/whql/hcl/win2000hcl.txt.

A Case for Small Business

Through the use of the built-in permissions of Windows 2000 Server (more on this in Chapter 12) and the features and functionality of its built-in web server (IIS 5.0), I was able to create a self-supporting system that created an attractive return-on-investment (ROI) for a small Japanese-based manufacturing company. The integrated Terminal Services and VPN capabilities introduced secured access from the company's Asian and European satellite offices, opening access to information and applications previously unavailable. Windows 2000 created unification of all corporate locations that the company never had before. It also made it easier for the company's customers to do business with it because, prior to Windows 2000 Server, its legacy web site application didn't offer a cost-effective way for its customers to look up forgotten passwords. Instead, there were many daily phone requests for inventory information.

Within a week of notifying its customers about its new intranet, which now listed real-time inventory data, the company's phone requests dropped by about 50 percent, increasing employee productivity substantially (daily shipments increased by 20 percent). This estimate was derived from a comparison of the average number of direct calls per day the one month prior to the deployment of the Windows 2000 Server system, and the one month after the e-mail and fax notification went out informing customer of the new service.

Although the company had warehouses in the United States and Europe, it was difficult to determine how much business was lost due to unsuccessful inventory inquiries after business hours (it was now available 24/7), but we all agreed on a conservative estimated ROI of 220 percent over the course of the following year (this estimate included assumptions provided by its accounting firm and the sales history of the organization and one of its competitors).

You never hear about the little guy's success with Windows 2000 Server, but there are many more of these successes than the high-profile case studies you read about in the industry magazines. My point is how can you not afford it.

See Figure 1-1 for an example of a server.

Figure I-I
A cutaway illustration of our server

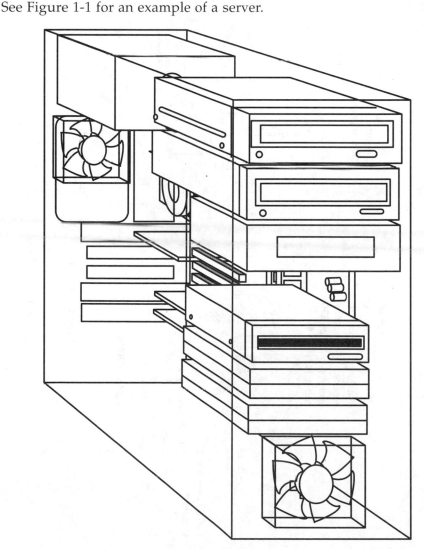

The server is made up of the same type of components as a computer, with the exception of server-centricities. The close-up is shown in Figure 1-2.

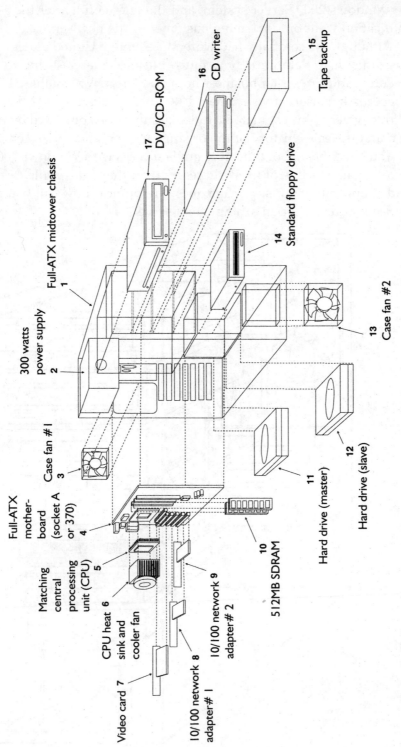

Figure 1-2
An exploded view of the server shown in Figure 1-1

Piece-by-Piece Close-up of the Server

It's the new operating systems, business software updates, and interactive games, with their heightened sophistication and requirements, that drive a computer's slow and miserable death. The workstations that are exclusively for word processing or basic accounting functions are still productive machines—but if you try to push their limitations and ignore minimum system requirements, the experience can be very frustrating, to say the least. Those invisible incompatibilities can become quite the nightmare (more on this in Chapter 2). They can force you to spend excessive time troubleshooting rather than doing something more productive. That's when it may be time to buy a new computer, but the rate at which technology and power-hungry software continue to advance means buying a new computer every 18 to 36 months. Even if that's economically possible for you, there's no guarantee of compatibility with your current software applications. This is what drove me to a solution that I'll share with you—how to build a modular, super server for under $400 (with monitor), which includes all the most compatible and upgradeable components. I've found this to be a more cost-effective alternative to spending a fortune on the latest name-brand system with a lifespan of about two years. Together, we'll build a machine that will give you the flexibility to keep up with technology, and, most important, your business.

Future Proof

Technological innovations continue to drive the future of computing. However, computer-related technology, including processors, memory, and software, appears to become obsolete faster than the latest television sitcom. Someone, somewhere is working on building a better mouse-trap and not giving us enough time to get used to the one at hand. Usually, new software drives this obsolescence—new software engineered to handle designated tasks faster and easier. Very little in computer technology is "future-proof." Fiber optics, with its seemingly unlimited supply of bandwidth, is "future-proof," but it is hard to imagine what that really means in an industry moving to cut all wires and move into increasingly wireless solutions. It was Bill Gates, the co-founder of Microsoft, who once said 640K would be all the memory we would ever need in a desktop computer.

Building a server requires assembling a variety of components, similar to building a bicycle. Many of the server components may be foreign to you, and you may feel bewildered at the prospect of assembling all of them to build a working server, but I'll break down the process into smaller, interconnected modules, with graphics and step-by-step instructions you can easily follow.

Keep in mind that my goal is not to train you for certification, but rather to show you how and why these components work, and how to put them together. When you purchase a bicycle, you're not interested in how it works; only that it works after you put it together. I'll give you tips on where to find some great prices on those components and make the idea of building a computer that nobody "uses" but everybody uses more attractive to management, who may only understand using a computer as a workstation, making employees more productive. What you're building is not a workstation, and nobody should be using a server as a workstation; it's just a server, a box that sits there and lets the software do its thing, without human intervention.

Locking the Server for Better Performance

Making a server accessible as a workstation for someone to come by and print a large document, because it's directly connected to the best printer and their own system is down, will greatly degrade its performance for the multitude of other people trying to use it. This machine will run various server software applications that support many workstations, so the server should be locked away to "serve" the many and not the one.

For me, this hunt to build my own servers began at a supercomputer show and continued throughout the world (actually, the World Wide Web), in search of those exceptional new and used components. It was a matter of economics. It may be difficult to justify spending a few thousand dollars on a machine that literally just sits there. (Most entrepreneurs outside the field of information technology may not understand that "just sits there" doesn't mean it isn't being productive.) Most larger cities host a computer show at least once a month; and if you're looking for a specific component, chances are that you can find it at such a show (see Chapter 2). These shows have become a haven for administrators, serious PC gamers, and hobbyists.

Table 1-1 lists the basic components that will make up our server. I'll provide details regarding some of the places I've found these parts and more, with specific hints, tips, and deals that I've discovered that can keep you within the $400 budget. To reiterate, this is a server, not a workstation. I do not recommend having a server double as a workstation, for the following reasons:

❏ You don't want anyone at the console of a server, and you want to access it remotely, because it contains sensitive data and should be under lock and key (more on this in Chapter 12).

❑ Using a server as a workstation will degrade its performance substantially by eating up resources the server needs to fulfill its obligations.

❑ If you use a server as a workstation, you run the risk of infection from viruses, since most workstations have Internet and e-mail clients that can download harmful viruses and Trojan horses that can take down the server and the entire network.

Component	Cost
ATX tower case with 300 watts power (new)	$26.00
Tyan Trinity KT	$20.00
AMD Duron 900 MHz (200 MHz FSB)	$35.00
Cooler fan and heat sink (new)	$7.00
Voodoo 3 3000 2x AGP 16MB	$10.00
30GB hard drive (generic)	$40.00
Backup 30GB hard drive (generic)	$40.00
Seagate TapeStor internal backup tape drive (used)	$45.00
TapeStor tape cartridge (new)	$30.00
Belkin 10/100 network adapter (new—with full rebate)	$0.00
GigaFast 10/100 network adapter (new)	$5.00
3.5-inch floppy drive (used—includes cable)	$5.00
52x CD-ROM drive (used—includes cable)	$15.00
Polaroid CD writer 24x 10x 40x	$30.00
NEC 15-inch SVGA monitor (used)	$25.00
512MB RAM	$70.00
Miscellaneous cables and accessories	$15.00
Total	$418.00

Table 1-1
Cost of Server Components for My Server (Cost of Your Parts May Vary)

The costs listed in Table 1-1 are actually costs for parts purchased through various outlets, as described in Chapter 2. They may also include shipping and applicable taxes.

One way of keeping people away from the server console is to turn off the monitor and disconnect it from the server after installation, thus leaving it unusable. There is a monitor listed in Table 1-1; it should be temporary as you will access the server's desktop through remote administration in Windows 2003 or Server 2003 Terminal Services (more on this in Chapter 11). You should just borrow a monitor for the installation and configuration process.

The Chassis

The standardized form factor for a computer case is ATX as opposed to the older AT style, which stands for "Advanced Technology." The ATX case is simply an "extend- able" AT case, turning the motherboard 90 degrees to make room for more expansion slots. I recommend an ATX midtower for our chassis, with at least a 300-watt power supply. This gives you six drive bays, room enough for two CD-ROM/DVDs, a tape-backup drive, a floppy drive, six expansion cards, and up to three hard drives. I found this computer case on sale at a local computer show for $26 (see Figure 1-3), and another at a local wholesale outlet for $22 (see Figure 1-4). This included a 300-watt power supply, which is the minimal we'll need for our server. The tower case is a taller, vertical unit, as opposed to the traditional desktop. This tower case gives you more room to work and ample capabilities for expansion. Power supplies usually range from 150 watts for the smaller, micro-ATX cases, up to over 500 watts for multiprocessing servers. I picked up a full server tower (see Figure 1-5) from eBay for about $45, including shipping. It's a monster case with eight drive bays, which I don't think I could fill in my lifetime. Hard drives are over 200GB now, so bigger doesn't mean better, just heavier.

Figure I-3
This $26 ATX midtower includes six bays, enough room for a CD-ROM drive, CD writer, tape backup, floppy drive, and three hard drives.

Figure 1-4
Here's another option (at $22), with more room for hard drives

Figure 1-5
A full server tower with eight bays

The Motherboard

The motherboard (also referred to as a main board or system board) contains the computer's core circuitry and components. On the typical motherboard, identification and configuration information is silk-screened on the planar surface. The embedded circuitry is on a chip or permanently soldered onto a board. The most common motherboard design for computers is the ATX, based on the original IBM AT motherboard. The components you'd find on both designs include the following:

❏ A CPU or microprocessor

❏ Memory

❏ Basic input/output system (BIOS)

❏ Expansion slots

❏ Interconnecting circuitry

❏ Jumpers

❏ CMOS (BIOS) battery

Figure 1-6 shows the full-ATX motherboard on the left and the micro-ATX motherboard on the right. The smaller size of the micro-ATX means less expansion slots and limited expandability. These two boards may appear to have the same processor slot (upper left with the extension brackets), but they are different. The motherboard on the left is the AMD "Slot A" and the motherboard on the right is the Intel "Slot 1."

Figure 1-6
A full-ATX
motherboard (left)
and a micro-ATX
motherboard (right)

Figure 1-7 displays three flavors of the ATX motherboard, which can include onboard video and audio (top); or with onboard audio, but video dedicated to an expansion card (middle); or little onboard functionality, leaving the other necessary components for the expansion slots (bottom).

Figure 1-7
Three types of ATX motherboards

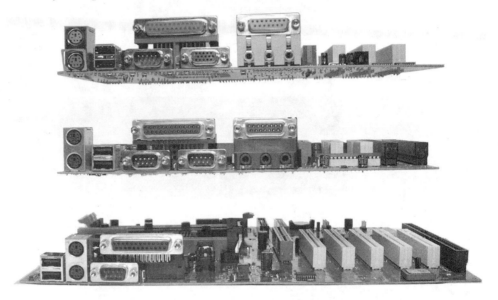

The CPU

All systems need a CPU to operate them. With CPUs, the general rule is the faster the better, but typically an increase in speed corresponds to an increase in price. AMD and VIA are the only commercial competitors to Intel. The Intel Pentium and Celeron CPUs hold their value, even when used for at least two years after their first release. The Pentium Xeon is Intel's flagship server processor. It offers better performance on enterprise-size servers, but at the cost of hundreds of dollars. The AMD family of CPUs includes the Athlon and Duron. The Duron is considered a direct competitor to the more economical Intel Celeron chip. However, even with the same processor speed, the Duron's front-side bus (FSB) is twice as fast as the Celeron's FSB (200 MHz vs. 100 MHz), making it an infinitely better bargain because the Celeron is usually more expensive (even used). The FSB is a more direct link to the system's memory, and thus a higher FSB increases the system's performance (discussed further in Chapter 4).

At first glance, the two CPU sockets on these two motherboards may appear to be the same.

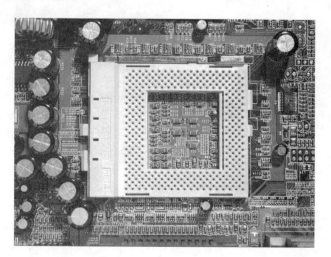

However, a *side-by-side* analysis reveals that they are two different species of form factors; the left is the AMD Socket A, and the right is Socket 370, typically used for Intel Processors. The VIA C3 chips also use the Socket 370 form factor.

There are specific motherboards for matching CPUs. Depending on its age, an AMD Athlon or Intel Pentium sold on eBay doesn't necessarily mean that they'll fit your motherboard (see Figure 1-8). Here's a short list of the most popular CPUs and their dedicated sockets:

❏ The newer Pentium 4 chips use either Socket 423 or Socket 478, while Pentium III chips (which also came in two flavors) originally used

Slot 1, and then moved to the more compact Socket 370. That's also true for the Intel Celeron.

❏ The newer AMD Athlon and Duron processors, from about 800 MHz and up, use Socket A. However, there is some overlap with the older Slot A (see Figure 1-9). You can purchase an AMD Athlon 800MHz processor in both Socket A and Slot A. These are two very different forms.

❏ The form factor for the VIA Cyrix C3 processor (600 MHz to 1 GHz) is also Socket 370, and is usually compatible with any motherboard that accepts an Intel Celeron.

❏ The only processors capable of working on a dual-processor motherboard are the Pentium III, Pentium 4, and Athlon MP. The socket may match other processors, and you may be able to use, for example, a Celeron on a dual Pentium motherboard, but only one. There are a few Socket 370 Celeron motherboards, but they're not the best choice for dual processing because of limited FSB speed.

Pentium 4 and AMD Athlon XP chips may cost over $100 alone, so consider your needs: Is this a file server with minimal workload, or do you plan to install the corporate materials management application on it, too? Do you need that much speed? The cost of dual processing is easily justified when working with applications that require high processing, such as those that perform 3-D graphics rendering, videoconferencing, or DVD encoding, or when working with databases that are queried hundreds of thousands of times a second. That coupled with a high-speed Small Computer System Interface (SCSI, pronounced "scuzzy") drive will take almost anything you throw at it—but do you need it?

A dual-processor motherboard and a few high-speed CPUs will run you in the hundreds of dollars alone (Figure 1-9). True, I'm all for more power and speed, but the accountant usually doesn't see it that way. Let's follow specifications based on Table 1-1 for our hunting excursion. I'll also consider speed and power and let you know when and where a dual-processor motherboard or a SCSI hard drive may benefit you.

Figure I-8
The AMD Athlon Processor: "Socket A" on the left and as the older "Slot A" on the right

Figure 1-9
Dual-processor
motherboard

Simply put, dual-processing capability requires a machine that uses twin processors. One could be dedicated to, say, maintaining the power to stream a training video throughout the corporate intranet, while the other could continue with maintaining the other necessary functions of the server (such as security, web sites, and so forth). In a development environment, dual processors are used in video editing and 3-D rendering workstations. Of course, if you're doubling the number of processors, you're also doubling the cost, and the motherboards can be very expensive. These are large workhorses specifically designed for demanding systems, and can be a potential solution for future expansion, but at this time could single-handedly exhaust your $400 budget.

Heat Sink and Cooler Fan

Any CPU you buy should include a heat sink and cooler fan, whether it comes with your CPU or you purchase it separately. Typically, although the heat sink and fan are two different components, they do come as one package. Don't run the processor without it. This is to keep the processor running cool and extend its life; without one, you will burn up your CPU quickly.

Memory

Random access memory (RAM) also comes in a few flavors (see Figure 1-10). The most popular types include synchronous dynamic RAM (SDRAM, pronounced "es-dee-ram"), which is a 168-pin dual in-line memory module (DIMM). The single in-line memory module (SIMM) was the DIMM predecessor. The DIMM effectively doubled the amount of memory chips there were typically on a SIMM. While the last of the SIMMs were either 30-pin or 72-pin circuit boards that you'd plug into the motherboard, the more microchips on the DIMM effectively increased its size to 168-pin, and 184-pin for double data rate (DDR) modules. The most common modules used are the SDRAM 168-pin DIMMs and the 184-pin DDR modules. Anything else is much too old, and could potentially cause compatibility problems with Windows 2000 or Server 2003.

Figure I-10
The evolution of RAM, from the top down, is the 30-pin SIMM, the 72-pin SIMM, the 168-pin DIMM, and the 184-pin DDR module.

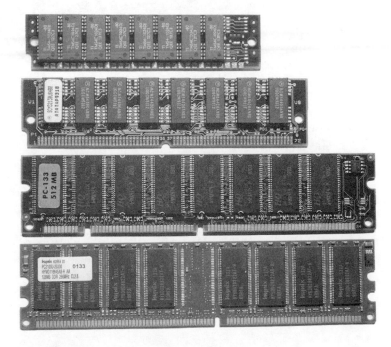

It's a universal fact that the more memory your system has, the better the performance. You can pick up a single 256MB 168-pin DIMM for less than $30 at OfficeMax (www.officemax.com), Memory4Less.com (www.memory4less.com), and Crucial Technology (www.crucial.com). I also picked up a 512MB PC133 module at TigerDirect.com (www.tigerdirect.com) for less than $50, and prices will continue to drop.

The Hard Drive

There are a few common types of storage devices: hard drives (the most common), DVD-ROMs, CD-ROMs, floppy drives, and tape backup units. The most common of the hard drives is referred to as Integrated Device Electronics (IDE), based on an old industry standard; but most of the computers sold today use Enhanced Integrated Device Electronics (EIDE), which is a faster version of IDE (see Figure 1-11).

The more popular is the standard electronic interface, used between the computer motherboard's bus (communications path) and the computer's disk storage devices (including CD-ROM, tape backup unit, and DVD-ROM drives).

Figure 1-11
The IDE (bottom) is more popular hard drive technology among PCs, with a 40-pin connector, while the faster SCSI drive pictured includes a 50-pin connection, but can go as high as 80 pins in the ultra-wide SCSI high-speed drives.

The other choice is the SCSI drive. An IDE drive may go up to 7200 RPM (revolutions per minute) when reading and writing to the hard disk. The SCSI can reach over 10,000 RPM and is typically in high-end enterprise servers and workstations that demand more speed. I'll discuss the various types of SCSI, hot-swappable hard drives, and RAID controllers in Chapter 6.

I found a generic-quality 20GB hard drive running at 7200 RPM for $37. You'll need at least one good-sized hard drive for the system to hold any backup files. A 20GB hard drive may be adequate, depending on your plans for backup, but you can always expand if you need more. In a file sharing server, with automated backups, you'll fill up those drives sooner than you think.

Expansion Cards and the Network Adapters

The following are the three most common expansion slots on a motherboard (see Figure 1-12):

❑ **Accelerated Graphics Port (AGP)** Designed for a high-speed connection between the CPU, memory, and video adapter for graphics- and video-intensive applications.

❑ **Peripheral Component Interconnect (PCI)** The most common type of slot, PCIs are used to add network adapters, modems, sound cards, video adapters (in the absence of onboard video or AGP), and controller cards, to add more hard drives. This interconnection between a microprocessor speeds up the operation, much like the AGP slot, but not as fast. The AGP slot runs at double the speed as the traditional PCI (66 MHz vs. 33 MHz).

❏ **Industry Standard Architecture (ISA)**   The original bus interconnection architecture for the older PCs' motherboard, which ran at 16 MHz. You'll rarely find one of these on a new motherboard, which is usually loaded up with PCI slots and the single AGP.

Figure 1-12
Expansion slots 101

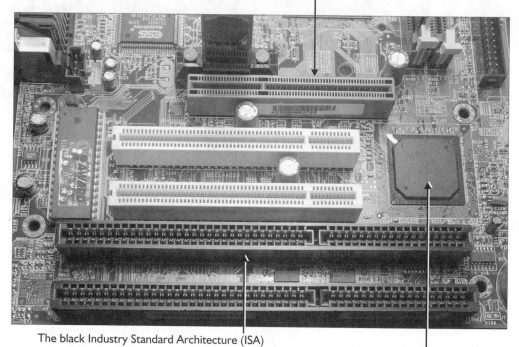

The brown Accelerated Graphics Port (AGP)

The black Industry Standard Architecture (ISA)

The white Peripheral Component Interconnect (PCI)

Network Adapter

The Ethernet 10/100 Mbps network adapter is the PCI expansion card (see Figure 1-13) to set up your computer to communicate on a local area network (LAN)—or, linked to other computers within your offices, a wide area network (WAN) that extends to other office locations—and become a communications gateway to the Internet, setting up Internet sharing and firewall security. Windows 2000 Server can handle multiple network adapters. If you wish to set up this server as an Internet gateway, thus sharing an Internet connection with your LAN, you'd need two network adapters—one for the Internet and one for your internal network (more on this in Chapter 5).

Figure 1-13
The network adapter
provides connectivity
to and from the server.

AGP

The AGP card is a high-speed port designed for the display adapter (video card) only. It provides a direct link between the card and memory, and there's only one slot of its kind on the motherboard. Introduced as a higher-speed alternative to the standard PCI-based adapter, the AGP makes for smoother graphics or video-intensive applications. If you're planning to use streaming media or videoconferencing from your web server (another built-in function of Windows 2000 Server), you'll need to consider a high-performance AGP card, rather than onboard video.

Figure 1-14 shows a few of the many choices in video adapters. Centered is a dual monitor, TV-out, 128MB 3-D graphics accelerator, great for PC gaming or digital video production, but do you really need it on a server? Considering that you'll be using Windows 2000 Server Terminal Services to remotely administer your server from your laptop or from home, pick an inexpensive option (but make sure it's compatible), something in the range of 16 or 32MB. At the top of Figure 1-14 is my choice, a 16MB Voodoo3 3000 graphics accelerator, which I picked up for $10.

Figure 1-14
A few examples of
video adapters

If your motherboard doesn't already have onboard video, you can also pick up an inexpensive (and compatible) Matrox MGA video card (see Figure 1-15) for a few dollars—an inexpensive alternative to today's high-performance (and expensive) hardware graphics accelerators, and many of them do have Windows 2000 support.

Figure 1-15
The Matrox MGA
4MB video adapter
is one of the
older Windows
2000–compatible cards.

Sound Card

Most motherboards now come with onboard audio, and because we are building a server with limited need for any stereophonic sound, the onboard audio is more than enough. If you end up with a motherboard that requires a sound card, and you decide you need one (99 percent of the servers I've worked on do not have sound cards), you can get one at a low price. I picked up a SoundBlaster Live card at a computer show in Washington, D.C. (with a 30-day warranty) for $5.00.

Floppy Drive

The floppy drive is an out-of-date legacy device, but is still a necessary emergency boot component of any computer system. If the computer crashes for whatever reason, an emergency boot disk in the floppy drive can bring it to life for surgery. It's also valuable for upgrading the BIOS on your machine. I've picked up many "lots" of floppy drives off of eBay—usually three of them for about $10—but if you don't need more than one, you can pick one up for about $8 to $12 at a local computer show or wholesaler.

Compact Disc Drives

If anything were to replace the legacy floppy diskette, it would surely be the CD-ROM. Today you can periodically get up to 100 CD-Rs at OfficeMax for free (after mail-in rebates). I've been an advocate of picking up free discs, and the

CD-ROM since the "multi-media computer" (computers with CD-ROM drives) reached mass-market proportions in the mid-1990s. With up to 650MB of space, the vast majority of your software comes on a CD-ROM, and many of Microsoft's multi-disc sets are also available on DVD-ROM (DVD-5), with up to 4.7GB of space. The DVD-5 is called a "single-sided/single-layer" disc, referring to the physical encoding scheme. The largest DVD-ROM (DVD-18) holds up to 17GB of data and is "double-sided/double-layer" encoded.

DVD-ROM/CD-ROM

A DVD-ROM drive can read any compact disc—DVD-ROMs, DVD movies, CD-ROMs, music CDs, and CD-Rs. The DVD-ROM drive can read data nine times faster than the equivalent CD-ROM drive; the data on the DVD is more closely packaged and thus doesn't need to "spin" as fast. For example, a 1x DVD-ROM drive can read the same amount of data as a 9x CD-ROM drive, which is about 1.35 Mbps. This makes the data transfer rate of the newer 20x DVD-ROM drives equivalent to 180x CD-ROM drives, or 27 Mbps. The tightly packed data on the DVD will force the extinction of the CD-ROM, because the reading technology can't keep up any longer.

I purchased a 12x DVD drive (including all the cables) on eBay for $30; only weeks before, DVD drive manufacturers introduced rebates that dropped the price to under $20. If you find a DVD-ROM drive for a deal, grab it—but keep in mind that the most use it may get is holding the master in the duplication of CD-ROMs and installing new software, so don't go out of your way and beyond your budget to grab one. The CD-ROM drive can handle your needs at about $15–$30 for something comparable to a 52x.

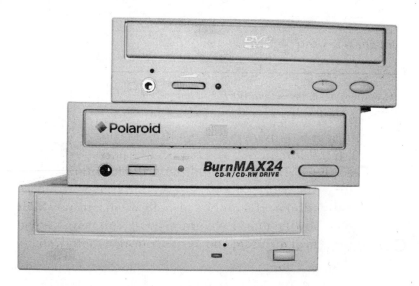

CD Writer

I broke down a while ago and decided to buy a faster CD writer (32x) to add to my server at home, for the same reason I installed one at work. Now, with a 32x (write), 10x (rewrite), 52x (read) CD writer in my servers (at home and the office), I don't have to worry about scheduling time with "Bob" in Accounting to burn a series of CDs. I can drop a CD-R in the drive and, through Terminal Services, burn a CD-ROM in about three minutes. My original 4x took about 45 minutes. However, keep in mind that this eats up resources.

Tape Backup System

Although the ever-dropping price of hard drives makes it an attractive alternative to traditional tape storage drives, the typical large-capacity tape drive offers a few advantages. The tape is easily removable and transferable, and more economical than the hot-swappable hard drives, which are hard drives that can be pulled out of a machine without having to turn off and open the machine first. Even your hot-swappable hard drives are still electronic devices that can crash and fail. A tape cartridge is a universally proven solution, and thus will be an optional part of our machine. If a tape drive is within your budget, you may wish to add one to your server. I have found that a protected and well-maintained hard drive can do the trick, and it doesn't need to be one located in the same building.

Some of the miscellaneous parts include an audio cable for the DVD-ROM/CD-ROM to the sound card (either on the motherboard or the expansion card), another IDE cable for the hard drive (unless it came with one), a three-pin to two-pin Power LED connector adapter for the motherboard (if it doesn't offer both options), and chassis cooling fans. The four types of cables that link drives to motherboards are (shown from left to right in Figure 1-16) SCSI; IDE, with 80-wire and 40-pin (for larger and higher-speed hard drives) and the older 40-wire, 40 pin IDE; and the 3.5-inch floppy drive cable.

Figure 1-16
The four cable types that link drives to motherboards

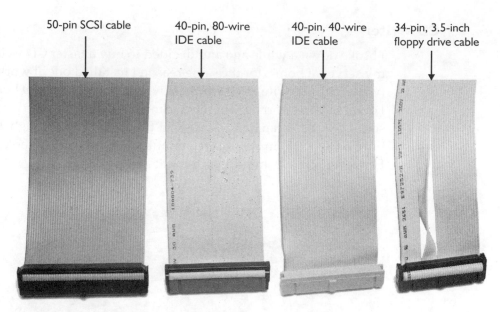

50-pin SCSI cable

40-pin, 80-wire IDE cable

40-pin, 40-wire IDE cable

34-pin, 3.5-inch floppy drive cable

Computing Without a Monitor

Windows 2000 and Server 2003 offer the ability to work without a monitor and mouse. This is accomplished by using Terminal Services, an embedded application that opens the server's actual desktop within any workstation's desktop (see Figure 1-17). Figure 1-18 shows how you can log into your server from a laptop computer, either at the office or from home, eliminating the need for the server to have input peripherals.

Figure 1-17
Logging into Server from a ThinkPad

Figure 1-18
Microsoft's Terminal Services opens the server's desktop on another computer.

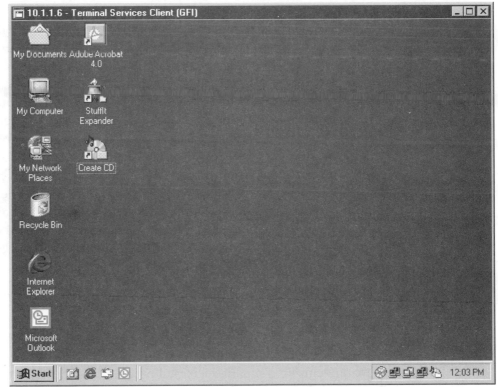

If you decide to purchase a monitor for this server (rather than borrowing one for installation and configuration), keep in mind that this is not a workstation, so any SVGA monitor will do, even the ones in the bargain bin at the next computer show. I found a new keyboard at Micro Center in Westmont, IL, for $5.00, and clean used ones for about $2. They also had a basket of used mice for 99 cents. My file/web server at the office doesn't even have a mouse or monitor attached. It sure saves a lot of space because without a monitor, keyboard, and/or mouse, there's no need for a desk.

Build It and They Will Come

Some of my friends think I'm crazy. Oh, they agree that the concept of building a great, inexpensive server is possible; many of them use a few I've built daily, so I've convinced them of that. The continued skepticism is about time and grief. It did take me many hours of research, analysis, troubleshooting, hunting, buying, and building to put together my servers. It's difficult for them to justify that amount of time and grief when you can buy a new Dell server (with an operating system installed) advertised nowadays for under $1000, instantly—or as long as it takes to pull it out of the box and put it together. But it's just not the same thing. If you "customize" a configuration closer to what we're about to build, you're talking about $2500 (without an operating system).

There are also the smaller, entrepreneurial companies that decide to pick up a PC and use that as a "file server." What they don't understand is that when they buy a PC to do a "server's" job, the underlying technology is still that of a PC—not a server. It lacks security, tools, administrative components, and functionality to really perform as a server. What we're building here is a server, not a PC. There is a lack of the necessary memory, limited space, and no expansion capabilities. Most of your inexpensive PCs today are the smaller, micro-ATX towers, with only two or three PCI slots, and one or two expansion drive bays for sharing CD-RW, DVD, or tape drives. Our goal here is not to build a PC, but rather to build a box that can effectively use either Windows 2000 or .NET Server. Why invest so much money on a machine that may shortchange the operating system to operate effectively?

I've done most of the research, hunting, analysis, and hair pulling for you, and with these components, it'll take you about an hour to put it all together. First, we need to find those pieces of our puzzle. The hunt is on!

TESTING 1-2-3

❏ The value of using a client/server environment includes scalability, better security, shared resources, and centralized administration. I explained how a Japanese manufacturing company increased production and shipments by upgrading a legacy Manufacturing Resource Planning (MRP) system to Windows 2000 Server, and opened up information to foreign satellite offices and inventory information to their customers. My goal is to show you how to build your own server for about $400, with helpful hints about the components you'll need and which of those you can salvage from older computers.

❏ Midtower computer chassis or cases with six bays for CD-ROM, DVD-ROM, floppy, and hard drives are available at $20 to $30 at computer shows and wholesale outlets (more on this in Chapter 2). The Motherboard and CPU have coupled form factors, and you also need to be aware of the different types of the same brand and speed processors, as well as the various types of RAM for your motherboard.

❏ There are two different kinds of hard drives—the SCSI and IDE—and you need to be aware of their different flavors and compatibilities with your choice in motherboard and operating system.

❏ The server exists not to serve one person as a workstation but many as a server. To avoid having someone sit down at the server and slow it down for the rest of the network, I'll show you how to use Windows 2000 and Server 2003's Terminal Services to administer the server without any peripherals and from any internetworked computer, anywhere.

Chapter 2

The Hunt

I frequently participate in hunting excursions, not with a rifle out in the woods, but with cash and a credit card at a computer show. There are a flood of other hunters fighting for the same game. Busily hustling through the doors like a flock of Velociraptors encircling vendors and their deals for the day. They're early, believing the old adage "the early bird gets the worm." This may be true, but it's also often the second mouse that gets the cheese.

One Man's Garbage Is Another Man's Gold

There is a way to survive and flourish within this jungle of microprocessors and cable. I hope to pass that knowledge on to you, by pointing out some survival tips and by enlightening you to some fascinating data and deals. For me, this hunting adventure began with local computer shows and then led me online to seek out those exceptional new and used components that will give us the ingredients to build our server. It can be done for about $400, and I'm going to show you how.

The following are a few core ingredients to bargain hunting success, whether you're at a computer show or searching the online auction houses:

❏ **Patience**   Waiting for the right part at the right price

❏ **Knowledge**   Understanding of the right part and its compatibility

❏ **Caution**   Realizing some people are selling real garbage and bad lots

❏ **Timing**   Knowing when it's time to move in for the kill

There is truly a plethora of components at these computer shows. Some of my best deals have included a new 15-inch cathode ray tube (CRT) monitor for $50, a used 17-inch CRT monitor for $35, 2GB hard drives for $15, a used LS-120 floppy diskette drive and new network cabling for a buck, video adapters and sound cards for $5, and computer chassis (with power supplies) for under $30.

There is a long list of variables that can cause flaky behavior from electronic equipment like computer components. So, buying anything used is risky, but many of the vendors will guarantee a component is functional or offer an exchange (see Figure 2-1). In addition to damaged or unstable goods, there's also other variables in human error, including

❏ Incompatible bus speeds

❏ Incorrectly set jumpers (shunts)

❏ New BIOS or drivers needed (which can be difficult to add if a motherboard doesn't boot up)

❏ Not enough power from the power supply or wrong type of power supply (for example, Pentium 4 requires new connectors)

❏ Wrong type of cables and harnesses

Figure 2-1
One of the dealers at a local computer show attempting to tame the hunters

The list goes on. You could very easily troubleshoot a new motherboard, hard drive, or memory module until you're blue in the face, it finally works, or you surrender and admit defeat. In some cases, the problem may be something beyond your control. For example, I picked up an FIC (First International Computer, Inc.) SD-11 full-ATX motherboard with a new Slot A AMD Athlon

600 MHz processor as a combo unit on eBay for $60 (see Figure 2-2). Unfortunately, although rated very highly in reviews during its first release (1998), it's not designed to handle today's newer, power-hungry 4x AGP cards or PC133 memory (discussed further in Chapter 5). Therefore, I had a perfectly good motherboard and processor, but no video adapter or memory for it. This is why doing research before purchasing anything is important. You don't want to get stuck with a drawer full of useless parts.

An easy way to avoid buying something you don't need is to visit Google (www.google.com) and type the motherboard model in the search field along with "issues," "problems," or "won't boot." This will bring up not only the reviews, but also technical support message boards and the manufacturer's own documentation. Another resource is motherboards.org, which is an exceptionally valuable resource for data on the motherboard you may be considering. Unless your motherboard is an antiquated obscurity, you'll no doubt find someone somewhere who's had problems with it. The question is, is the solution something you're prepared to handle?

Figure 2-2
The FIC SD-11
motherboard

Keep in mind that whatever you see or I suggest in this book I've tested with a specific configuration and brands of components. If you've picked up the same pieces and are having problems, check my configuration and see if you have a wildcard that may be the culprit.

Electrostatic Discharge

Static electricity happens when two objects connect and one becomes positively charged and the other negatively charged. This is *electrostatic discharge (ESD)*. We've all experienced ESD when walking across a carpet and touching a metal doorknob; the positive charge transfers to the metal doorknob, creating sparks of hot static electricity. Although this isn't anything like a lightning bolt to us (the extreme example of ESD), to electronic components, it is a lightning bolt. The shock we feel overshadows the heat that dissipates from the event, but the microcomponents of an expansion card, hard drive, or memory module can literally melt. There's also a *latent defect*, where the component may continue to function for a while, but with a shortened lifespan.

ESD kills most computer components and is difficult to diagnose in used equipment. You can avoid frying your own parts by taking a few precautions. First, get into the habit of discharging any possible static electricity by touching something metal that's earth-ground before touching any computer components. Second, set up an antistatic workstation because eventually you'll forget to discharge yourself before handling components. You can also pick up a wrist strap with the Megohm resistor to help dissipate ESD. A megohm resister is a device that will limit the current flowing through your body to less than 0,5 mA—not enough to generate ESD.

It's also a good idea to wear antistatic footwear to ground you, an antistatic mat to cover your workstation, and/or enclose all ESD-susceptible items in antistatic-shielded packaging while being either moved or stored. You can pick up a package of about ten Ziploc-like antistatic bags for about $6 at most computer stores, such as Radio Shack.

System Requirements

You need to decide what you want this server to do for you and your customers. Remember that your goal is to build a machine that can handle your requirements, including the server operating system and suite of applications. I have an HTTP web server that delivers nothing more than HTML pages and simple Common Gateway Interface (CGI) script on an old 20 MHz Macintosh. As long as a hundred thousand visitors don't stop by at one time, it should be fine. It's the software installed onto the machine that handles your needs, and not the machine itself. Just as you don't need to buy a Formula 1 racecar to commute to work every day, you don't necessarily need to buy the fastest computer system to meet your requirements.

I picked up a refurbished Tyan Trinity KT S2390 mainboard (see Figure 2-3) from Justdeals.com (www.justdeals.com) for $25. This isn't one of the newest boards out there, but it fit my needs. It came with some necessary cabling for a floppy drive and one IDE device (CD-ROM or hard drive), and a CD-ROM that includes some important drivers and software. The Trinity KT provides an automated CPU configuration, eliminating the need to deal with complex jumper settings (discussed in Chapter 4). The AMD 900 MHz Duron CPU for this board is from NewEgg.com (www.newegg.com) and cost me about $40. At a local show, I picked up another, similar deal: a 1 GHz AMD Duron with an ECS motherboard for about $100. This is considerably more than I paid for the Trinity KT, but the processor and motherboard were new and under a full year warranty (compared to 30 days on the refurbished one). This unit also came with cabling and a system CD-ROM with drivers and software.

Figure 2-3
The Tyan Trinity KT
full-ATX motherboard

The motherboard/CPU combo specials are inherently better choices because they are pretested for compatibility, so there's less research required on your part. I recently put together a server for my latest client location as a wireless access point for laptops, file and print sharing, a bridge between three different networks (all with required resources), and an authenticated intranet for customers to access and download sensitive documents. The traffic on this server is nominal, so I opted for a new discovery from www.shentech.com (a Yahoo! store), which offered a Soyo SY-7VEM motherboard with onboard video and audio, with a 700 MHz processor, heat sink, and cooling fan for $69. Upon doing further research at the Soyo Computer, Inc., web site (www.soyo.com) and a few posted reviews, I decided that this would be more than adequate (especially with 512MB of added memory). You still need to research each component, from the CPU to the memory and the chipset on the motherboard, to determine whether there's ample support for expansion. This motherboard can support up to a 1 GHz CPU, which leaves enough room for growth. If I need more, I can always upgrade later. It works great for now.

Buy It New

The cost of a new 1GHz CPU is under $40. At this price, there's no need to risk shopping for a used one that may be defective.

Where to Find Inexpensive Components

A work colleague and I usually like to compare bargain-hunting notes. This helps us find a wide assortment of deals from a multitude of outlets. One day he received an e-mail from OfficeMax detailing an offer for 256MB modules of SDRAM for about $25 and 128MB for $15, after mail-in rebates. He mentioned it haphazardly, but I happened to need one, so he decided to join me on a component excursion. Upon our arrival, we discovered that our local OfficeMax tacked on an instant store rebate, bringing the price of the 256MB module to $19 and the 128MB down to $8. Needless to say, we pay closer attention to their newsletter. This is how you find those exceptional deals, by keeping your eyes out for the right item at the right price. This holds true for any outlet, from a retail store to eBay to computer shows.

Computer Shows

A computer show can be much like a swap meet, or eBay under a roof, except all products are at a fixed price. I recently attended the Super Computer Sale Show at the Donald Stephens Convention Center in Rosemont, IL (www .supercomputershow.com). There were dozens of exhibitors with all kinds of bargains.

I found a choice display for $35: the Gateway EV700 17-inch monitor (see Figure 2-4). I also picked up a brand-new 4x DVD-ROM drive for $30 from the same seller, Kaboom, Inc. (kaboom@willinet.net), which was a great deal at the time. Prices for DVD-ROMs and CD-ROMs are dropping dramatically to make way for the newer, faster models and the latest combo technologies—DVD-ROM plus CD writer in one package.

At most of these shows were exhibitors that, for upward of $1500, would custom-build a computer to your liking while you wait. People were paying premium dollar for the privilege of seeing their computer built before their eyes, when in fact they could've found all the necessary pieces there to build it themselves for about $400. It was all there. I discovered TNS International (www.tnsusa.com), a local wholesaler who sold me a combination new 1 GHz AMD Duron processor and motherboard for $100. That's the core of the computer right there! TNS is where I picked up my chassis for $26 at the show ($30 at its store).

One other show I attended was the Giant Computer Show (www .giantcomputershow.com) show, located in the south suburbs of Chicago, which usually occurs every other month. The best way to find similar shows in your

Figure 2-4
A 17-inch monitor for $35 and a DVD-ROM drive for under $30

area is to check the Web, your local city commerce for an upcoming schedule of events, computer stores, and convention centers.

Figure 2-5
One man's garbage is another man's gold for sure. Here we have 1GB hard drives for $15, CD-ROM drives for $10, and mice for $1.

Online Auctions

The online auction houses have taken the concept of the local swap meet and perfected it with one simple change: they opened up the swap meet to the world. Unfortunately, it's very easy to get wrapped up in the auctioning and surpass the cost of purchasing the exact or similar new item. This is where doing your homework really pays off. Sometimes, when doing research on the value of a component you've contemplated bidding on, you find what you're looking for at a much better price.

Also, eBay is a fantastic outlet for *learning* about those components. When you have thousands of people posting the sale of computer components, most will post specifications, reviews, and even hyperlinks to the manufacturer's web site. Many times their configuration will also let you know that it's something to avoid, or to seek out. eBay is not only an auction house of computer components, it's also an electronic community and library for those components (see Figure 2-6).

Figure 2-6
There are about one million new items listed on eBay every day.

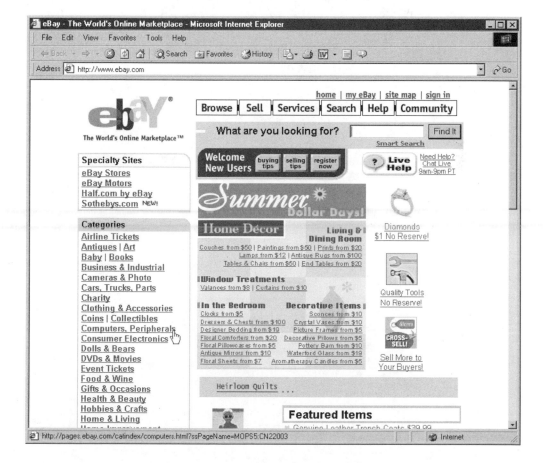

The first place I looked for components was eBay and uBid, both of which list for sale thousands of parts in a wide range of condition and prices. For those of you eBay addicts, you know that the best way to "shop" on eBay is by clicking "going, going, gone" in your desired category (see Figure 2-7). This takes you to auctions that are ending shortly, maybe with the perfect part at the perfect price. You'll no doubt be using eBay to buy parts for your server, so here are a few words from the wise:

❏ *The rating system is there for a reason, so check the seller's history and feedback.* Take it from someone who's been the victim of "eBay bandits" twice—if they're newly registered or have a large amount of negative feedback, do not bid on their items. I'm still waiting for a 1 GHz Celeron processor I "won" for $35 from a place called Ready2GoComputers. If it's *too* good to be true, it is!

❏ *Avoid sellers who insist on payment through money orders and cashier checks only—unless they have an incredibly positive feedback history.* Think of it as sending cash to a complete stranger with friendly referrals. Paying through a credit card or PayPal leaves a better paper trail.

Figure 2-7
Hunting for the right part in the very last minutes of an eBay auction can get you some great deals.

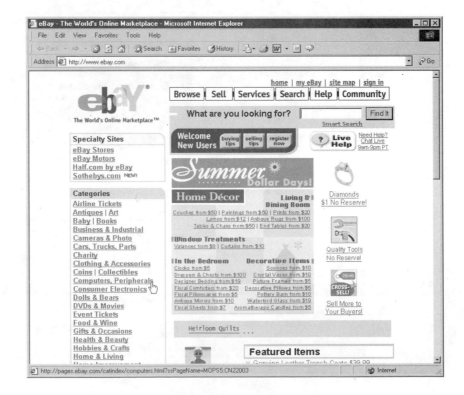

❏ *Do not bid on three or four of the same item if you need only one.* You may win them all. Be patient. When you discover an item that you desire, bid on that item and watch it. This is how you can get a new CHAINTECH Computer Co. LTD MX400 Nvidia 64MB graphics accelerator or a Legend 3D Eagle Eye 128MB 3D Thrill graphics accelerator for about $70, while purchasing comparable products at retail would be up to $300.

❏ *Don't get caught up in the competition.* Keep your maximum bid in mind. Winning an item at a great price is a better "kill" than winning the item at the price of a Ferrari. Remember your $400 budget.

The other online auction house that I've used extensively is uBid, as shown in Figure 2-8. The differences between uBid and eBay include the following:

❏ You bid and win most of the auctions through uBid, which processes the order and ships it to you directly, while on eBay you are dealing with the individual seller.

❏ The payment process automatically bills your credit card directly on uBid, but with eBay, you can use PayPal, an escrow-like payment service; a credit card, if the individual seller accepts them (many are actual retail outlets that also sell on eBay); or a check or money order, again sent directly to the seller.

Figure 2-8
uBid, an online auction site

❏ The number of offerings on uBid is considerably less, although still impressive. While eBay attracts over a million new auctions a day, I've rarely seen the total offering on uBid over a million.

❏ The auction doesn't close on the specified time and date on uBid, but rather when no more bids occur for a ten-minute period after the posted deadline. On eBay, the end is the end: if you don't get your bid in on time, you lost.

Originally, bidders would only deal with uBid and not individual sellers, as uBid was a conduit that provided excellent delivery (usually) at a price. Today, there are three choice sellers on uBid: the official uBid Preferred Partners, who are uBid-approved third-party merchants; the Consumer Exchange, where you can sign up as an individual seller (like eBay); or uBid itself. Another valuable service offered by uBid is the payment process. When you sign up as a buyer, you are required to provide a credit card number, to which all of your winning bids are automatically charged; whereas on eBay, you actually have to check out each item, using the seller's paying preference.

My tips for bidding on uBid are the same as for bidding on eBay. Overall, uBid has been a great resource for memory and hard drives, although they can be quite expensive with shipping and handling—so check before you bid, especially because the payment process is automated. You may win a 17-inch Sony Trinitron monitor for $35, but there's a hidden $50 shipping and handling charge, usually listed as "Standard Ground – $11.99, plus $0.99 per pound." That's about $50 for a 40-pound monitor, which for a server is overkill.

Online Retailers

Through eBay, I've discovered Justdeals.com (www.justdeals.com), where I picked up my Tyan Trinity KT S2390 motherboard. Other online stores worth mentioning are Directron, Inc. (www.directron.com); NewEgg.com (www.newegg.com); The Hard Drive Outlet (www.harddriveoutlet.com), where I purchased a 4GB SCSI hard drive for $5 (an eBay store); and the Yahoo store, Shentech.com (www.shentech.com), where you can buy a CPU and motherboard combo for under $70.

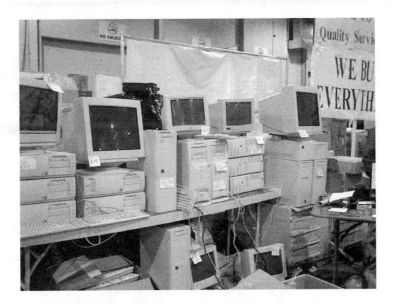

The online comparison portals, or "shopping agents," are also helpful, not only for helping you find new and used merchandise at the lowest prices, but also to check if the bid you're about to make is less than what you would pay to buy the product new. Dealtime.com will search hundreds of web sites for the best prices and give you a list of the retailers and a community-based rating system, much like the feedback profiles of eBay sellers.

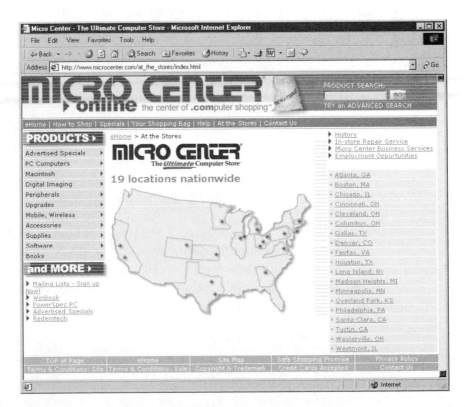

Micro Center and OfficeMax

When I discover an exceptional deal at a retail level, the risk factor diminishes greatly. It's a brand-new product, with warranty and an actual physical location where you can walk in and see and touch the product *before* purchasing it. This is why I'll go out of my way to grab a special at an OfficeMax or Micro Center.

Recently, I was at a computer show in Washington, D.C., where I picked up two used SoundBlaster-compatible PCI sound cards for $10. It was a great deal at the time, until Micro Center offered a special on their Inland SoundBlaster-compatible PCI sound card, marked down to $6.99, with a one-year warranty. I was fortunate that my two used sound cards work fine, but the extra $1.99 would've been worth it.

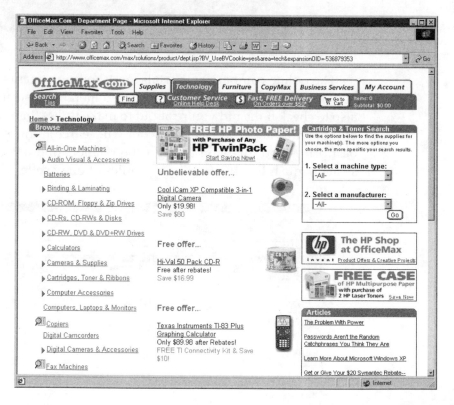

I've picked up multimedia speakers, network adapters, 100 CD-Rs, and 64MB of Kingston Memory from OfficeMax (www.officemax.com) for $0.00—zero dollars, but I wasn't shoplifting. OfficeMax routinely has promotions that offer a full rebate on the entire cost of products, so essentially they are free. OfficeMax has had promotions for memory modules, like I mentioned earlier, and more recently a 40x CD-RW drive for $19.95 (after rebates). You can also find specials for memory at Coast to Coast Memory, Inc. (www.18004memory.com) or at Crucial Technology (www.crucial.com), where at my last visit I was offered a $30 instant savings coupon on the memory I was looking for. In fact, I once asked the technicians at Micro Center about some obscure memory and they steered me to www.crucial.com, which offers a memory upgrade wizard that can help you choose the right memory for your specific motherboard or computer make and model (see Figure 2-9).

Figure 2-9
Crucial.com offers a drop-down menu wizard with which to find the right memory for your motherboard.

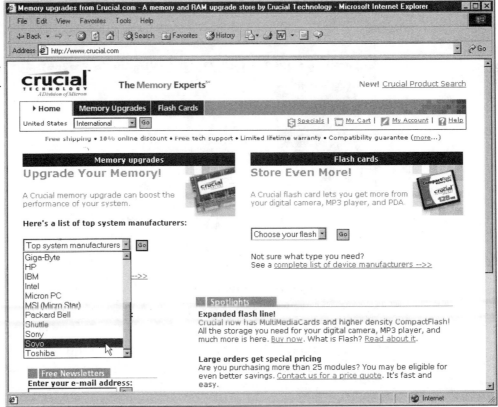

Micro Center has 19 locations nationwide, but is also available online at www.microcenter.com. Fortunately for me, one of its stores is conveniently located a stone's throw from the headquarters of Intellisys Technology, LLC, (www.intellisystechnology.com). This store offers everything at reasonable prices and has a clearance section that includes goodies from time to time. (I bought a 10/100 Mbps network adapter once for $5 and an internal fax/modem for $9.)

The standard Ethernet network connection requires a typical RJ45 Category 5 (Cat 5) cable and network adapter PCI expansion card. I picked up one of these at OfficeMax, taking advantage of one of its regular full-rebate specials. The adapter was $10 with a full $10 rebate, so essentially it was free! I picked up the GigaFast 10/100 Mbps at the local Micro Center, on sale for $5. I first discovered the Proxim Symphony wireless adapters on the clearance table at a local OfficeMax, but then rediscovered them on uBid, at www.justdeals.com, and at a few other outlets for under $15. At first, I decided to experiment, since I was skeptical about what I could get wirelessly for $10. I purchased one network adapter for one of my towers and one PC card for my laptop; both were on closeout for $10 apiece (regularly $150). It was simple to set up; and after downloading the Windows 2000 drivers from the Proxim, Inc., web site, I had both computers talking to each other, peer to peer and without wires, within minutes (technology is like magic when it works seamlessly). True, these discontinued items are limited to only 1.6 Mbps (you can get 11 Mbps wirelessly these days); but considering that the traffic throughput between the two computers is limited to online access at 1.5 Mbps, I found it exceptionally handy to cut the wires.

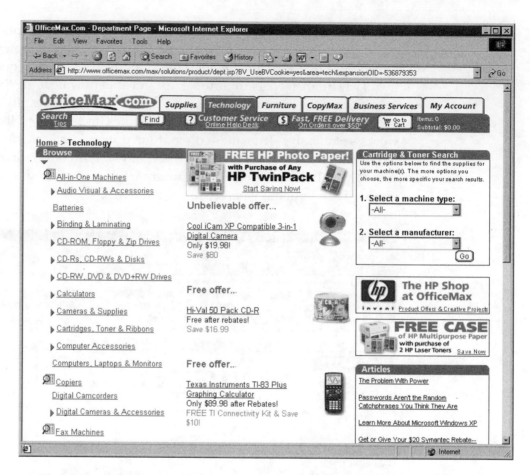

Thanks to the continued proliferation of wireless technologies, you can easily find products that can turn your server into a wireless Internet gateway. By configuring your server with a wireless network adapter and setting up Internet sharing for that adapter, you've effectively given anyone on your wireless network Internet access from anywhere—they no longer need to be chained to a specific desk and network RJ45 outlet (more on this in Chapter 10).

Dust Collectors

One of our early PC desktops at home was a 166 MHz OEM machine built by a computer technician friend named Manny back in the 1990s. This was an older AT-style system, midtower, with antiquated SIMM memory. Affectionately referred to as the "Manny Computer," it has had most of its components replaced over the years, until finally it couldn't keep up with the newer, more demanding software requirements. I ended up pulling out its guts, and used the floppy, network adapter, video card, and CD-ROM on the file/print server I built for home. Fortunately, the components were Windows 2000 compliant. These parts brought down the cost of the server to about $200, so don't write off those old systems entirely just yet.

Since the time I wrote this book, prices have dropped (and continue to drop) for components that are not quite out of date, and not necessarily future-proof. However, falling out of style doesn't make them useless. The computer industry, like any other industry, is driven by profits. They have a constant need to churn out new products and continue to garnish consumer dollars, sometimes offering new and exciting features that the vast majority of buyers don't need. A 1 GHz processor may not be as fast as a 2.5 GHz processor, but it doesn't mean it does the job any less effectively—just slower. They are more than enough for the server we have planned.

Here's a list of my hints and tips when you're out there shopping for components:

❏ To avoid any problems with compatibility, purchase a combination CPU and motherboard from a reputable source.

❏ The 1 GHz AMD Duron and Athlon processors are exceptional bargains at under $50. They also appear to be the most favorable with the greatest number of Socket A motherboards.

❏ Do not build an entire server from parts pulled out of junk machines. If you use those to build a single workstation, that's fine. If it goes down, you only have one person down. If a server goes down, it affects everybody in the company, so seriously consider the risk factor.

❏ There are many places online where you can find bargains, and the computer shows are always a great resource. Never stop looking!

❏ Stick with PCI expansion cards and/or an AGP card for your video adapter (if not already available onboard).

Chapter 3

The Network Operating System

The network operating system (NOS) is the brain of your server; without it, it's just a computer. The NOS offers applications and utilities that are designed to help users do business faster and better. Only a few NOSs are widely used: Novell, UNIX, Linux, and Windows 2000 Server and Windows Server 2003. All of these NOSs are very complex, as indicated by the variety of 1000+ page books written about each one. The goal in this chapter is to give you an overview of the choice of NOS that I made and the reasons why I feel it may be the best fit for your organization. In this case, I've chosen both Windows 2000 Server and Windows Server 2003 in a dual-boot system (more about dual-boot systems in Chapter 9).

The Evolution of a Robust Windows Network Operating System

I remember being at a Microsoft event several years ago at which the presenter (a Microsoft employee) defensively stated to the audience that you shouldn't have to reboot Windows NT more than once or twice a month. At a certification class, a Microsoft trainer called Internet Information Server (IIS) a "virus with documentation." I wasn't much of a Microsoft fan to begin with at the time, and the defensive nature of these comments only solidified my apprehension.

Then Windows 2000 Server was released, followed by Server 2003, which includes even more features (see Figure 3-1). These two NOSs changed my views entirely. They are two of the most robust NOSs on the market and are backed by a massive support structure. There are regular updates, patches, and service packs to deal with (and you need to, to keep the system healthy), but that's only because it's a very popular platform, with an incredible development and support community. The Automatic Update feature is an essential component to system maintenance,

Figure 3-1
Auditing shutdowns
are included in the
latest version of
Microsoft's NOS.

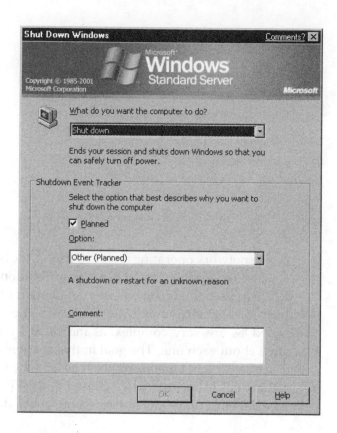

and you can configure the application to automatically download, update, and reboot the server while you sleep at night. Most of the updates and patches are for security vulnerabilities discovered by releasing the "final version" to the general public—in a sense, using consumers as testers. This is not unusual for software; the variables can be so complex that an attempt at replicating a live environment within a laboratory is unlikely.

Choosing the Right Technology

As a system analyst, my job often involves researching and analyzing various solutions and then reporting the outcome, including which solutions I personally recommend and why. One of the most attractive aspects of Microsoft products that I've discovered through my research and analyses is the monolithic support structure and community. Microsoft takes sophisticated tools and applications and makes them usable and affordable, so that companies of any size can take advantage of the best suite of server utilities and applications.

However, many people are biased toward Microsoft or simply do not like Microsoft—for whatever reason—and thus prefer other NOS over Microsoft's. One of my clients was the American Licorice Company (ALC), who a few years before my tenure there as a consultant chose a web servicing company called Web Design Group that slapped together an assortment of custom and obscure technologies to create four ALC web sites. Providing ALC with a shared Oracle database gave it a more cost-effective database solution, but negated its employees' remote access to the web sites for updating content (for security reasons, they were told) and locked ALC into the web services company.

ALC was not concerned about this arrangement until it found itself tied into multiple approvals and design changes to its web site at $200 an hour. ALC had paid for a SHREK movie tie-in for its Sour Punch candy line, which also included a web strategy with Burger King and Dreamworks, LLC (the producer of SHREK). This arrangement put even more demands on the marketing department, including the mandatory requirement by both Dreamworks and Burger King for ALC's web sites to become COPPA (Children's Online Privacy Protection Act) compliant before the release of the film and before they would link their web sites together.

The plan of the marketing department and the IT director was first to make the web sites COPPA compliant and then move them onto internal servers, where they could regain control. The marketing department had no concept of computer time, demanding results from the web services company within hours, while Dreamworks, ALC, Burger King, and a team of lawyers continued to fine-tune and make changes to content. I don't believe I'd be exaggerating by saying that the IT director just *hated* Microsoft and its products with a passion (there's one in every crowd). This prejudice steered the company to technologies that had no immediate support structure set into place. ALC had attempted to internally convert the original NOS, application server, and dynamically generated web sites from one non-Microsoft platform (Linux/Jrun/Java) to another non-Microsoft platform (Novell/WebSphere/Java), but the problem was finding a consultant with the appropriate skill set who was available immediately.

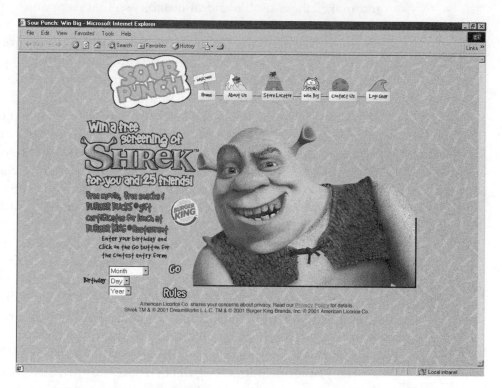

ALC, using an outside consulting firm, had searched and experimented, but with multiple dead ends. I walked into their building armed with a developer copy of Windows 2000 Server and asked for access to one of the targeted Hewlett-Packard machines and the designated interim IP address for the SourPunch.com web site. That was at about 1 P.M. By 5:30 P.M. (after some BIOS upgrading), I had installed and configured Windows 2000 Server, with Internet Information Server 5.0 set up to "serve" the new version of the SourPunch.com web site, including using Microsoft's Active Server Pages (ASP) to generate the dynamic components from a Microsoft Access 2000 database (later converted to Microsoft's more robust SQL Server to go live). ALC personnel were a bit bewildered at the rapid deployment. So much so, in fact, that they decided they needed to duplicate my procedures (using my notes) to confirm its viability. The new BIOS was already in place, so it took them less time.

The point of this example is that Microsoft offers widely used and understood tools that may be the best choice for small or midsize companies with limited time and resources (human and otherwise).

Features for Better Business

Typically, a networking environment opens up shared resources, such as files, printers, and an Internet connection. Windows 2000/ Server 2003 both provide a server configuration wizard (see Figures 3-2 and 3-3, respectively) that will get your file and print server up and running within minutes. Windows 2000 Server can also be a proxy server, controlling access not only to the Internet but also to internal resources.

The tools available in Windows 2000 Server and Windows Server 2003 that are new since Windows NT 4.0 are Remote Installation Services (RIS), which allows you to install software on multiple machines, unattended; the built-in Windows Terminal Services (WTS), which gives you access to the server's actual desktop from anywhere with a WTS client; the Group Policy Editor; and Plug and Play (as long as you have the drivers).

Other general capabilities include IP address filtering to limit the IP addresses that have access to the internal network, a web, FTP, Newsgroup, SMTP, and Application Server, all in one, using Internet Information Services (see Figure 3-4), and Internet Printing, which allows you to print to a printer at the office from any web browser, anywhere. You can assign disk quotas to specific personnel, integrate UNIX, Macs, and older Windows versions.

Figure 3-2
The Windows 2000
Server Configuration
Wizard

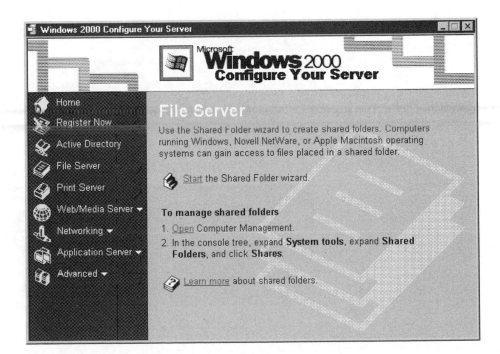

Figure 3-3
The Windows Server
2003 Configuration
Wizard

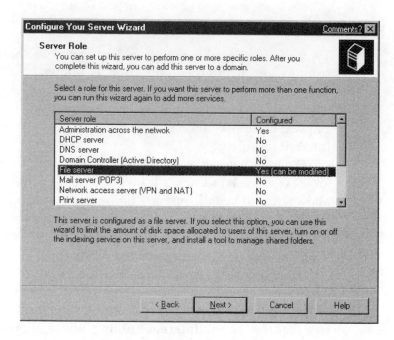

The list of some of the capabilities built into Windows 2000 Server and Windows Server 2003 is long. Table 3-1 has a few of the highlights.

Figure 3-4
Microsoft's Internet
Information Services
(IIS) is one of the most
popular web server
applications.

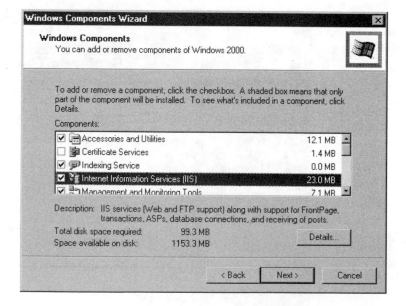

Component	Description
Active Directory	Microsoft's directory services, creating an environment that standardizes networking; uses domains.
AppleTalk network integration	Enables you to incorporate your Macintosh network.
Certificate Services	Built-in security for using public/private key encryption.
DHCP service	Dynamic Host Configuration Protocol assigns IP addresses automatically within a dynamic networking environment.
Disk Management	You can add hard drives, and then partition and format them through this application within the Administrative Tools/Computer Management part of the Microsoft Management Console (MMC).
Disk quotas	Enables you to limit the amount of disk space any individual is allowed on any system within the network.
Distributed File System (dfs)	Changes the appearance of physical locations of shared folders to become transparent to clients.
DNS service	The Domain Name Server (DNS) converts IP addresses such as 64.58.79.230 into a domain name like Yahoo.com. You can incorporate this naming convention within your own network environment.
Fault tolerance	Enables your system to continue functioning when part of the overall system fails, such as a disk failure, power outage, or corrupted operating system or system files, which can impact startup or even operations.
Group Policy	Enables you to create users who are members of groups (such as Power Users, Marketing, Accounting, and so on) and then determine the permissions for the entire group rather than for each individual.
Internet Authentication Service	Microsoft's version of a Remote Authentication Dial-In User Service (RADIUS) server, providing authentication for dial-in and virtual private networks (VPNs).

Table 3-1
A Few Capabilities of Windows 2000 Server and Windows Server 2003

Component	Description
Internet Protocol Security (IPSec)	Internet security that's based on the standards developed by the Internet Engineering Task Force (IETF).
Network and Dial-Up Connections	Using the server's network connection wizard, you can configure connections for shared Internet access, VPNs, dial-up connectivity, and routing.
Network Monitor	Enables you to monitor network activity, data paths, and so forth.
Remote Installation Services	Enables you to install an upgrade to all the workstations (and other servers) automatically, unattended.
Routing and Remote Access	A robust, customizable routing and remote access application.
Security configuration and analysis	A multitiered security architecture that includes access control, permissions, and sharing.
Smart Card setup	Use smart cards to lock up sensitive data or for login.
Telephony	Built-in support for integrating your overall communications systems, including video teleconferences.
Terminal Services	Enables you to open the server's desktop on any computer (with the appropriate client software) and manage the system remotely.
Virtual private network (VPN)	Enables you to create a secured path through the Internet that can be accessed only by select users.
Windows Backup	Automate the backup process using integrated software.

Table 3-1

A Few Capabilities of Windows 2000 Server and Windows Server 2003 *(continued)*

A Familiar Face

Besides all the wonderful attributes built into Windows 2000 and Server 2003, choosing Windows over Linux, Apple, or UNIX also offers intangible benefits. The fact that you are more than likely already working with the Windows interface helps a great deal (see Figure 3-5). I can't tell you how many times I've seen expert computer users move from one platform to another, only to become

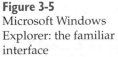

Figure 3-5
Microsoft Windows
Explorer: the familiar
interface

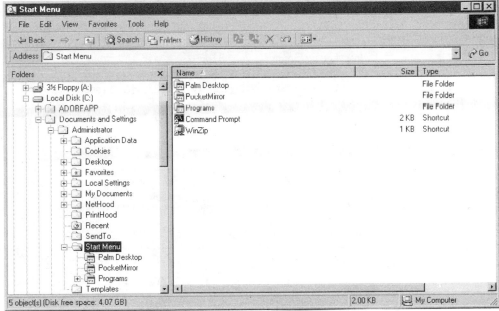

frustrated at its perceived inefficiencies; when the computer crashes, they usually blame it on the computer platform. I've done it myself, moving from Macintosh to Windows to Linux—each one has similar yet very different interfaces. In all three environments, windows pop up from a click of a mouse, but that doesn't mean they work the same way.

For example, to eject a floppy disk or CD-ROM from the Apple Macintosh, you can highlight the desktop icon that appears when you insert a new disk, and then choose Eject Disk from the Special menu or simply drag the desktop icon that appears to the trashcan. I've seen people repeatedly pushing the light on the CD-ROM drive on a Mac, cursing because they thought it was stuck. Linux requires any removable media to be "mounted" and "unmounted." Older versions of Linux required you to manually enter a command-line attribute to have the Linux operating system recognize a CD-ROM or floppy disk. This then, much like the Macintosh, places an icon on the desktop in order to remove the disk; you can choose "unmount" from a menu that appears when you right-click the icon. Linux also does not use lettered hard drives (see Figure 3-6), but instead uses a hierarchical directory structure within each partition (imagine Windows Explorer, without any specified hard drives).

The technology used to read data on hard drives is completely different between each operating system, whereas you would not be able to read, say, a Linux partition on a hard drive from either a Windows or Macintosh environment, without special

Figure 3-6
The Linux KDE
graphic user interface

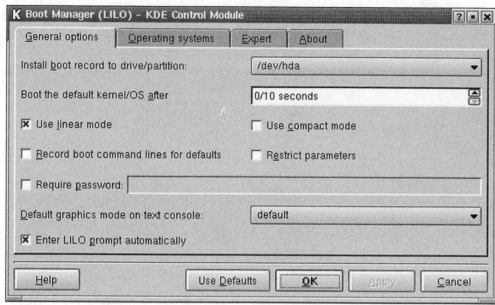

software and configuration. All three file systems do have the applications that are necessary to include the machines within a cross-platform environment, but in such an environment there are limitations with file naming conventions, encryption, and compression.

All three platforms run differently, like different models of automobiles. Whereas all automobiles have four wheels, windshields, steering wheels, and a dashboard, their interfaces, control panels, and engines are completely different. If you try to tune-up or configure a Chevy like a Mercedes Benz, you'll cause problems in the way the car operates. The same holds true for your platform; Microsoft's Windows environment is something you're already familiar with, and thus choosing Windows will benefit you in the installation, configuration, operation, and maintenance of the server.

Administrative Tools

Windows 2000 and Server 2003 come with a set of Administrative Tools that help you manage your server (see Figure 3-7), which is described in Table 3-2.

Microsoft Management Console

All of your system management tools are available in one group using the Microsoft Management Console (MMC) interface. The MMC standardizes an

Figure 3-7
Administrative Tools

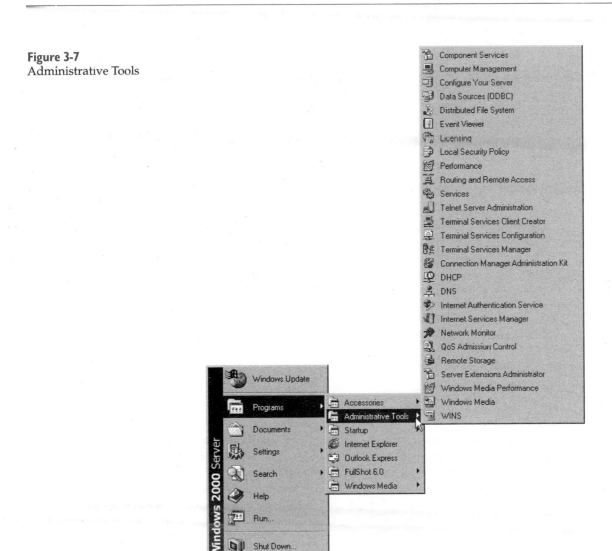

Administrative Tool	Brief Description
Component Services	Provides the ability to create a console of services for maintainability.
Computer Management	A very useful part of the Microsoft Management Console (MMC), giving you a view of many components and attributes.
Configure Your Server	The Server Configuration Wizard.
Data Sources (ODBC)	Sets up a link to a database using Open Database Connectivity.
Distributed File System (dfs)	Manages software distribution points used to install applications through the network.
Event Viewer	For managing and viewer audit logs for system, applications, and security.

Table 3-2
Descriptions of Available Administrative Tools

Administrative Tool	Brief Description
Licensing	For licensing the client access licenses for your Microsoft products.
Local Security Policy	Manages the security of the local computer.
Performance	Monitors performance for review.
Routing and Remote Access	Additional networking functionality and capabilities including network address translation (NAT) for Internet sharing.
Services	A complete list of all services running on the machine. This is where you can turn unused services off to tighten security.
Telnet Server Administration	If you don't plan on using Telnet, turn off the service as it can be a security vulnerability.
Terminal Services Client Creator	Creates the two floppy disks used to install a TS client on a workstation.
Terminal Services Configuration	Sets up your server as a Terminal Server.
Terminal Services Manager	Manages all your servers through Terminal Server.
Connection Manager Administration Kit	A network connection wizard and management console.
DHCP	Dynamic Host Configuration Protocol dynamically assigns IP addresses, subnet, router, and DNS servers to workstations.
DNS	Domain Name System resolves IP addresses to domain names.
Internet Authentication Service	Added authentication security and management.
Internet Services Manager	The management console for Internet Information Server (IIS).
Network Monitor	Captures network traffic data for review.
QoS Admission Control	Quality of Service mechanisms for data transmissions for Windows 2000 Server and Windows .NET Server. You can assign a specific amount of bandwidth to specific applications for better performance.
Remote Storage	Data management that will store infrequently accessed files to remote storage.
Server Extensions Administrator	Management of server-side installs for the web server.
Windows Media Performance	Monitors how streaming media is used on the server.
Windows Media	Manages and reviews media on the server.
WINS	Windows Internet Name Service for dynamically assigning IP addresses to NetBIOS computer names.

Table 3-2
Descriptions of Available Administrative Tools *(continued)*

MMC group (see Figure 3-8), called the Computer Management MMC, to support your most common management tasks. This list is customizable by entering the MMC and adding snap-in modules. To access the MMC, select Start | Run, type

Figure 3-8
The Computer
Management Console

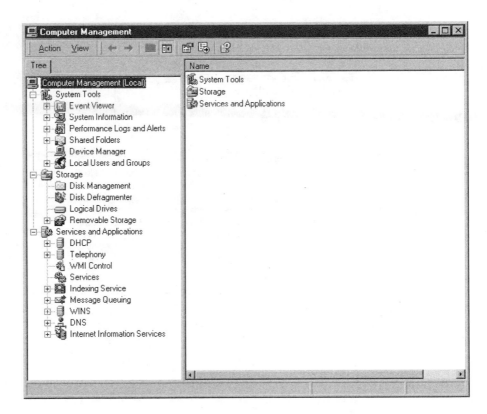

Figure 3-8
The Computer
Management Console

MMC, and click OK. A window pops up called Console1. From the menu at the top, choose CONSOLE. You then have a few predefined choices:

❏ C:\WINNT\system32\compmgmt

❏ C:\WINNT\system32\devmgmt

❏ C:\WINNT\system32\eventvwr

These represent, in order, Computer Management, Device Manager (discussed in Chapter 9), and Event Viewer (see Figure 3-9).

Scalability

Windows 2000 Server and Server 2003 include Active Directory (AD), Microsoft's directory service, much like Novell Directory Services (NDS), which standardizes distributed components over a network. While the typical file and print sharing setup in Windows 2000 Server and Windows Server 2003 is linked to workgroups, AD uses domains, much like the Internet, to create and maintain a networking environment. AD gives Windows 2000 Server and Windows Server 2003 the ability to create a domain enterprise environment, making the technology, location, and

Figure 3-9
Event Viewer

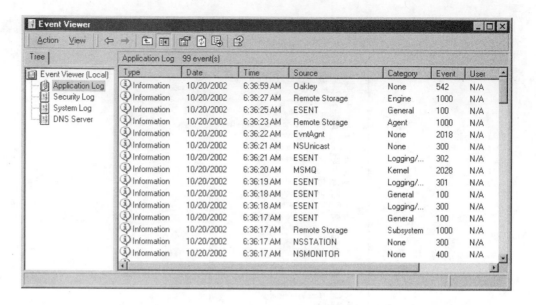

system invisible to the user. In addition, one of the most valuable capabilities of AD is the secure extension of network operations to the Internet, breaking down boundaries and making it easier to interconnect global offices. AD is the single access point of user accounts, workstations, servers, applications, and security, with an object-oriented approach to a hierarchical directory structure for simplified system administration.

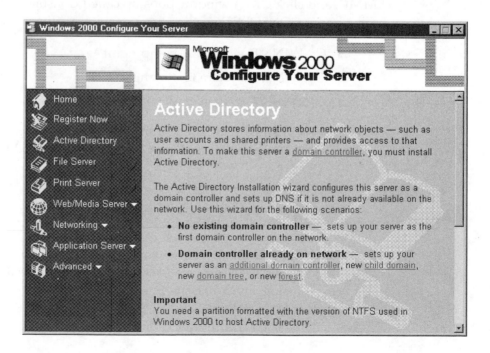

Expandability

Overall, Windows 2000 Server and Windows Server 2003 can deliver what you may need in a server. If your needs expand, so does Microsoft's arsenal of additional applications that can be purchased as add-on tools:

❑ **Application Center** For easy management of a group of servers

❑ **BizTalk Server** To build and deploy integrated business applications faster

❑ **Commerce Server** To build easy, e-commerce solutions from templates

❑ **Content Management Server** To build and easily manage content-driven web sites

❑ **Exchange Server** Offers 24/7 messaging and collaboration

❑ **Host Integration Server** To integrate the system from that new corporate acquisition, with legacy computing systems

❑ **Internet Security and Acceleration Server** A multilayered enterprise firewall

❑ **Mobile Information Server** To extend your enterprise and any mission-critical and line-of-business application to mobile devices

❑ **SharePoint Portal Server** To instantly create a component-based corporate intranet portal designed for corporate-wide collaboration

❑ **SQL Server** Microsoft's robust commercial database program

The majority of these server applications resides on top of Windows 2000 Server and are merely extensions of its capabilities. Most of these applications you may never need, but they are there, giving your system the potential extensions to keep up with your business.

Business Integration

The NOS is one of the resources that keep the wheels turning within your company. It may provide automated services that most of us take for granted (until it stops working), such as printer sharing, e-mail, and access to the Internet. These solutions intertwine within your company and become important components that keep it moving. Table 3-3 presents various business processes, and lists components of the Windows 2000 Server and Windows Server 2003 suite of applications that can help you handle those business processes, and describes how those components add value to those processes.

Item	Component	Advantages and Added Value
Geographic considerations	IIS, Terminal Server, Remote Desktop, Active Directory	Gives select authenticated access to partners, vendors, satellite offices, and remote administrators
Personalization	IIS, Active Directory, Local Security Policy	Offering/limiting user customization of workstation
Order processing/logistics *Inventory control* *Shipping* *Notification* *Status inquiry* *Policies* *Returns*	IIS	Centralization for better data communications and control
Customer service *Telephony integration*	IIS, Telephony, Terminal Server	Online 24/7 support
Multiple workstations *Maintainability* *Solution deployment*	Remote Installation Services (RIS)	Centralization of virus protection updates, patches, service packs, and so on, no matter where the workstation is located
System integration	Active Directory, DHCP, DNS, Network File & Print Services, IIS, dfs, TCP/IP	Interfaces to existing systems, creating a cross-platform network for access to resources previously unavailable due to location and/or platform
Security *Customer security* *Business security* *Physical security* *System security*	Granularity to Local and Group Policies, and/or Domain Policies with Active Directory; IIS, Microsoft Certificate Server (with Active Directory), Proxy, Secured Sockets Layer (SSL), and multiple security options	Multitiered authentication, permissions, and accessibility controls
Accountability *Reporting* *Maintenance* *Performance*	IIS	Tracking traffic, participation, login, and so on

Table 3-3
How Windows 2000 and 2003 Can Help Your Business

Item	Component	Advantages and Added Value
Scalability	Active Directory, IIS, Load Balancing, Clustering	Provides extendibility rather than replacement
Marketing	DHCP, Terminal Server, IIS	Plug and Play networking and remote accessibility to valuable data
Backup and recovery	Microsoft Backup, Active Directory	Disaster recovery

Table 3-3
How Windows 2000 and 2003 Can Help Your Business *(continued)*

Your server will change certain business processes, usually for the better. For example, as a manufacturer of widgets, you may have the simple yet all-important process of checking widget inventory. Typically, in a non-client/server environment, one or two people are in charge of inventory control. These people get constant stock queries synchronously and asynchronously via telephone, voice mail, e-mail, and fax, requesting inventory information. Upon receiving a call, they return to their desk and open some application that maintains inventory information, such as Microsoft Access or Excel—inexpensive yet effective. They update this application manually, periodically. They then provide that data and move on to the next caller or back to updating inventory. Anyone in the company has access to this information by simply calling these people and asking them for it. Whatever the procedure may be, there is a current process in place for this business requirement and set rules that govern. Today, any non-automated isolated process to access inventory data has room for improvement (see Figures 3-10 and 3-11), providing a means of giving people more dimensionality.

In a client/server environment using Windows 2000 Server or Windows Server 2003, the data within the Excel workbook or the Access database can be quickly made available to authenticated, authorized personnel and customers, through the ubiquitous web browser (currently a standard addition to any operating system). This can be done using IIS or Terminal Server (more on this in Chapters 13 and 14). Moreover, having a networking environment also opens up enterprise software possibilities for the future. Integrating each department can update the inventory automatically when a shipment arrives.

Baby Steps

Once you've chosen the network operating system, the first steps that I will show you (using Windows 2000 Server and Windows Server 2003) will be smaller ones, focusing on file, print (Chapter 10), and Internet sharing (Chapter 12). Then, in Chapter 13, I'll show you how to set up your own intranet web site and/or Internet web site.

Figure 3-10
Old-world
"silo" customer
relationship

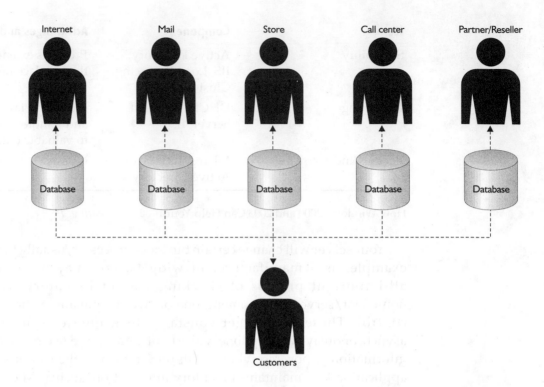

Figure 3-11
New integrated
enterprise

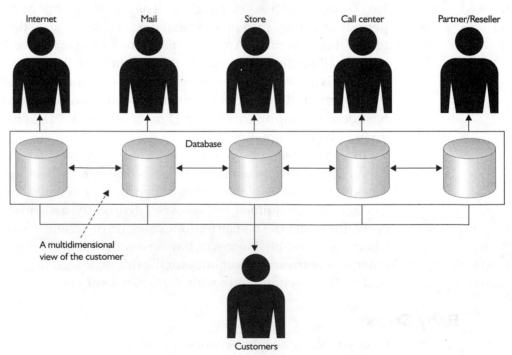

A few things to keep in mind when choosing your network operating system:

❏ Choose a network operating system you're familiar with, and if you've never installed and configured a server before, Windows 2000 Server and Windows Server 2003 will at least give you a familiar interface to start with.

❏ The network operating system should have plenty of functionality and security features.

❏ There should be software support, from an extensive online knowledge base to help diagnose problems, to the ability to actually call an expert for advice.

❏ Most non-automated business processes have room for improvement, and those improvements can be done using network operating system functionality and add-ons.

❏ If you're not familiar with creating a client/server environment, take it slow and ask for help.

Part II

Step-by-Step
Building Instructions

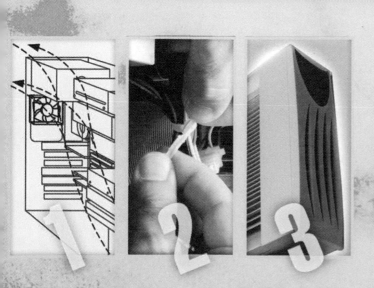

Chapter 4

The Heart of the Machine

Tools of the Trade

Precision screwdriver set
Needle-nose pliers
Antistatic sleeves
Heat sink compound
Electrostatic-free environment

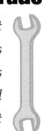

The components you'll need for this chapter include

❑ An ATX midtower chassis

❑ Minimum of 300-watt ATX power supply

❑ A central processing unit (CPU)

❑ A full-ATX motherboard (matching the CPU form factor)

❑ A compatible heat sink and cooling fan

The motherboard is a multilayered electronic device that is the heart of the server. It contains embedded circuitry and soldered components, and includes the ability to add on expansion parts. If you take a close look at a motherboard, you'll see a series of microscopic imprinted wire-like channels that carry data from one place to another. It's one of the most sophisticated and delicate components you'll be handling.

When you are looking for the motherboard, you have to know the type of central processing unit (CPU), also known as a "microprocessor," you've planned to purchase. Each CPU has a form factor that's unique to specific boards. Usually, you can tell the age of the system board by the CPU socket type. Older Pentium processors (75 to 200 MHz) are usually Socket 5 or Socket 7. The boards for these processors are cheap, typically ranging from $1 to $20. There is not much room, power, or compatibility with these systems. A 200 MHz computer has little use, other than a simple word processing workstation. Since they can't handle much of today's software, I do not recommend them for a server. The new Microsoft .NET Server has a minimal system requirement of 166 MHz as a processor speed, but that's recommended only if you're planning to take a nap between mouse clicks. Server applications require more power; I wouldn't drop below a minimal processor speed of 550 MHz, and at least a 100 MHz FSB. Thus, I suggest staying away from any motherboards that are pre-Socket 7 and stick with either Socket A or Socket 370.

The CPU and Motherboard: AMD vs. Intel

In the early 1990s, Intel chairman Andy Grove and his team at Intel decided to bypass the computer manufacturers of Intel's microprocessors. The "Intel Inside" marketing campaign, featuring the metallic-suited character, pushed AMD into the background. This simple yet very effective marketing campaign forced the original equipment manufacturers (OEMs) to buy Intel, because the end consumers demanded "Intel Inside." However, for our purposes, AMD's microprocessors are a better bargain because they're not only less expensive than the Intel Pentium or Celeron, but also faster. The actual CPU *clock speed* refers to the oscillator pulses per second, which sets the tempo for the processor. Clock speed is measured in *megahertz (MHz)*, millions of pulses per second, or *gigahertz (GHz)*, billions of pulses per second. Intel and AMD offer competitive clock speeds.

Although clock speed can make a difference in computer "power," that doesn't necessarily equate to better performance. If you upgrade your 1 GHz processor to a 2 GHz processor, but leave only 128MB of RAM and use an 8x CD-ROM drive and a 5400 RPM hard drive, you'll see little difference. What really makes the difference is the type and speed of your CPU; its bus architecture (more on this later, in the section "Jumpers"); the amount of RAM; and the type of data instruction.

Remember that hardware like hard drives and CD/DVD-ROMs all work in milliseconds while your RAM works in nanoseconds. For example, older hard drives have "average seek time" or "access time" of about 10 milliseconds. Seek time is the amount of time that it takes the actuator to position the read and write heads to execute a local request between tracks. If the hard drive is new, with little use and data, the hard drive can "find" that data along adjacent tracks and you can have a seek time of about one millisecond. However, a heavily used drive must write new data where it can find space. That's sometimes randomly spread out where you've deleted periodically saved data. So, the hard drive needs to find a number of bits and pieces randomly saved and then read them, piece them together, and deliver them as a whole, which can take up to 9 milliseconds, even with today's hard drives.

There's also the rotation latency, which is the amount of time it takes for a hard drive to spin into action once it's found all the data bits. That's measured in revolutions per minute (RPM). The relationship between Rotation Latency and RPM is also measured in milliseconds. Typically, a 7200 RPM hard drive will take about 4 to 5 milliseconds to spin into action—on top of the seek time.

A millisecond is slow compared to the speed of the RAM and the CPU. Typical RAM has an access time of six nanoseconds, which is about a million times faster than a typical hard drive; theoretically, a 1GHz CPU could execute about 1 million instructions during that same time period. Therefore, if you're building a file server, for example, which will be used specifically for storing files onto a hard drive, it doesn't make sense to buy the fastest CPU on the market because it'll sit there and twiddle its thumbs waiting for the electrical-mechanical hard drive to spin up.

Disconnect Power

Whenever you're working on the motherboard, always pull out the power cord from the power supply. Many power supplies, and motherboards, retain power after the system is shut down; some for several seconds, others at all times. Either way, no matter how long, or how little the current, changing any component and any jumper settings while power is flowing through the motherboard can cause serious damage!

Motherboards have Intel- or AMD-specific cavities. The 1GHz AMD CPU uses a "Socket A," while Intel uses the "Socket 370."

Socket A

This is unique to the newer AMD Athlon and Duron processors, with clock speeds over 1.9 GHz. The front-side bus speed is an impressive 200 MHz, as opposed to the 100 MHz bus speed of the popular Intel Celeron (up to 1.6 GHz).

Socket 370

This is a popular socket, with Pentium III, Celeron, and even Cyrix having available processors with speeds upward of 1.3 GHz.

There are many choices available in system boards for these three CPU models, but always make sure that they are specific to these sockets. There are older Athlons for a completely different "Slot A" socket and an older Pentium and Celeron for a "Slot 1" socket (refer to Chapter 1).

I've purchased and tested several processors, and dozens of motherboards. This wasn't a benchmarked speed test, but rather a compatibility and usability test. I simply swapped processors I purchased from various locations—eBay, Micro Center, NewEgg.com, and so on—with a similar mix of form factor–compatible motherboards. My hands-on research and testing of these components will save you loads of time. My goal was to find the processor/motherboard combinations that gave me the least amount of incompatibility problems. These issues included specific memory speed, type, or even little things like the proper connections for the power switch, power LED, fans, and speaker.

When purchasing the processor and motherboard separately, the AMD Athlon and Duron seemed to be the most adaptable. This could be due to good luck with my choice of boards; but I tested a few Celerons (the least expensive of the Intel line) on several system boards, and I had to consider much more than the socket size. We don't need to get into the details, but if you decide to go the Intel route, make sure that the motherboard matches the type of CPU—exactly.

TIPS OF THE TRADE

PPGA vs. FC-PPGA

There are two types of Socket 370 Intel CPUs, beyond the two models (Pentium and Celeron). These differences can cause some confusion and grief if you haven't considered this fact when buying your components. The first type is the PPGA (plastic pin grid array) design. The PPGA Celeron puts the silicon core of the microchip facing down toward the computer motherboard, which must support the VRM 8.2 specifications. The other design is the FC-PPGA (flip-chip plastic pin grid array), which flips the silicon core on the other side. If you've picked up one of these Celerons, the motherboard must be FC-PPGA or VRM 8.4 compliant.

Front-Side Bus Speed

Essentially, an AMD 1 GHz Duron, with a bus speed of 200 MHz, would run faster and have higher performance than the Intel Celeron 1 GHz, with only half the bus speed. An FSB speed is what synchronizes the processor with your memory and AGP slot (for your video adapter). Therefore, at 200 MHz, you have double the communications speed between the three. The newer Pentium 4 and AMD XP CPUs have an FSB of 400 MHz and 533 MHz, respectively. Incidentally, the reason for my lack of interest in the Intel CPUs is that even used, they tend to be more expensive components. Again, if our $400 budget is not an issue, go for it, but make sure you have the right motherboards for those CPUs. You can get more information on that at www.motherboards.org.

Choosing the Right Motherboard

Many of the newer system boards include automated CPU configuration, which eliminates complex jumper settings (described later this chapter, in the section "Jumpers"). For example, my Tyan Trinity KT s2390 includes automatic CPU recognition (with no jumpers and switches to adjust), and even though the documentation states a maximum processor support of 800 MHz, it immediately recognized my 900 MHz AMD Duron without any trouble. The only configuration that I needed to perform was to connect the chassis cables to the control panel jumpers, which usually consists of the connections for a power switch, power LED, hard drive LED (to show that the hard drive is "thinking"), speaker, and reset switch.

All the Socket A and Socket 370 motherboards have an ATX form factor. You can also purchase motherboards with most of what you would ever need built onboard. In Figure 4-1, the ATX motherboard (bottom) has built-in connections for the keyboard, mouse, printer, audio extensions and two serial ports. Many of the older-style "AT" motherboards (top) only provided an onboard connection for a keyboard. The mouse is connected via an add-on serial port or expansion card.

Figure 4-1
The older "Advanced Technology" or AT motherboard, at top, and the "extended AT," or ATX motherboard at the bottom

TIPS OF THE TRADE

Motherboard Parts

When deciding on a motherboard, here are a few tips that will save you the grief I've lived through:

❏ Buy a motherboard (new or used) only from a reputable source that can provide you with some documentation and/or support.

I purchased a used, obscure Socket 7 motherboard for a server I built from Douglas Kankiewicz, an eBay seller who was more than happy to help me with my specific CPU and RAM configuration. The obscurity and age of the motherboard made it next to impossible to find adequate documentation to understand how to configure the many jumper settings. After several e-mails, he helped me discover that the problem I was having was how I was configuring the jumpers; I was reading the jumper numbering upside-down. My jumper settings were backward, so nothing worked. This brings me to my next tip.

❏ If you do choose to purchase a used motherboard, make sure the product you buy comes with documentation; not everyone is as nice as Douglas is. The manual is a necessary resource when you're manually trying to configure the board to recognize your CPU and memory speed. It's even more important when troubleshooting, if any problems arise.

❏ A great way to avoid compatibility issues is to purchase a CPU/motherboard combo kit. This somewhat guarantees that the processor and motherboard are compatible and will work together out of the box. You can buy a 1 GHz AMD Duron CPU

TIPS OF THE TRADE

and a compatible full-ATX motherboard for under $100. If our $400 budget isn't an issue for you, you can pick up the new AMD XP or Pentium 4 combo kits for about $200–$400.

❏ Select a full-ATX motherboard, not a micro-ATX version (for a visual comparison, refer to Figure 1-3 in Chapter 1). The TYAN Trinity KT motherboard I purchased will not fit inside a micro-ATX chassis, which usually fits a motherboard that's only 8×9 inches or less (full-ATX is about 9×12 or 13 inches). A micro-ATX motherboard is not extendable, and thus is limited. Micro-ATX motherboards usually have only two PCI slots, which, inside a server, you'd fill up immediately with two network adapters, leaving no room for anything else.

❏ Do not buy any motherboard "as is" from any place or anyone. We're talking about a multilayered electronic device that may not ever boot up for you and would be worthless. The minimal guarantee for online auctions is "not DOA," which stands for "not dead on arrival." Motherboards sold "as is" are intended for parts on the component level. Don't buy one expecting it to work in a system.

❏ Make sure that the motherboard BIOS can handle the speed of the CPU you have in mind. An easy way to determine the maximum speed is to check online documentation. Many motherboard manufacturers are from Asia, so don't be surprised if their first web site is in Kanji (Chinese letters). Most of them have English versions of their web sites—just look for the British or U.S. flag, or an "English" label.

❏ Make sure the motherboard takes either 168-pin DIMM or 184-pin DDR memory. DIMM goes up to 133 MHz maximum speed, while the newer DDR jumps to over 266 MHz (but, again, we're on a budget). The DIMM modules are usually a better bargain (see Chapter 5 for more details on memory).

So, to summarize what you're looking for are the following: a full-ATX chassis case; a full-ATX motherboard with a Socket A for either a 900 MHz to 1.2 GHz AMD Athlon or Duron; or a full-ATX motherboard with a Socket 370 for an Intel Pentium III or Celeron processor. Whichever you choose, it must accept 168-pin DIMM or 184-pin DDR memory modules (more on this in Chapter 5).

Jumpers

When today's motherboards automatically configure the CPU, through their Plug-and-Play capabilities, those invisible adjustments include setting the bus speed frequency, core voltage, and the multiplier ratio. On older motherboards, this type of manual configuration was done using jumper settings. A jumper is a pair of prongs that are electrical contact points set into the computer motherboard or an adapter card (see Figure 4-2). By placing a small plastic shunt on a set of contact pins, you could close a circuit and change the way the motherboard operated.

Figure 4-2
The numbered pins of a jumper block are critical to successful configuration.

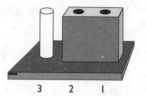

3   2   1

Motherboard Bus Speed and the CPU

The bus speeds for older motherboards are usually 66 MHz or 100 MHz. Most of your newer boards begin at 133 MHz and go up from there, depending on the type of RAM you use (see the next chapter for more on RAM). The FSB speed is the clock rate speed at which the processor communicates with memory and the AGP expansion card, so the faster the speed; the better the system handles heavy 3-D graphics and video. In order for a manually configured motherboard to work with a clock rate speed of 800 MHz or 1 GHz CPU, you need to first make sure you have the right type of processor and that it works at the same bus speed as the CPU (for example, both work at 133 MHz), and adjust the jumper settings as determined within the product documentation. This is not a mandatory requirement, as there are motherboards that will adjust for different speeds, but I've discovered that some motherboard manufacturers recommend this synchronization.

The Core Multiplier Ratio

You also need to know the core multiplier ratio, which is a configuration that sets the motherboard to run the bus speed at the clock speed of the CPU. The motherboard must know how much the bus speed needs to be "multiplying" to reach the CPU clock rate speed. For example, the multiplier setting on a motherboard running an AMD Duron 1 GHz processor with a 200 MHz bus speed would be ×5, or 200 MHz × 5 = 1,000 MHz or 1 GHz. On a non-automated board, this would be done through a specific jumper block, as shown in Figure 4-3.

When you set a shunt, you place a plug on the prongs that completes a contact. Jumper settings tell the computer motherboard what the current CPU setting should be, if it does not have the capability to do it automatically. Computers come with the jumpers preset, with instructions so that you can reset the jumpers for new equipment.

Figure 4-3
A set of jumpers on a motherboard

Small charts are silk-screened onto motherboards for your convenience. Many times, you need to go digging on the Web for this information; usually, you must visit the motherboard manufacturer's web site for a similar set of tables and visit the CPU manufacturer's web site for compatibility issues, such as whether a motherboard with a 66 MHz bus speed will work with an 800 MHz processor.

The Highest Core Multiplier Ratio

You can determine the maximum CPU clock speed a motherboard can handle by checking the bus speed times the highest core multiplier ratio. For example, a motherboard with a maximum bus speed of 66 MHz and a core multiplier of ×8 would have a maximum CPU compatibility of 528 MHz. Therefore, the fastest CPU it can handle is a 500 MHz or maybe a 533 MHz CPU.

What will happen if you get it wrong? Nothing will happen—no boot, no beeps—nothing but the spinning of the CPU fan. Jumper misconfiguration can also damage the motherboard, so be careful and double-check your findings before you set a board to a core voltage that is too high.

Core Voltage Regulator

The second set of important jumpers, also appearing in older motherboards, is the core voltage regulator. The core voltage is the amount of circuit that runs through the CPU. A wrong core voltage setting can cause serious problems. If it's set too low, then your system may hang or stop booting consistently. If you have the core voltage set too high, your CPU will run hot, thus reducing the life expectancy of the processor. The proper core voltage setting is something your CPU documentation will clarify, either the documentation you've received with the CPU or documentation on the manufacturer's web site. However, instead of downloading the "technical specifications" of a CPU (with all its complex engineering data), check the frequently asked questions (FAQ) or "quick guide" first.

Coming to Life

I've configured and set a multitude of motherboards, and I can tell you that when a motherboard comes to life (even if its just the spinning CPU fan), after lying silent through many attempts, it's like music to your ears. At this point, without any RAM, a motherboard wouldn't be able to boot up, but this is how the motherboard and CPU come to life.

TIME CHECK

Although motherboard documentation may suggest clearing the CMOS memory by switching the CMOS jumper for about 10 seconds, I've found a minimum of 60 seconds is more effective across many systems.

Power-On Self Test

When you turn on your computer, before the operating system boots up, the system needs to determine whether its drives, memory, keyboard, and other hardware are functioning properly before it even begins to look for an operating system. This process is called a power-on self test (POST). This is the initial set of diagnostic testing sequences, run by the basic input/output system (BIOS).

CMOS (complementary metal-oxide semiconductor) is a very low-power semiconductor technology used in most of today's computer microchips, including the BIOS chip, an example of which is shown in Figure 4-5. CMOS stores the BIOS information (the terms often are used interchangeably) and is powered by a battery that usually lasts about three to seven years. All motherboards have a CMOS jumper that allows you to reset the CMOS memory to its default settings. The CMOS jumper is one you'll find on every motherboard—typically, with proper settings silk-screened onboard (see Figure 4-4).

In the event your CMOS memory becomes corrupt by misconfiguration or noncompatible hardware, you can force a "reset" of the CMOS to its factory default settings by switching the setting on the CMOS jumper.

Figure 4-4
Many motherboards have the proper procedure for clear CMOS silk-screened directly on the board.

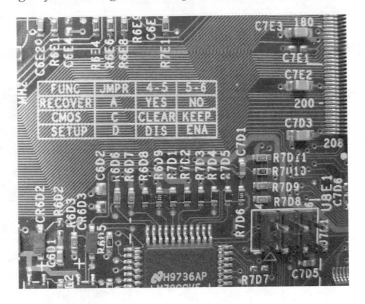

If you're working with a motherboard that isn't reading specified hardware (100 MHz × 7 = 700 MHz), and no matter what you try, it just isn't working, then clear CMOS, usually by moving a jumper from pins 1 and 2 to pins 2 and 3 (see Figure 4-6). Although the motherboard manual may suggest that 10 seconds will do, I've found that 60 seconds, plus, is really the trick.

Figure 4-5
An AWARD BIOS chip on the motherboard

HEADS UP!

Pull Out That Battery

If resetting the CMOS jumper doesn't clear the CMOS memory, try pulling out the CMOS battery for about 60 seconds, and then replacing it. Make sure to pull out the power cord from the power supply. See Figure 4-6 for a picture of a CMOS jumper.

Figure 4-6
The Clear CMOS jumper is typical of most every motherboard (behind the battery).

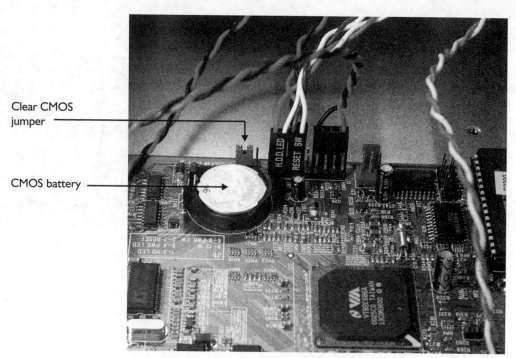

Clear CMOS jumper

CMOS battery

To give you a better idea of how to configure the CPU frequency, let's look at an example. Figure 4-7 shows the jumpers for the bus speed frequency, and Figure 4-8 shows a set for the multiplier. The documentation for the motherboard indicates that to configure the proper frequency for a 700 MHz processor, you need to set the JFREQ1 jumper to 100 MHz. That's done by setting the four rows of jumpers to CLOSE, OPEN, CLOSE, OPEN. The yellow jumpers have "closed" the circuits of the first two pins and the third set of pins. The six rows of jumpers for the core multiplier need to be set at 7.0, or shunts closing the connection on the fourth and sixth set of jumpers, shown here:

Status	OPEN	OPEN	OPEN	CLOSE	OPEN	CLOSE
Jumper Row Set	1–2	3–4	5–6	7–8	9–10	11–12

Figure 4-7
The jumpers for the
bus speed frequency

Bus speed frequency jumper block

Figure 4-8
The jumpers for the
core multiplier

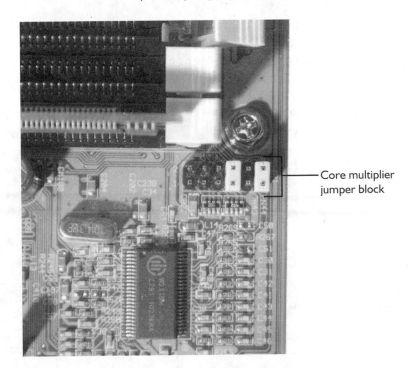

Core multiplier
jumper block

You can get a great deal on an older motherboard with a top CPU speed of
1 GHz, but you'll need to configure it manually. If you decide to go this route,
there are a few things you should keep in mind:

❑ Make sure it comes with documentation, even if it's silk-screened
onto the motherboard itself.

❏ Research the board thoroughly before buying, checking particularly for compatibility issues.

❏ I've seen the jumpers labeled JP13, JP14, JP15, and JP16 in the manual, but on the board itself, they appear as JP13, JP16, JP15, and JP14. It was confusing to say the least and most likely a breakdown in language translation. The three items to clarify are the bus speed, the multiplier ratio, and the CPU type and core voltage regulator. If you get your hands on this information, you can easily change the shunts with a pair of tweezers or needle-nose pliers.

The systematic instructions on installing the motherboard, CPU, heat sink, and cooler fan inside your computer case follow.

Installation Instructions

To successfully install your motherboard and CPU within the ATX chassis (as shown in Figure 4-9), you need a Phillips screwdriver, a pair of needle-nose pliers (valuable when handling some smaller components), and an electrostatic-free workstation.

Figure 4-9
The ATX chassis with a secured ATX motherboard, with onboard video and sound

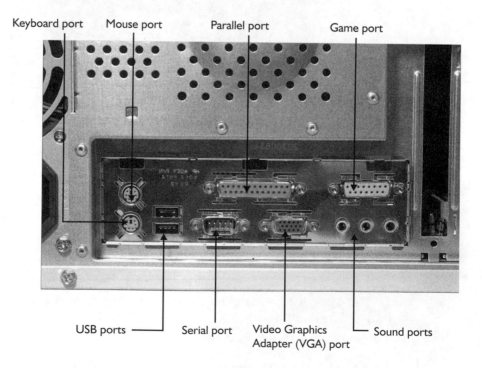

Keyboard port   Mouse port   Parallel port   Game port

USB ports   Serial port   Video Graphics Adapter (VGA) port   Sound ports

The ATX computer chassis has the form factor of the motherboard, as shown in Figure 4-9. ATX improves the original AT motherboard design, which has a single hole used for the keyboard, with the rest of the components having separate locations. The AT motherboard is rotated, shifting the layout by 90 degrees, thus offering more room for expansion cards.

Many motherboards have a label that makes pin 1 easy to recognize (as shown in Figure 4-10), but sometimes you'll need to check the documentation to find "pin 1" and continue with the installation process.

Figure 4-10
The Socket 370 and Socket A CPUs both have a pin 1 that needs to be positioned correctly in order to successfully install your CPU without damage.

To install your CPU, simply lift up the lever pin alongside the socket. This opens up the pinholes for your CPU.

Make sure you've aligned pin 1 on the CPU with pin 1 on the socket on the motherboard. The pins on the bottom of the CPU should easily drop into the pinholes if they align correctly. Once the CPU is in place, pull down the lever pin and snap it back into position, thus locking the CPU into its socket. Apply some heat sink compound (a few dollars at Radio Shack) to the processor. This is to help dissipate the heat generated by an active CPU.

The bottom of the heat sink gives you a guide to how the units attach it to the CPU. One side of the bottom of the heat sink is inverted to fit the raised-bar side of the motherboard CPU socket.

Two hooks that connect on opposite sides secure the heat sink and cooler fan. First, clamp the smaller loop of the heat sink onto the protruding hook on the side of the socket. Keep in mind that the beveled portion of the heat sink fits on top of the bar side of the socket.

This can be a bit tricky, but clamping the loop onto the hook before setting it onto the CPU makes it easier.

Now comes the most dangerous part of the installation! You need to get the loop on the other side, down and onto the pictured hook, without causing any damage to the motherboard. One slip and your screwdriver will hit the motherboard hard enough to damage the microcircuitry.

The best way is to take a small flat-head screwdriver, and gently push down on the loop until the heat sink clamp hooks on. If this isn't working for you and your heat sink and cooler fan connector, don't get too anxious: the screwdriver may slip off and scratch the motherboard (not good). You may want to grab needle-nose pliers and, once you've pushed the loop down as close as possible, push the loop onto the hook from the outside.

After the heat sink and cooler fan are securely in place, you need to connect the fan's power cord in the appropriate socket on the motherboard. Typically, the three-pin socket is labeled for a CPU fan and is designed to accept only the fan connector.

You've now successfully installed your CPU!

Figure 4-11
The fully and successfully installed CPU

Now you need to install the motherboard into the ATX case. To do this, you need to screw in the standoffs that came with the case. If you picked up the TNS International case that I have (or comparable), it actually has the holes labeled for either standard ATX or micro-ATX. Count how many holes are in your motherboard and screw in the standoffs where labeled for a full-ATX motherboard.

After you've screwed all the standoffs into their appropriate holes to accommodate your motherboard, insert the whole motherboard into the chassis case. Simply follow the form factor, pushing the outside ports through their place in the case.

Secure the motherboard with the appropriate screws supplied with the chassis case.

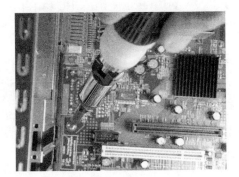

The motherboard connector (sometimes referred to as a control panel) comes with the following connection cables:

❑ A power switch, to turn the computer on

❑ A reset switch, for when you need to do a hard reboot of the system

❑ A power LED connector, which illuminates when the power is on

❑ An H.D.D. LED, which illuminates when there's activity on the hard drive

❑ A speaker connector

These connections are different on every motherboard, and if labels are not included on the motherboard itself, the manual will have an easy diagram to follow. A few other connectors may be included for a lock, sleep button, and sleep LED.

The last connection is for the power. If you wish to connect it to the motherboard and turn it on to validate that the motherboard is getting power (usually by witnessing the CPU fan spinning), then go ahead. However, without memory or (if you have this same motherboard) a video adapter card, you won't be able to boot it up until you have followed the instructions in Chapter 5.

The memory will "hold" the initial boot sequence, and the video adapter will let you see what's happening during the boot process. If you do plug in the power connector to the motherboard now, leave the power cord out of the chassis power supply until you're done. This is very important, since some motherboards retain power, even when the power is off. Adding and subtracting components to a motherboard with power flowing through it will damage the motherboard or the components.

The older "AT" power connector and chassis power switch (shown next) are not compatible with any ATX motherboards and use a different scheme for powering up the motherboard.

**TESTING
1-2-3**

The computer chassis, motherboard, and CPU all conform to a specific and unique form factor. It's important not only to match the form factors, but also to guarantee that all components are compatible. A recommended combination includes an AMD 1 GHz + processor and a full-ATX Socket A motherboard.

A few suggestions and precautions to be aware of follow:

❑ Use an electrostatic-free environment.

❑ Be sure your motherboard comes with or has documentation available.

❑ Avoid anything marked "as is" when purchasing used motherboards.

❑ Make sure the motherboard can handle your chosen CPU clock speed.

❑ Whenever working with any electronic component, unplug the power cord.

Chapter 5

Memory and Video

Tools of the Trade

Anti-static sleeves
Electrostatic-free environment
Compatible RAM modules (minimum of 512MB preferred)
AGP or PCI video adapter

In Chapter 4, I touched on how each component has its own speed limit. Hard drives and CD-ROM drives work in milliseconds, or one millionth of a second, and 1 GHz CPU can support upward of one million instructions during the time it takes a hard drive to spin into action. Memory works at one billionth of a second—nanoseconds, not milliseconds—so whatever the instruction, if it resides in RAM, it'll open up almost instantly, as opposed to waiting for it to be read off the hard drive. This is why you can never have enough RAM.

Working at the Speed of Thought

Computers have many different types of memory, used for different purposes, but all working together to make the interaction work seamlessly and faster.

The system's first access to memory happens even before the operating system boots up. The computer BIOS (basic input/output system) is stored in CMOS (complementary metal-oxide semiconductor) memory, which is powered by a lithium 3-volt battery when the computer is shut down (refer to Chapter 4). The small CMOS

95

memory chip enables the computer to retain your basic configuration information (date, time, and so forth) while your computer is turned off, so that your configuration is the same the next time you turn on the power.

CMOS is *nonvolatile memory*, which also includes all forms of read-only memory (ROM), such as programmable read-only memory (PROM), erasable programmable read-only memory (EPROM), electrically erasable programmable read-only memory (EEPROM), and flash memory. Typically, a battery powers nonvolatile memory, sometimes referred to as *nonvolatile RAM (random access memory)*. The BIOS EEPROM (see Figure 5-1) holds just enough data to do a self-test, then load the operating system into RAM when you boot up the computer.

Random Access Memory

Although RAM is stored inside a microchip, it doesn't permanently write itself to that chip or any other hardware. It's a virtual place where all software is first loaded after you boot up the computer or double-click an icon. This makes it easily accessible by the CPU. RAM is very important for your computer's performance, simply because reading and writing to RAM is much faster than reading and writing to the hard drive. Unlike the hard drive, RAM only exists while the power is on. When the computer shuts down, all the data held in RAM disappears. When you boot up your computer, all of your software (including your operating system) is loaded once again into RAM from your hard drive.

Figure 5-1
The Award BIOS chip

Two of today's most popular flavors of RAM are the 168-pin dual in-line memory module (DIMM) and the 184-pin double data rate (DDR) module. Both are considered synchronous dynamic RAM (SDRAM). A DIMM is double the original 30-pin and 72-pin single in-line memory module (SIMM). Each one of these iterations has RAM chips soldered onto a small circuit board with pins that connect to the motherboard. DDR improves memory clock speed by doubling output.

HEADS UP!

Numbered Memory Slots

The memory slots on a motherboard are numbered. Make sure that a single module is in the first slot, typically labeled BANK1 or 0, or DIMM or DDR 1 or 0.

RAM 101

There's a limit to the amount of RAM you can add to any system. The more memory slots (known officially as *banks*) that a system has, the better; but if you're going to use only one initially, make sure you insert it in the first slot—they're usually numbered beginning with 0 or 1, and labeled either as Bank0, Bank1, Bank 2, or DIMM1, DIMM2, DIMM3, and so on. If you've mistakenly placed the single module in a bank other than the first one, the system will most likely not see any RAM and not boot, or give an alarm (usually a continuous beeping, once every second).

Think Inside the Box

It's very important to stick with the system's design bus speed and not mix 66 MHz, 100 MHz, and 133 MHz flavors of SDRAM, or 266 MHz, 333 MHz, and 800 MHz and up of DDR. If you are successful in booting up the computer with a concoction of RAM, it will most likely eventually become unstable.

Most PCs allow you to add additional RAM modules, but up to a limit. My ThinkPad i1300 has a maximum memory capacity of 192MB, while my new HP Pavilion can be expanded up to 1GB. At 192MB, the ThinkPad was more than adequate to handle simple Microsoft Word documents, but it struggled with most graphics files and any Word document loaded with images. The machine slowed to a crawl at times, and if I configured Word to auto save (always a good idea), then a 50MB document would take up to five minutes to save. The lack of memory resources during this RAM-hungry process also locks out any other attempt at using the machine. Although you won't be working on client-based applications on a server, the applications that serve the many, rather than the one, can be even more demanding as more and more requests hit the server.

Crucial.com

One of the best ways of finding compatible RAM for your system or motherboard is through the Crucial Memory Selector at Crucial.com. This provides a documented guarantee of RAM compatibility with your motherboard.

The Pagefile

The reason my ThinkPad was struggling is simple: if you're opening a 50MB Word document, the system opens it the quickest way—in RAM. If there's not enough RAM, then the system begins writing to the hard drive in the form of a *pagefile*, an allocated space on the hard disk that is used as an extension of RAM. If you open a file that requires more space than readily available, the system will begin to write any idle data to the hard drive. This process itself can eat up RAM and time, depending on the operating system, processor, and how fast your hard drive can write, which, as I've mentioned, is far slower than RAM. How long does it usually take to copy a 50MB file to your hard drive? The only advantage to a pagefile is that it keeps the data in one large file, which makes accessing it later faster than trying to recollect it all from its original locations, which could be scattered all over the disk. Servers that are running many server-side applications also add more "services," or background apps, that can be memory hogs. These services monitor the functionality of the programs, preparing them for further instructions. In the event an instruction comes in, and there's not enough RAM to support it, the server will begin writing to the hard drive, effectively bringing the effort down to a crawl.

At 512MB of RAM (on my new HP), my documents can auto-save in the background, giving me more room to multitask.

The "random access" of RAM is a misnomer that originally distinguished it from memory read off drives or tapes. RAM is not as much "random" as it is "linear," with the ability to directly access any storage location. RAM is organized and controlled for the most efficiency in writing and reading directly to specific locations.

Video RAM

For hardware graphics accelerators, with their own exclusive video RAM, the technology is similar to your system RAM, except that while the processor writes data into video RAM, the video controller can simultaneously read from RAM to refresh the graphics display. Older hardware graphics accelerators shared memory with the system memory, essentially stealing a percentage to improve the video performance. Today, an Accelerated Graphics Port (AGP)

Memory and RAM

There are many speeds, sizes, and flavors of memory. The two most popular, DDR (left column in Table 5-1) and SDRAM (right column in Table 5-1), include registered, nonregistered, error correction code (ECC), ECC registered, Parity, and Nonparity. ECC and Parity Checking both examine the memory for errors. While Parity Checking will only see the errors and report them, ECC will see them and correct them, instantly.

Registered memory is RAM that will hold and "register" the data for one clock cycle before passing to the motherboard. This process increases reliability (and the cost), and is typically used in high-end servers handling mission-critical applications, where proper handling of data is essential.

You must take all of these factors into account when purchasing RAM for your motherboard. The motherboard must be able to use the size and features of the RAM; otherwise, it may not work at all, leaving you with a silent motherboard, and unusable RAM.

DDR (Double Data Rate) PC2100–266 MHz   SDRAM 168-Pin PC133–133 MHz

DDR (Double Data Rate) PC2100–266 MHz	SDRAM 168-Pin PC133–133 MHz
DDR 128MB	PC133 64MB
DDR 256MB	PC133 128MB
DDR 512MB	PC133 256MB
DDR 128MB ECC	PC133 512MB
DDR 256MB ECC	PC133 ECC 128MB 16×72 nonregistered
DDR 512MB ECC	PC133 ECC 256MB 32×72 nonregistered
DDR 256MB ECC registered	PC133 ECC 256MB 32×72 registered
DDR 512MB ECC registered	PC133 ECC 512MB 64×72 nonregistered
DDR 1000MB ECC registered	PC133 ECC 512MB B 64×72 registered
DDR PC2700 333 MHz	PC133 ECC 1000MB 64×72 registered
DDR 128MB 333 MHz	PC100 SDRAM 168-pin 100 MHz
DDR 256MB 333 MHz	PC100 64MB
DDR 512MB 333 MHz	PC100 128MB
RAMBUS(RIMM) 800 MHz	PC100 256MB
RAMBUS 64MB	PC100 512MB
RAMBUS 128MB	PC100 512MB registered
RAMBUS 128MB	PC100 ECC 64MB
RAMBUS 256MB	PC100 ECC 128MB
RAMBUS 256MB	PC100 ECC 256MB
RAMBUS 512MB	PC100 ECC 512MB
RAMBUS 512MB	PC100 ECC 512MB registered
RAMBUS 128MB ECC	PC66 ECC 64MB
RAMBUS 256MB ECC	PC66 ECC 128MB
RAMBUS 256MB ECC	PC66 ECC 256MB
RAMBUS 256MB ECC	
RAMBUS 512MB ECC	

Table 5-1
Sample List of DDR and SDRAM Modules

expansion card comes with more than 128MB of its own share (more on this, in the section "Here Comes the Bus").

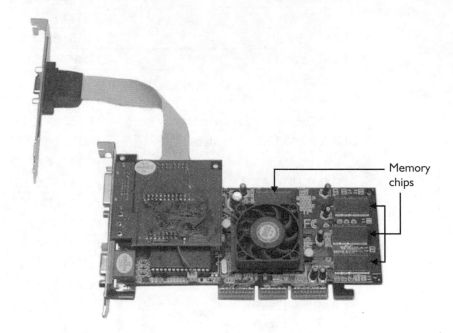

Memory chips

The Chipset

When shopping for a motherboard, you'll come across a line item called the *chipset*. A chipset is a group of microchips on a motherboard, designed to work together to perform one or more related functions. Typical chipsets are manufactured by VIA; Intel and SIS are used on motherboards running AMD or Intel CPUs (see Figure 5-2).This two-chip chipset provides the *interconnect bus controller* and is designed to optimize the front-side bus (FSB) for memory and graphics and the back-side bus (BSB) for speeding up PCI, USB, and ISA transactions.

Here Comes the Bus

The bus of a motherboard is a circuit arrangement that attaches devices to a direct line, allowing all signals to pass through each one of them. The signals are

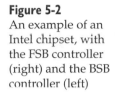

Figure 5-2
An example of an
Intel chipset, with
the FSB controller
(right) and the BSB
controller (left)

unique to each particular device, so the devices only understand their own signals. Figure 5-3 provides a diagram of the system bus architecture.

Most PCs today have a dual independent bus (DIB): the FSB is the data path and physical interface between the processor, AGP, and RAM, and the BSB is an interface between the processor and the level 1 (L1) and level 2 (L2) memory (or cache). If the data resides in L1 or L2 cache, the CPU doesn't need to even look in RAM, thus saving even more time in operation. Both the FSB and BSB can function simultaneously, allowing the processor to accomplish more with its own designated clock speed. The clock speed (or clock frequency) is its advertised "speed," specified in megahertz (MHz) or gigahertz (GHz).

When adding more RAM to your system, choose the same speed and type of RAM. It's also best to complement the CPU's bus speed, as this will greatly improve performance by taking full advantage of the system's bus speed. For example, if you have an AMD Duron (with a 200MHz bus speed), but the motherboard's bus speed (the channels between the CPU and other expansion cards) is limited to 33 MHz, you won't be able to take full advantage of the 200 MHz

Figure 5-3
A simple diagram of
the architecture of the
system bus

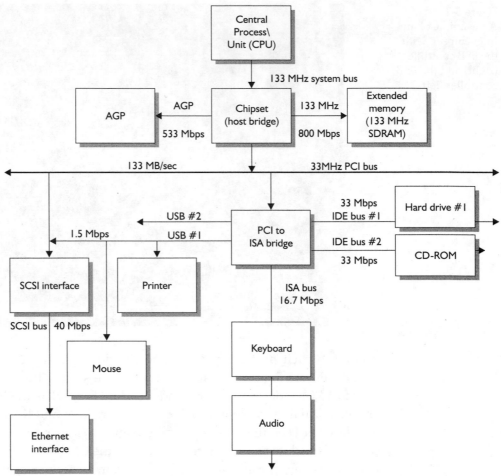

bus speed of the CPU. However, if your motherboard accepts DDR modules
with 266 MHz speed (as SDRAM has a ceiling of 133 MHz), you will be able to
take full advantage of the 200 MHz bus speed of the AMD Duron.

Two Buses Are Better Than One

Before Intel introduced the Pentium Pro processor (around 200 MHz), both the L2
cache and RAM were accessed using the same bus, creating an occasional bottleneck
and reducing the overall throughput of the computer. Beginning with the Pentium
Pro, the L2 cache is packaged on the same module or chipset as the processor. Intel's
DIB design separates and coordinates accesses between the processor and RAM and
accesses between the processor and the L2 cache. The FSB operates at anywhere from

66 to 100 MHz for the pre-1.7 GHz Intel Celeron, to 266 MHz for the AMD Athlon, and up to 533 MHz for the Intel Pentium 4. This is also dependent on the chipset—as I mentioned before, a 533 MHz processor will not reach its full potential on a motherboard with only a 400 MHz system bus. In the Pentium Pro, the BSB (to the L2 cache) operates at the same clock speed as the processor. In the Pentium II, the BSB operates at one-half the processor clock speed.

Memory Errors and Corrections

There are two types of memory errors: *repeatable* (or *hard*) errors and *transient* (or *soft*) errors. A hard error always occurs from something physically, such as loose memory modules, broken or blown chips, and motherboard defects. These are easier to diagnose because there's a repeatable pattern. The soft errors are much more common and more difficult to diagnose, since a bit may return the wrong value once, and then seemingly function correctly subsequently. Soft errors can also be caused by physically bad or defective memory, but usually are caused by a poor-quality motherboard, incorrect memory system timings, or ESD shocks. On a system without error detection, soft errors may appear as operating system bugs or random glitches.

Parity and Nonparity

Two line items that you may encounter when shopping for SDRAM and DDR memory are *nonparity* and *parity*. *Nonparity* is the most common type of memory. It adds a single bit of memory for every bit of memory stored. Parity memory stores an extra bit for every byte (or 8 bits) of data. For example, DIMMs contain a 64-bit width. There are 8 bytes within 64 bits, so the stored data measuring 64 bits would in fact be 72 bits—adding an additional 8 bits, one for each byte. These extra bits are for error detection. Bits are a series of 1's and 0's. If a 1 bit is returned as a 0, but should be a 1, those extra bits will be able to determine that and correct it.

Error-Correction Coding

Parity checking detects single-bit errors, but it doesn't have any way to correct them or to detect any errors more than a single bit. Error-correction coding (ECC, sometimes called error-correcting code) can both detect and correct single errors. ECC accomplishes this with more bits—7 bits for 32 bits or 8 bits for 64 bits; effectively a bit for every 32 bits. ECC also can detect multibit errors, but it cannot repair them. Instead, it instructs the system to shut down, to avoid corrupting any data. Memory errors that involve 2 or more bits are very rare.

Direct Memory Access

Direct memory access (DMA) is a capability provided by most computer bus architectures that allows direct data transmission from an attached device (such as a disk drive) to the memory on the computer's motherboard (see Figure 5-4). The microprocessor is then free from involvement with the data transfer, thus speeding up overall computer operation. A portion of memory is typically designated for DMA. The ISA bus standard allocates up to 16MB of memory for DMA, while PCI can double that.

You can find information on the assigned DMA channels by opening the System Information application in Windows 2000 (select Start | Programs | Accessories | System Tools | System Information) or by changing the View option in the Device Manager to Resources By Connection. You can access the Device Manager by right-clicking My Computer; choose Properties, then Hardware and Device Manager, and then select the View Devices By Connection radio button.

Video Controllers

Computer displays, up until the 1970s, were monochrome, used for word processing and text-based systems. It wasn't until 1981, when IBM introduced the Color/Graphics Adapter (CGA), that color graced the computer screen. CGA provided four colors with a maximum resolution of 320 pixels horizontally by 200 pixels vertically. CGA added additional color to the checkerboard, but it wasn't enough for any sophisticated graphics requirements.

IBM continued the evolution with the Enhanced Graphics Adapter (EGA) in 1984, with 16 different colors and a resolution of 640×350. Today, the minimum standard is Video Graphics Array (VGA), first introduced by IBM in 1987; it offers

Figure 5-4
DMA devices increase performance by bypassing the CPU for certain tasks.

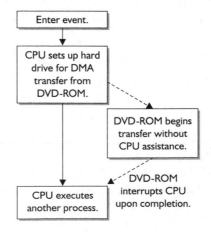

16 colors at 640×480, and 256 colors at 320×200. Every PC that runs Windows supports this minimal standard. In 1990, IBM enhanced the graphics display further with the introduction of the Extended Graphics Array (XGA) and a later version called XGA-2, both of which offer 800×600 pixel resolution in "true color," or 16 million colors, and 1024×768 resolution in 65,536 colors. XGA-2 is the most popular method of displaying imagery on a computer monitor today.

The Video Electronics Standards Association (VESA) established newer specifications, which ultimately offer more pixels horizontally and vertically for higher resolution for any graphics-hungry application. However, these VESA specifications—Super Video Graphics Array (SVGA), Super Extended Graphics Array (SXGA), and Ultra Extended Graphics Array (UXGA)—require dedicated video RAM to hold all that additional data.

The term VGA represents the connection for a traditional computer monitor. The 15-pin VGA connector is for a cathode-ray tube (CRT) monitor, which is your average computer monitor. Digital Video Interface (DVI) is a newer standard designed to support both analog and digital signals. It recognizes the difference and adjusts the signal accordingly. Most flat-panel displays must use the DVI connector because it's specific for digital signals.

There are three ways to attach a monitor to a computer:

❑ Use a built-in onboard video controller, with a connector built onto the motherboard.

❑ Add a PCI expansion video card.

❑ Add an AGP expansion card.

These add-ons can be specific to improving your interface experience, and not just for playing PC games better. I don't recommend using any exception for a server, especially if you'll be administering it remotely with Terminal Services and no display. However, I have discovered a few non-entertainment-oriented uses that take advantage of the benefits an AGP expansion card offers. Video RAM can increase the reaction time of your input devices and Windows in general. I discovered this fact while working on two different ThinkPads: my old i1300 at 650 MHz Pentium III, with 192MB of RAM and without any added video RAM—just a plain video adapter—and someone else's ThinkPad T20, with a 600 MHz Pentium III, 256MB of RAM, and an added 16MB ATI hardware graphics accelerator. After working on the T20 for a while, I noticed that the mouse moved faster and smoother and the windows opened and closed faster than on my ThinkPad. I was astonished when I discovered that the machine had a slower processor than my own ThinkPad.

The following are some other business workstation benefits for added video RAM:

❑ Better handling of any graphics-oriented programs, such as Microsoft Visio, Microsoft Project, and Adobe Photoshop, to name a few

❑ Frees up your computer's normal RAM when you're printing larger graphics files

❑ More flexibility with screen resolution and size

❑ Enhanced videoconferencing performance

❑ Better resolution for projected presentations

Overall, if you're planning to use the machine as a workstation, increasing video RAM is beneficial; but for a remotely administered server, there is nothing that I know of that warrants the added expense of anything more than 16MB, which you can find for about $10. However, when purchasing a video adapter for your server, here are a few important tips:

❑ Check whether there are drivers for the OS of your choice. If there are no software drivers to link your hardware to your OS, it may not work at all.

❑ Make sure that there is continued support for the brand of adapters. I'm using a 3Dfx Voodoo3 3000 video adapter with 16MB of RAM that I picked up for $20. I've also purchased a Matrox MGA Millennium, with 4MB of RAM, for about $10. The driver was built into Windows 2000.

❑ Stay away from ISA video adapters. Most of them are not plug-and-play capable and require manual jumper settings (and good luck trying to find any documentation to help support one!).

The AGP Mystery

I upgraded an older Gateway 400c tower from a 400 MHz Pentium II with 4MB of built-in video RAM, to a 1 GHz AMD Athlon with a CHAINTECH 64MB, NVIDIA AGP card. The change in my son's PC gaming experience was dramatic, to say the least. The jump in video memory provided more textual detail, higher resolution, faster playing time, and further virtual distances within the game (rather than watching the horizon drawn as you move closer).

The motherboard I chose is a new full-ATX ECS Elitegroup K7S5A (see Figure 5-5). It provides support for an AMD Athlon or Duron up to 1.3 GHz, with

Figure 5-5
Some motherboards come with the option of using either DIMM or DDR, but you cannot use them simultaneously.

a choice of either two SDRAM 168-pin 133 MHz DIMMs or two PC2100 184-pin 266 MHz DDR modules. When I first installed it, I used two 256MB 133 MHz DIMMs for a total of 512MB of RAM. It now cuts through high-intensity graphics like a hot knife through butter. The difference is so dramatic, visitors comment on the visual representation.

Based on these results, I thought, if two DIMMs can provide such a marked improvement, what about DDR modules, with speeds over and above the Athlon's 200 FSB speed? I picked up two Hyundai 256MB DDR modules, with which even the K7S5A manual confirmed compatibility. I opened up the chassis, carefully pulled out the two DIMMs, and inserted the DDR modules. I sealed the chassis and connected the peripherals—mouse, keyboard, monitor…the usual, and all original—and pushed the power button.

Nothing.

I pushed it again. Still nothing.

I checked the monitor connection, keyboard, mouse, and power cord—both on the back of the computer and in the surge protector. Everything seemed to be in order. Nothing changed but the Hyundai memory modules.

I pulled out the power cord and took it downstairs into my "laboratory." I opened the case again and checked the CHAINTECH AGP card, and, as Figure 5-6 shows, it was clearly set in place by the rear guard. I gently pushed down to make sure it was firmly in place and there was no give—it was properly set in place. However, sometimes all you need to do is reseat a component, so I grounded myself, unscrewed the securing screw, pulled out the card, and then immediately reseated it. I was positive it wasn't loose and, once again, it was set firmly in place.

Figure 5-6
The small latch that
locks the AGP card
into place

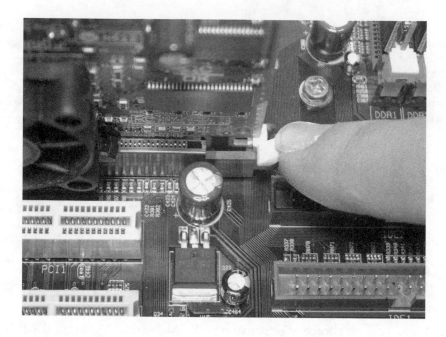

I confirmed the power cord was disconnected before I added a keyboard, mouse, and monitor to the unit, and I was grounded from any ESD. But then I thought, could I have accidentally zapped the new modules with static electricity and fried them? Although I was sure I hadn't, I decided to switch the modules back to the DIMM modules. I plugged in the power cord and pushed the power switch. Nothing...again.

Carefully, I unplugged the power cord and switched the memory back to the known good DIMM module, and then inserted the power cord and pushed the power switch.

Nothing.

I double-checked the seating of the memory modules, which appeared to be fine. I took the DDR modules and plugged them into another motherboard I was working on—and yes, that system booted up immediately, with a passing memory test.

I checked the compatibility of the DIMMs and tested them on another system—which seemed ridiculous in hindsight; they worked great before. They were perfectly okay.

What was it? The power supply? Check. The video card? I swapped in an older 16MB Voodoo3 3000, and that still didn't work. Just in case it wasn't compatible with a 2× AGP card, I pulled a 4×128MB from my video workstation, and still nothing. Could it need a BIOS update, however unlikely (it was working fine before), but I checked and it was running the latest BIOS.

At this point, if it were a used motherboard, I may have been convinced that it suddenly went bad; but this was a new one. I purchased a used ASUS MEW-AM, which had onboard video that eventually stopped working, but all I had to do was add a PCI and/or ISA video adapter, and it booted up fine. This didn't accept anything at all.

Finally, being completely at a loss and realizing I did everything I could possibly do to get the motherboard to boot up again, I went to the Web. That's where I discovered the astonishing truth, deep in the message boards of the Internet.

At first, I couldn't believe it—the solution couldn't be that simple, but it worked. It appears that the new ECS Elitegroup K7S5A has a quirk. Christened by the "geek nation" as a design flaw, the motherboard sometimes just doesn't hold the AGP card correctly and you need to use a special device to secure it into place: your finger.

Simply pushing down on the video adapter (any video adapter) during the system boot gives the motherboard that something special it needs to recognize it.

The computer booted immediately. I switched the modules back to DDR. It was the act of snapping the modules down into their banks that pushed down on the motherboard enough to pull the AGP card out of its slot—even though it appeared to be well seated, it was not. Mystery solved, and whenever a video adapter doesn't boot up, one of my new troubleshooting steps is to hold the adapter down.

Fortunately, we live in the Internet age. What are the chances that, without the multitude of resources available at my fingertips, I would've discovered this simple solution? The Internet gives you access to so many other people that, somewhere out there, someone likely has experienced the same problem you're having. If all else fails when troubleshooting a problem, research the issue thoroughly online. Sometimes I find the answer immediately, but other times it takes me an hour—but I do find it.

If your motherboard supports an AGP expansion slot and needs a video adapter, use the AGP slot for video, as opposed to a PCI slot. This will keep the PCI slot free for future expansive needs.

Memory Installation Procedures

It can be quite frustrating when working with sensitive electronic components that seem to be defying logic. Keep in mind that most of the time, if you've done the right research, you can insert the memory module or video adapter, and the magic happens without any major obstacles. If the computer doesn't boot up the first time around, here is a list of very important troubleshooting tips:

❏ Make sure you have power:

   ❏ Check the power cord connections.

   ❏ Check any switch on the power supply itself.

   ❏ Confirm the proper power switch connection on the button control panel on the motherboard.

   ❏ Check that the power connection is connected to the motherboard.

❏ Confirm proper configuration:

   ❏ Does the motherboard automatically set up the speed, frequency, and voltage?

❏ How about the RAM speed? Are you using 133 MHz SDRAM on a motherboard that doesn't support it? Make sure your RAM is the same speed and that your motherboard can support that speed. Older motherboards may only be able to support 66 MHz or 100 MHz SDRAM (like my FIC SD-11).

❏ Secure the modules:

  ❏ Don't be afraid to press harder if necessary (just make sure you have the notches lined up, as discussed following this list). Micron Technology (the world's largest manufacturer of memory) believes it can take 20 to 30 pounds of pressure to install a module.

  ❏ The side clips should snap into place on their own. If you have to move the clips into place by hand, your module may not be compatible or installed properly.

❏ Check the internal cables and component. Like the video adapter in my ECS motherboard, you may have inadvertently unplugged something.

❏ Check that your BIOS is up to date by checking the manufacturer's web site for instructions on finding and updating your BIOS (only if necessary).

❏ Make sure your AGP card is compatible. Besides the velocity, 1×, 2×, 4×, and even 8×, AGP cards also require different voltages and power. Adding a 4×128MB AGP card to a micro-ATX chassis with only 145 watts of power is questionable, and it may not even boot up. If using an AGP, be sure about compatibility with its velocity, as newer video adapters may demand more power than the motherboard can handle.

HEADS UP!

Beware of Static

It's very important to make sure you're working in an electrostatic-free environment when handling sensitive electronic components. Memory modules and expansion cards, such as an AGP video adapter, are especially vulnerable.

Figure 5-7
The DIMM form factor includes two notches.

Your first step is to ensure you have the right type of RAM. Earlier in the chapter, Figure 5-5 shows a motherboard with the option to use either DIMM or DDR modules. DIMM modules have two notches in their design (see Figure 5-7), while the DDR module has only one, off-center notch (see Figure 5-8) to help distinguish the correct way to insert the modules properly.

Figure 5-8
DDR includes only one off-center notch to help guide proper installation.

Each end of the memory module fits into a channel on the insert slot, shown here:

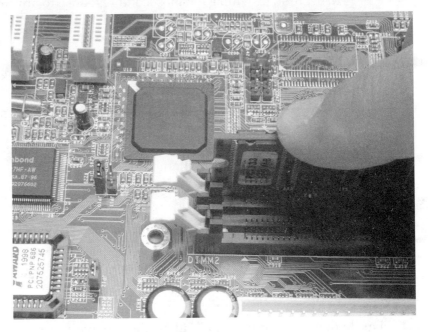

When inserting the module, avoid sticking one side in first. You should install it parallel to the slot, with both hands pushing each end firmly into place.

Usually, but not always, a successful installation of a memory module ends with a "snap." The side clips should snap into place on their own. If not, double check that the module is properly seated.

If you're installing a single module, make sure you're installing it in the slot labeled first. Some motherboards label it 0, while others label it 1.

Even with the latest in hard drive technology, and a lightning-fast CPU, it will most likely go unnoticed without enough RAM. All instructions open in RAM first, providing a nanosecond response to any application instruction, as opposed to the milliseconds of a hard disk.

The AGP slot is exclusively for the video adapter function. It introduces its own RAM used solely for video and graphics depiction, and should be used (if the motherboard doesn't have onboard video) to keep the PCI slot free for future expansive needs. RAM and AGP cards are exceptionally delicate components. If purchased used, make sure it's from a reputable source that will provide at least a fair exchange in the event they're dead on arrival. Many outlets will not accept refunds on such components because they're delicate and a simple electro-static discharge can destroy them.

TESTING 1-2-3

A few suggestions and precautions to be aware of follow:

❑ Use an electrostatic-free environment; memory is very susceptible to damage.

❑ Handle memory modules and video adapters with care.

❑ Be sure your memory is compatible with your motherboard chipset before purchasing it.

❑ Make sure all your memory runs at the same speed (133 MHz, 266 MHz, and so on).

❑ For better performance, add as much RAM as budgeted and use RAM with speed faster than the FSB speed.

❑ Your server will be a remotely administered, monitor-less computer— you don't need an expensive high-powered graphics accelerator.

❑ If using an AGP, be sure about compatibility; newer video adapters may demand more power than the motherboard can handle.

❑ Whenever working with any electronic components, *unplug the power cord* from the chassis power supply.

Chapter 6
The Drive Way

Tools of the Trade

Precision screwdriver set
Needle-nose pliers
Anti-static sleeves
Electrostatic-free environment

The components you'll need for this chapter include

- ❏ Two hard drives
- ❏ Floppy disk drive
- ❏ CD/DVD-ROM or CD-RW
- ❏ SCSI host bus adapter (for SCSI drives)
- ❏ IDE host bus adapter (for optional third hard drive)
- ❏ Cabling

The drives of a server—or any computer, for that matter—are the more permanent residence for your data. While information only stays in RAM as long as the system is running, the hard drive will still hold that data, even when shut down. Removable media—such as CD/DVD-ROMs, backup tapes, floppy disks, and Zip disks—are all mediums created to move data from one place to another. CD/DVD-ROMs typically will hold the software you'll need to install, as well as patches, upgrades, and service packs. Backup tapes provide a means of creating a failsafe copy, and floppy disks (originally used for software installation) and Zip media are also to transport data from one place to another.

Even the hard drive can be made mobile; but using a "hot swap" tray (under lock and key) that will allow you to pull the hard drive out of one server and plug it into another, or pull a hard drive at full capacity out and load in another, without shutting down, gives the hard drive similar capabilities of a tape backup unit, only with infinitely more capacity and speed.

Of course, in addition to file and print sharing, your server could also provide drive sharing. Rather than having a single DVD-ROM, for example, in a desktop for one person to use, you can add this drive into the server and have it serve the many, instead of the one. The DVD-ROM becomes another storage unit within the server to share. Keep in mind while building your server requirements that the amount of use can greatly diminish the performance of the other roles the server plays.

Choosing Your Drives

Typically, any server (file, web, or print) includes one or more floppy, CD-ROM, and/or hard drives. When installing and configuring your system, these three very different drives will actually work together. The floppy disk drive is a random access, removable, magnetic, data-storage medium. Originally, the drive supported 5¼-inch disks that were soft and flexible, or "floppy" (hence the name). These disks were half the thickness of today's 3½-inch floppy disks, which were developed about 20 years ago by Sony. These floppy disks have a maximum capacity of 1.44MB, which limits their usefulness.

Thanks to the development of networking, network users rarely use floppy disks as a method of file transfer; besides, there are few files under 1.44MB these days. In fact, Apple Computer has eliminated the floppy disk drive from its iMac series, and Gateway Computer offers to consumers the choice of whether or not to have a floppy disk drive in their new computer. However, I believe a floppy disk drive is an important part of the maintainability of your server—mainly because of network operating systems (NOSs) like Windows and Linux, that in a recovery situation recommend the use of an Emergency Repair Disk (ERD) or boot disk.

When the server starts its boot process from a cold start, the motherboard is initialized. After a self-aware initialization, the BIOS in the motherboard then looks for a valid drive and operating system. Typically, the A drive is the default and is reserved for the floppy disk drive. If the floppy disk within the drive holds the bootable MS-DOS IO.SYS file, BIOS will boot the system to an A:\ prompt. Windows 2000 Server or Windows .NET Server require a CD-ROM for an emergency boot process, but you can create a series of four floppy disks that you can use in the event of a mishap.

Believe me, the floppy disk drive comes in very handy when troubleshooting a problem with motherboards, memory, hard drives, the OS, or any server component.

The floppy disk drive is like a stalwart guardian, always there and always ready. It doesn't need any additional drivers to run, nor does it need any special software. If a motherboard refuses to initialize, or doesn't find the OS to launch, the floppy disk drive is there, ready to boot your system to the A:\ prompt and give you access to the boot drive. For example, if after installing a new 120GB hard drive you get the Blue Screen of Death (BSOD), and later discover that you need to update the BIOS to handle that hard drive, the floppy disk drive is available. I've also used the Windows 2000 Emergency Repair Disk (on a single floppy disk) on a few occasions. Sure, the floppy disk drive is slow and becoming slower relative to faster speeds of newer devices, but when nothing works, accessibility is more important than speed.

Eventually, CD-RW discs, which are dropping in cost dramatically, are sure to replace floppy disks. Also, computer hard drive technology has become more sophisticated since the introduction of the floppy disk, and now provides seamless, uninterrupted operations and new ways of improving the meantime between failure (MTBF), which is the measure of hardware reliability, so the stalwart guardian may find the need to retire. Computer components are thousands or tens of thousands of hours between failures. Anticipating those potential failures and preparing redundancy options reduces any possible downtime.

TIPS OF THE TRADE

Emergency Repair Disk (ERD)

During the process of installing Windows 2000/Server 2003, you're given the option to create an ERD. If your system doesn't boot into your OS or you get the BSOD, this simple floppy disk can be a real lifesaver. Unless you have an EEPROM burner handy, the floppy disk drive is also the only way to update your system BIOS. If some new hardware is causing some bad reactions, pull out the culprit, clear CMOS by using the jumper or pulling out the CMOS battery for about 60 seconds (refer to Chapter 3), and then boot to the A:\ prompt using a boot floppy disk. Next, download the latest BIOS from the motherboard manufacturer's web site and, using the appropriate flash utility (see your motherboard documentation), flash (update) the BIOS from the floppy disk.

The floppy disk drive is typically the default first boot device, which is why it's an important part of system maintainability—it's always on. It's a surefire way to access the computer's information and data. If your hard drive fails, it would be rather difficult to access information by way of the OS if it is on the hard drive that failed.

- ❏ **AUTOEXEC.NT**   Copy of autoexec.nt
- ❏ **CONFIG.NT**   Copy of config.nt
- ❏ **SETUP.LOG**   Contains the locations of system and application files and cyclic redundancy check (CRC) information used during the repair process

If you skipped the procedure to create an ERD during installation, or your ERD is lost or damaged, you can still create an ERD of the system by following the ERD wizard within the Windows 2000 or Server 2003 Backup utility. This is located by selecting Start | Programs | Accessories | System Tools | Backup. Be sure to have a clean floppy disk on hand.

If the opportunity to use the ERD presents itself, you first need to boot the computer with the Windows 2000/Server 2003 CD-ROM or the set of four boot floppies. You can create these by running /bootdisk/makeboot.exe on your Windows 2000/ Server 2003 Installation CD-ROM (more on this in Chapter 10). The Windows 2000/Server 2003 setup will begin and take you to the option of Install or Repair. Select Repair and follow the onscreen instructions.

ATA vs. SCSI

The computer hard drive exists because most of your data needs to be stored in something more permanent than RAM. Even if you turn off the computer for days or years, the data on the hard drive will sit there waiting to be accessed. The following are the two most common types of hard drives being used today, ATA and SCSI:

❏ **Advanced Technology Attachment (ATA)**   The official name given by the American National Standards Institute (ANSI) for the Integrated Device Electronics (IDE) or Enhanced Integrated Device Electronics (EIDE) hard drive, the most popular for desktop computers.

❏ **Small Computer System Interface (SCSI)**   Apple Computer, the innovator who gave us the universal serial bus (USB), first introduced the faster and more expensive SCSI (pronounced "skuzzy") drive. SCSI is a standard high-speed interface that enables peripherals to communicate faster than they could with previous interfaces.

Both the ATA and SCSI interfaces support a wide variety of devices, including hard drives, CD-ROM drives, tape drives, and RAID. The latest SCSI standard, Wide Ultra-3 SCSI, can transfer data at a rate of 160 megabits per second (Mbps); while the latest ATA standard, Ultra ATA133, bursts speeds of 133 Mbps. SCSI accommodates up to 16 daisy-chained devices on a single 12-meter cable connected to one channel on the motherboard, whereas ATA is limited to only two devices on a single cable and channel. The hard drive speeds go up to 15,000 RPM for SCSI and 7200 RPM for ATA. The most significant differences between ATA and SCSI are cost, complexity, and compatibility, as discussed next.

Cost Comparison

The built-in higher-performance features make SCSI drives more than twice as expensive as their ATA counterparts. Therefore, determining whether you really need that higher performance should be your first step in determining whether or not to choose or migrate to SCSI devices. You may discover that the less expensive ATA fills your requirements initially, if not forever, and you can always make a later assessment.

Complexity

Configuring SCSI drives is more complex than configuring ATA drives. An ATA device (hard drive, tape drive, or CD-ROM/DVD-ROM) must be either a *master* or *slave*. ATA devices also provide the option of *Cable Select*, which configures the drive in the middle of the cable as the slave and the drive at the end of the cable as the master. However, the drives, cable, and IDE controller must all support the Cable Select jumper setting, or it will not work. I recommend avoiding this potential problem by simply configuring fixed jumper settings for master and slave. The boot hard disk can only be the master; whereas with SCSI, you can configure any device to be a boot device.

All SCSI devices need to be assigned a position in a chain, or an ID, usually from 0 to 7 or 0 to 16, depending on the type of SCSI drives. Most SCSI drives contain two sets of *jumper blocks,* much like the jumpers on a motherboard. A shunt is placed over a set of two pins to configure the SCSI drive's ID. SCSI drives also need to be *terminated,* or the chain of devices must be closed. This usually requires another jumper block and setting on the device.

On a SCSI chain, you must close (terminate) the ends of the chain (see Figure 6-1) and determine the order of the IDs between the ends of the SCSI chain (see Table 6-1).

Figure 6-1
The SCSI terminator encapsulates the SCSI chain of devices.

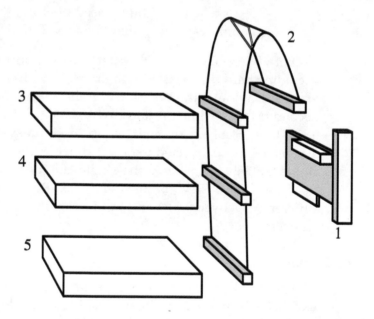

Device	ID	Configuration
Host adapter (#1 in Figure 6-1)	ID = 7	Terminator ON
SCSI hard drive 1 (#3)	ID = 2	Terminator OFF
SCSI hard drive 2 (#4)	ID = 1	Terminator OFF
SCSI hard drive 3 (#5)	ID = 0	Terminator ON

Table 6-1
Example of SCSI ID and Termination Configuration

The SCSI host adapter typically will provide you with a BIOS option to configure which device you can boot from.

Setting SCSI Jumpers To set the jumpers for a SCSI drive:

1. Find the jumper block for setting the SCSI drive's termination and ID by looking at the jumper label, which is either a sticker on the drive or etched directly on the drive. If you're not sure about the proper configuration settings, or the device itself has no labels, check the device documentation.

2. Check the SCSI ID numbers used by the other SCSI devices on the SCSI chain by identifying them onscreen during system boot or through the device documentation, and then set the drive's SCSI ID to a free number. See Table 6-2 for more.

SCSI Drives Up to 15,000 RPM	Transfer Speed	Number of Devices	Cable
SCSI (SCSI-1)	5 Mbps	8	50-pin
Fast SCSI (SCSI-2)	10 Mbps	8	50-pin
Fast Wide SCSI (SCSI-2)	20 Mbps	16	50-pin
Ultra SCSI (SCSI-3)	20 Mbps	8	68-pin

Table 6-2
Hard Drive Transfer Rate, Device Capacity, and Cables

SCSI Drives Up to 15,000 RPM	Transfer Speed	Number of Devices	Cable
Ultra Wide SCSI (SCSI-3)	40 Mbps	16	68-pin
Ultra-2 SCSI (SCSI-3)	40 Mbps	8	68-pin
Ultra-2 Wide SCSI (SCSI-3)	80 Mbps	16	68-pin
Ultra-3 SCSI (SCSI-3)	80 Mbps	8	80-pin
Ultra-3 Wide SCSI or Ultra160(SCSI-3)	160 Mbps	16	80-pin
Ultra320 (SCSI-SPI-4)	320 Mbps	16	80-pin
Ultra640 (SCSI-SPI-5)	640 Mbps	16	80-pin

Table 6-2
Hard Drive Transfer Rate, Device Capacity, and Cables

Compatibility

It pays to check out Microsoft's Hardware Compatibility List (HCL) before you pick up a used hard drive. The HCL is included on the Windows 2000 or Server 2003 CD-ROM, and the most up-to-date version is located at www .microsoft.com/hwdq/hcl/. An incompatible hard drive will cause an installation failure, so it's better to check the HCL before you start instead of after the third failed installation attempt (more on this in Chapter 9).

A recent compatibility problem that I encountered existed because Windows 2000 and Server 2003 are now true Plug-and-Play operating systems, whereas Windows NT Server, the predecessor to Windows 2000 and Server 2003, is not. If you are installing this Plug-and-Play NOS on a machine with non-Plug-and-Play devices, as is true with many systems designed for NT, the installation will fail. Non-Plug-and-Play devices include drivers that "hard-code" specific system resources, such as IRQs, to those devices. When installing a Plug-and-Play NOS, it will automatically recognize and assign resources through virtual drivers to those devices throughout the installation process. The legacy ISA device or older SCSI drive may be fine during the first part of the installation process, but at the tail end, when trying to reshuffle resources, the resulting conflict causes an installation failure. I learned to check the HCL when I attempted to install Windows 2000 on a seemingly adaptable 9GB SCSI hard drive inside an IBM Netfinity 3000 Server running Windows NT.

Other factors when using SCSI devices include jumper configurations and limited system BIOS support. There are many standards, variations of speeds and connectors (50-, 68-, and 80-pin), and no common software interface.

Any ATA device (hard drive, CD-ROM, or tape drive) has a 40-pin connector. There may be a single pin missing on the newer ATA66, ATA100, and ATA133 80-wire, 40-pin cables, but the classic ATA33 IDE cables have only 40 wires and 40 pins (see Table 6-3). Many of the faster 80-wire, 40-pin high-speed ATA cables have a single pin missing, with the coordinating hole plugged on the connector, as shown at the bottom of Figure 6-2. Be careful not to force one of these 80-wire, 40-pin cables into a "classic" 40-wire, 40-pin connector socket—effectively trying to punch the extra pin through the plug.

Figure 6-2
Each drive requires
a special cable.

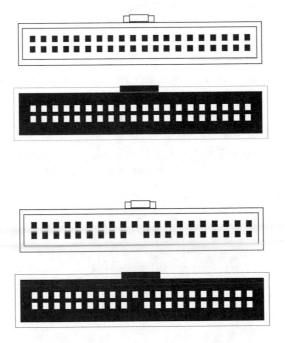

EIDE Drives (ATA) Up to 7200 RPM	Transfer Speed	Number of Devices	Cable
ATA33	33 Mbps	2	40-pin (40-wire)
ATA66	66 Mbps	2	40-pin (80-wire)
ATA100	100 Mbps	2	40-pin (80-wire)
ATA133	133 Mbps	2	40-pin (80-wire)

Table 6-3
Speed and Proper Cabling for ATA Devices

Partitions and Volumes

You have a few choices of setup applications that will help you when you're setting up a new hard drive. Although these choices are described in detail in Chapter 9, a brief mention of them is appropriate here. New name-brand hard drives include setup applications such as EZ Drive for Western Digital or Max Blast Plus from Maxtor (available as a free download at their respective web sites). Both still require a Windows boot floppy disk for formatting the drive for usability. The second and older choice is to use MS-DOS, which includes the applications FDISK for partitioning and FORMAT to format (more details on using MS-DOS are provided in Chapters 9 and 10).

Host Bus Adapters (HBAs)

There are two ATA hard drives (one master and one slave), connected to the only channel available for hard drives on most ATA motherboards, with the assigned master drive at the top, the assigned slave below, and the longer extension of cable leading to the motherboard (see Figure 6-3). The secondary channel is typically dedicated to removable media devices, such as CD-ROM, tape backup, or Zip drives. I've offered a scenario in which two CD/DVD drives are used: one as a simple read-only device and the other as a CD-RW, to back up CDs or files on external media. This fills the capacity of the typical ATA motherboard. For any additional devices, such as the optional tape backup drive, you would need to find another alternative, and that's where expansion controller cards come into play.

Figure 6-3
The longer extension of the ATA cable is connected to the motherboard.

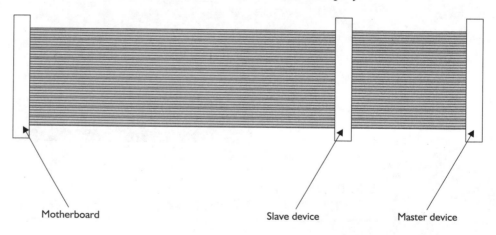

Motherboard   Slave device   Master device

RAID

RAID stands for *redundant array of independent* (or *inexpensive*) *disks* and has nothing to do with killing bugs. There are many versions of RAID, used to improve performance, provide failsafe mechanisms, and reduce MTBF. If one disk fails, the redundantly stored data is accessed elsewhere, without any downtime.

A series of RAID hard drives may appear as a single logical hard disk to the operating system, but it may be a logical drive made up of parts, or *stripes*, from multiple discs. These stripes may be random bits and bytes of information, but the OS calls them in the order requested.

RAID first appeared around 1988 at the University of California at Berkeley in papers that defined several data protection and mapping models for disk arrays. These include striping with parity and *mirroring*, which duplicates data (such as an NOS) on multiple discs for redundancy, speed, and maximum uptime. Striping without parity is used specifically for speed. Although there are many categories of RAID, RAID 0 through RAID 5 tend to be the most popular.

Some RAID highlights are

❏ **RAID 0**   Offers striping without parity for added performance, but no reliability or redundancy.

❏ **RAID 1**   Introduced mirroring/duplexing, which are for redundancy. Mirroring is slower than duplexing, which uses two controllers for added speed.

❏ **RAID 5**   Introduced striping with parity, which is fast and redundant but requires three or more drives and one disk for parity. Its only drawback is the cost of having one more extra drive.

❏ **RAID 10**   Combines mirroring with striping, or RAID 0 and RAID 1.

HBA controller cards essentially add more channels to your system. They can be used for additional ATA hard drives, tape backup drives, RAID, or even SCSI drives. These controller cards range in cost, depending on what you need. For example, an expansion ATA controller card sells for about $30 to $50. I have a PCI Promise ATA66 and another ATA100 (see Figure 6-4), which offer me channels for up to four more IDE devices. My PCI SCSI Tekrom HBA gives me channels for up to 16 total SCSI devices.

Figure 6-4
The Promise ATA100 host adapter adds up to four more ATA devices to your server.

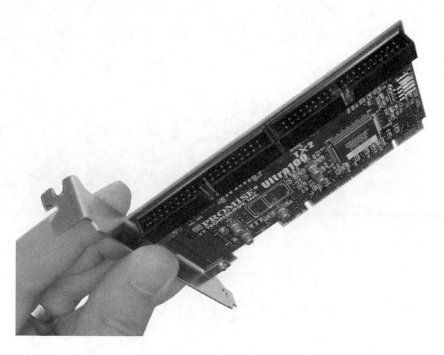

Of course, most ATX cases have space for only a few hard drives, usually underneath the floppy disk drive compartment, so you'd need to add any additional drive securely within the upper 5¼-inch drive bays. If you need more than four hard drives, you may consider moving to a full server tower (refer to Chapter 1), which gives you more bays. However, keep in mind that the more hardware you add, the more power you may need. A 300-watt power supply would be sufficient for up to seven devices, if you're not using any power-hungry AGP or SCSI card, in addition to an IDE HBA controller.

CD-ROMs, DVD-ROMs, and CD-RWs

In the mid-1990s, "multimedia" computers (computers with built-in CD-ROM drives) reached "mass-market" status—an installation base of over 50 million customers. Today, according to the Photonics Industry and Technology Development Association (PITDA), there are over 118 million worldwide shipments of CD-ROM, CD-RW, and DVD-ROM drives every year. In addition, about 5.7 billion CD-R discs will be sold this year, further expanding the market and reducing the cost of writable discs everywhere. CD-R's are a great and very economical way of backing up specific data and delivering proposals, presentations, and reports, many of which can barely fit on a floppy disk anymore.

Drive Installation Procedures

Before you dive into installing a drive into your server, you must take two steps to ensure proper installation: find the location of pin 1 on the device and configure the jumpers for master and slave. The master device is the first one that is checked by the BIOS for an OS. If the hard drives are not configured properly, the system may attempt to boot up from the slave (thinking it's the master) or not recognize anything at all, in which case you'll get one or two of a variety of responses, including

- ❏ A No Operating System Found error message
- ❏ A Cannot Find NTLDR or NTDETECT error message
- ❏ A No ROM Basic error message
- ❏ The Blue Screen of Death

❏ A message about hardware corruption or a virus

❏ The system hangs

Even if you have an OS on the slave (in a multiboot environment), it still may not boot because the Master Boot Record (MBR) is on the master drive (more details about this are provided in Chapter 10).

Pin 1

When installing a cable to a hard drive, either a CD-ROM or floppy disk drive, the red end of the cable must be at pin 1 of the appropriate socket. The location of pin 1 can be distinguished in several ways. It may be a blatant label, as in Figure 6-3, or more elusive as shown next. There may not be any sign at all, and you may need to check the device documentation for the correct location of pin 1. Typically, in a hard drive or CD-ROM drive, pin 1 is next to the power connector.

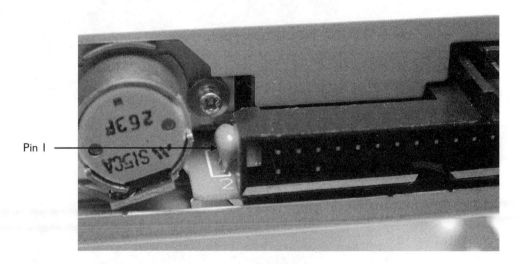

Pin 1

Master and Slave

Most ATA hard drives will include a diagram or label for the proper configuration as master or slave. This diagram can determine the proper configuration for master or slave, "MA" signifying Master, "SL" for Slave, and "CS" for Cable Select.

Master, Slave, and Cable Select

Floppy Disk Drive

You can install the floppy disk drive in either of two ways. You can install it from the rear of its carriage.

Or, you can install it through the front; either way, you need to remove one of the 3½-inch blanks from the front of the chassis.

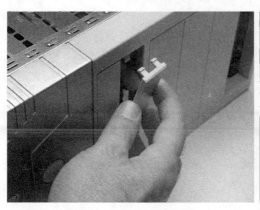 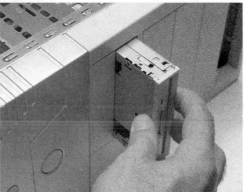

The bay for the floppy disk drive is usually marked, although it tends to be the top or single 3½-inch bay. Unlike the hard drives and CD/DVD-ROM drives, the standard floppy disk drive does not use the Molex connector for power and uses a special 34-pin cable, with a twist on the end connected to the drive itself. The power connector is also a 4-pin AMP connector, but it's smaller than the

Molex and can be cumbersome to connect. The carriage that holds the floppy disk drive includes rails that help guide it into place.

Secure the floppy disk drive in place with two screws. We'll take care of the opposite side when we're done with the installation.

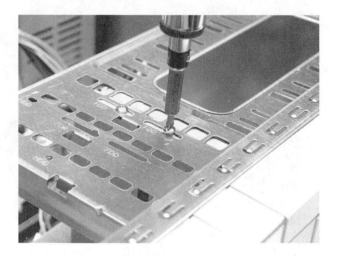

The floppy disk drive is typically the only device that uses the smaller 4-pin power cable.

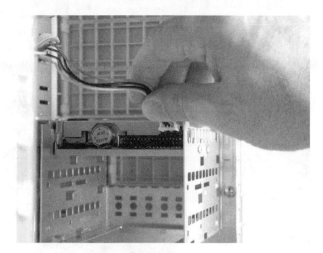

The floppy disk drive is also the only device with a unique 34-pin cable and a crossover midsection within the cable end installed into the rear of the floppy.

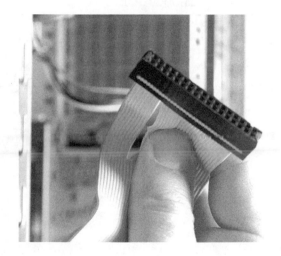

Once you've determined where pin 1 is located, insert the master end of the cable into the socket on the rear of the floppy disk drive. The red stripe should be on the pin 1 side.

The ATA motherboard typically has three specific sockets for drives: a 34-pin socket for the floppy disk drive (usually by itself somewhere); and two 40-pin IDE sockets labeled primary IDE0, IDE1, or first, for the hard drives, and secondary IDE1 (with IDE0), IDE2, or second, is for the CD-ROM, tape backup, or Zip drives.

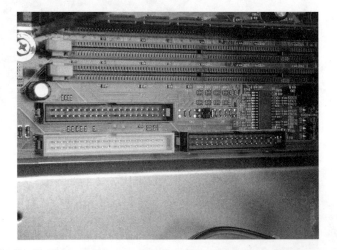

Aligning the red stripe on the side of the cable to pin 1 on the motherboard socket, carefully insert the tail end of the floppy cable into the FDD socket on the motherboard. There is a single 34-pin connector on the motherboard, usually marked as FDD or FLOPPY.

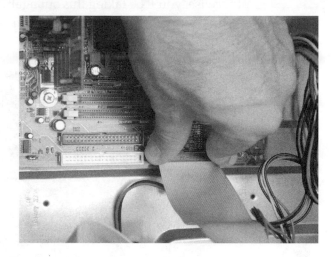

Hard Drives

Installing the hard drive is similar to the floppy drive, mainly because they usually share the same compartment. Although hard drives are the same size as floppy drives (4 inches wide), they do use very different connectors. While the floppy accepts a unique AMP 4-pin power connector, the hard drive (and CD/DVD-ROM) uses a standard 4-pin Molex connector.

Follow these steps to install the hard drive:

1. The first hard drive slides inside the bay just below the floppy disk drive.

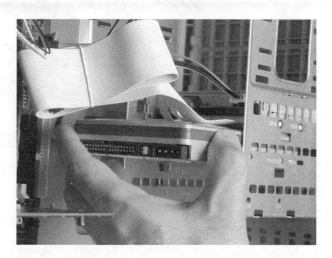

2. Secure the hard drive with two screws on this side of the chassis. Make sure you've configured the jumper setting on the hard drive as master— otherwise, you'll be taking this out again, if incorrect, to change it. Again, we'll take care of securing the opposite side when we're done with the installation.

3. Attach an 80-wire, 40-pin connector to the rear of the hard drive, aligning the red stripe side of the cable with pin 1.

Most power supplies have a single power cable that has a large four-pin Molex power connector linked to the smaller 4-pin AMP connector for the floppy disk drive. This is usually the best choice for the first hard drive, which is just below the floppy disk drive.

4. The 80-wire, 40-pin connector for modern hard drives includes a notch and a missing pinhole, in addition to the red stripe, to assist in proper installation. Again, as with the floppy drive, align the red stripe side with pin 1.

5. Insert the hard drive connector into the primary IDE socket on the motherboard.

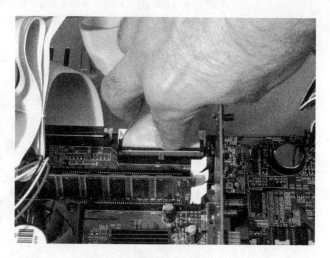

6. Slide the second hard drive into the carriage slot just below the master hard drive. The jumper setting for this one should be configured as the slave.

7. Secure the hard drive into place with two screws.

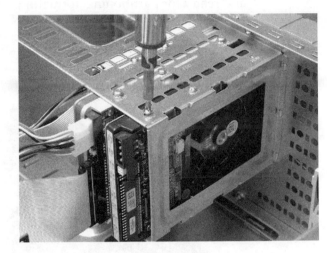

8. Insert the secondary slave connector from the hard drive cable into the rear socket of the hard drive.

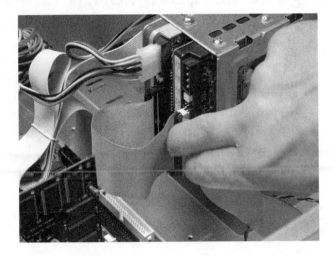

9. Plug in another power cable, and you have two hard drives installed and ready for partitioning, formatting, and installation.

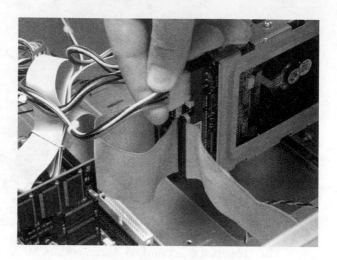

Installing a CD-ROM, DVD-ROM, or CD-RW drive

In my server, I've chosen to add a DVD-ROM drive as the master and a CD-RW as the slave. This requires the top two 5¼-inch bays and a single 40-pin cable. Incidentally, the reason CD/DVD drives are often in the top two bays isn't necessarily so that reaching them is more convenient (if planted on the floor next to your desk), but rather because they're typically the longest of the drives and may intrude on motherboard space. If you've run out of power connections, you can pick up a Y cable that will split one connection into two (see Figure 6-5). As with the hard drives, make sure your two CD devices are properly configured as master and slave.

Figure 6-5
The power Y cable can create two power connections out of one.

To install the master CD-ROM or DVD-ROM drive, pull out the top 5¼-inch bay blank.

1. Slide in the drive.

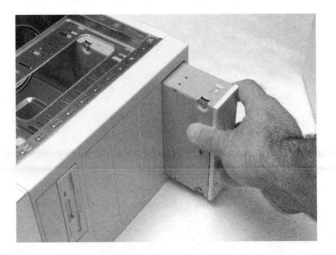

2. Secure this side of the drive with four screws (we'll get to the other side later).

It's very important to use four screws on each side, as any vibration from the drive spinning insecurely may cause read (and write) errors.

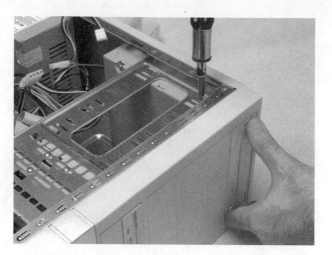

The 40-pin IDE cable for the CD-ROM or DVD-ROM drive is identical to the cable for the hard drive. The only difference may be that it has 40 wires rather than 80 wires, depending on the speed of the drive.

3. Insert the top master connector on the 40-pin cable to the rear of the drive—again, align the red stripe side with pin 1.

4. Plug in one of the large four-pin power cables.

5. Insert the tail end of the cable to the remaining IDE connection (secondary or 2nd) on the motherboard.

6. To install the slave CD-RW, follow the same procedures for installing the slave hard drive device. Set the jumper setting to slave, and then insert the CD-RW into the bay just below the master.

7. After you've secured it into place with its four screws, insert the secondary slave connection of the cable from the master drive.

Additional Hard Drives

Unless the computer chassis you purchased has built-in space for more hard drives, the only other option that you have available (for a standard midtower chassis) is to use one or two of the unused 5¼-inch bays. You can pick up from most computer retail outlets bracket adapters (see Figure 6-6) that enable you to install a laptop drive into a desktop and a typical hard drive into a 5¼-inch bay.

The drives you install within your server will provide different levels of value based on how you're planning to use your server. If a file server is what you have in mind, then the more hard drive space, the better. A print server will have very little use for two 20GB hard drives, but you can most likely fill up the space quickly as an FTP or web server, providing outside access to data and

Figure 6-6
Bracket adapters (about $8) can convert your extra laptop drive into a desktop drive and prepare your extra desktop hard drive for insertion into a 5½-inch bay.

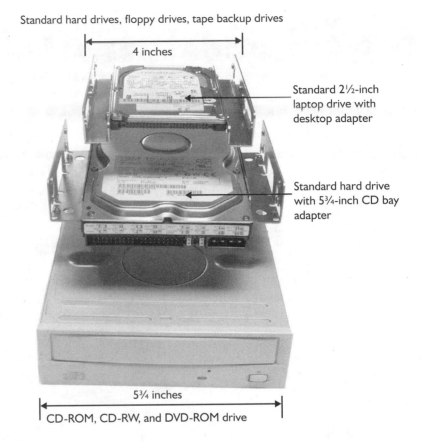

Standard hard drives, floppy drives, tape backup drives

4 inches

Standard 2½-inch laptop drive with desktop adapter

Standard hard drive with 5¾-inch CD bay adapter

5¾ inches

CD-ROM, CD-RW, and DVD-ROM drive

documents. Overall, it would be a good beginning. Whatever your choice, these are my suggested absolute minimum drive requirements for your server:

❏ A floppy disk drive, for better maintainability

❏ A single CD-ROM or CD-RW drive

❏ A minimum of two 20GB hard drives: one for your content, and the other for backup and system recovery (see Chapter 10)

If an extensive file server is your plan, you may want to pick up a few larger hard drives; but also keep in mind that the larger the drives, the hotter they may operate. We'll cover keeping the system cool, and a few other final touches, in the next chapter.

TIPS OF THE TRADE

Laptop Drive Installation

You can use any laptop hard drive inside your desktop or server by using a 2½- to 3½-inch desktop adapter. This unit comes with an adapter that creates the standard 40-pin connector and a male Molex power connection. There are two primary reasons for using laptop drives. They are rugged, designed for mobility; and although they are slower than standard hard drives, run a lot cooler, too. The reason, obviously, is space. (I do not recommend using a laptop drive as your primary drive.)

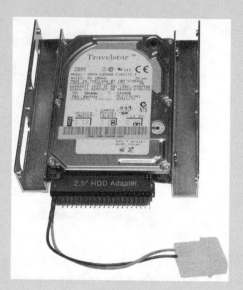

1. To install a third hard drive, pull out another blank from the 5½-inch bays.

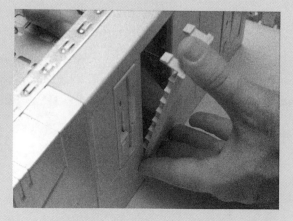

2. Slide in the 3½-inch hard drive, with attached 5½-inch bay adapters.

3. Secure the hard drive in place with four screws.

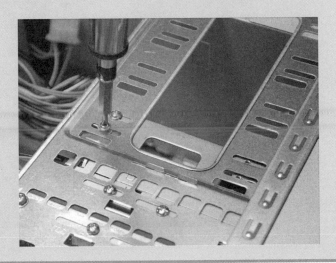

**TIPS OF
THE TRADE**

4. Replace the blank cover on the bay.

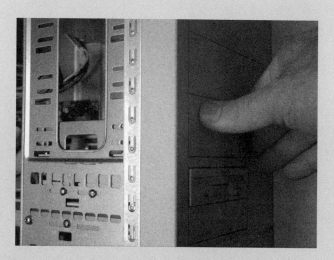

5. Insert a PCI IDE controller card into an open PCI slot.

TIPS OF THE TRADE

6. Plug in the cable from the third hard drive.

TESTING 1-2-3

❑ The floppy drive is, usually used for maintainability purposes after the initial hard drive installation.

❑ The CD/DVD-ROM drive, typically used for installing software, and a DVD-ROM drive can also be a shared device, much like a printer.

❑ The primary and secondary IDE controllers on the motherboard will only hold a maximum of two devices in each, one as master, and one as slave.

❑ You can add SCSI drives to a motherboard, with an open PCI slot, using a SCSI host bus adapter, or additional IDE devices using an IDE host bus adapter.

Chapter 7

Final Touches

Tools of The Trade

Precision screwdriver set
Needle-nose pliers
Anti-static sleeves
Electrostatic-free environment
Nylon or plastic ties
Rubber bands
Two 80mm case fans
Keyboard
Mouse
Monitor

At this point we have built the majority of our server, with the exception of the network adapters, which are covered in Chapter 8. In this chapter, we need to add a few critical final touches to ensure the longevity of the overall system, and then make a final detailed examination of our creation. The state of the server's interior depends on the amount of devices you may have, the size of your chassis, length of cables, and design of your motherboard, among others. Chances are the inside of your server looks like the Amazon jungle, so there are several precautions you need to be aware of before even booting up the system.

It's a Jungle in There

Many of the additions I propose are redundant, duplicating efforts, but I've found that spending this extra effort (and dollars) does extend the life of your server and its components. A final analysis of the system will also uncover any inconsistencies and missing pieces that may create mysterious problems later during installation or actual operation.

Temperature

The thermal engineers at AMD have determined that using an 80mm or larger exhaust fan at the upper rear of the internal chassis, just below the power supply, coupled with the bottom inlet fan of the power supply, creates the best airflow to keep the CPU coolest (see Figure 7-1). The typical 80mm case fan is available at many different outlets, from eBay and uBid for as little as $5.00 (with free shipping), to over $20 at many retail outlets.

Figure 7-1
The recommended placement of the exhaust fans in the computer chassis to create the optimal airflow

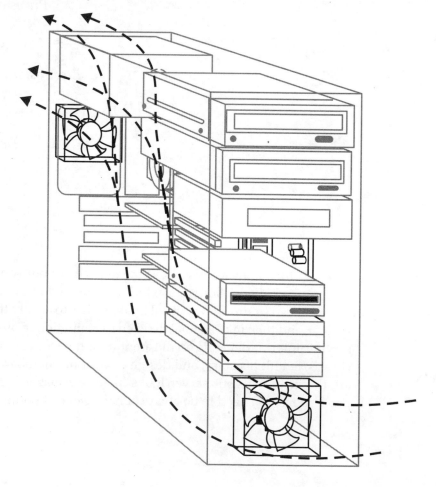

An overheating system can become unstable and somewhat unreliable. The components of any computer (server or workstation) that runs hot will have a shorter lifespan. This was the case for one of my early OEM computers. I didn't recognize this problem at first because, well, it was in the hands of another professional system administrator who probably should've known better. Within the first two years of the purchase, the hard drive died and needed to be replaced. Then the CD-ROM drive died, followed by the floppy drive, and finally the entire computer itself. I dug it up recently and, while examining the interior, discovered that the lack of ventilation was largely due to lengthy cables cluttering up the small, confined midtower. Also, no case fans were ever installed. Not surprisingly, the system runs much better with proper ventilation, even with newer devices installed that run hotter.

Extreme temperatures are slow death for electronic components. This is even more evident in a system stuffed with multiple components, running 24/7, 365 days a year. An overheating system will become unstable, and its components will eventually need to be replaced. I cannot stress the importance of keeping your server within the proper temperature requirements—both inside and out. Diagnosing an overheating server may be difficult, since the symptoms may appear to be caused by something else entirely. Random lockups, grinding noises, device misreads, and flickering video are all symptoms of a badly overheated system.

To keep your server cool, you must follow these guidelines:

❏ Install a CPU fan and heat sink that are the proper size.

❏ Use heat dissipation compound under the heat sink.

❏ Include at least two exhaust fans to keep air flowing.

❏ Avoid placing the server in a hot or humid area.

❏ Avoid placing the server in direct sunlight.

❏ Do not use oversized cables.

❏ Do not pack extra-large hard drives (80GB+) together in the typical hard drive carriage.

The typical 80mm case fan is shown here:

The addition of a CPU heat sink and fan that are the proper size may protect your processor from overheating and shutting down the system. However, because of the steady growth of the acceleration of RAM, hard drives, and even CD/DVD-ROM drives, many other components may generate excessive heat. This became all too clear to me after I built a dual-processor, digital-video workstation. I installed three hard drives in the traditional hard drive carriage, just below the floppy disk drive. The system became somewhat erratic at one point, and, upon opening up the chassis, I discovered that the aluminum carriage that held the hard drives was hot to the touch—not "warm," but just a few degrees below burning hot.

I had installed the ventilation according to the AMD recommendations, which controlled airflow from the front bottom of the chassis (near these three drives), up past the CPU, and out the "back door" fan just below the power supply. The front fan, which blew air inside the chassis, was just below the drives. I could feel that some of the airflow brushed against the lower drive. In an ordinary workstation that uses a single drive or even two, this may have been adequate. However, the three drives I installed were 120GB, 80GB, and 60GB in size. They run very fast and very hot. I had to do some redesigning of the system for better heat dissipation. I spread the hard drives to different locations and added hard drive and bay coolers (more on this momentarily).

At first, as usual, I blamed the problems I was having with the system on Windows, which is easy to do when the operating system appears to hang, or crashes. However, this was a "clean" system; in other words, being a fresh install, on a system that was running Windows 2000 Professional fine beforehand, there was little chance it was the OS. I suspected something else.

TIPS OF THE TRADE

The Hard Drive Cooling System

The advent of today's larger hard drives that run hotter, yet are still confined within the same chassis space, has prompted companies such as ANTEC to develop something more than a bottom dual fan attachment. This hard drive cooling system is an enclosure that secures the hard drive within an aluminum casing. The specially designed case provides better heat dissipation using dual fans in the front of the unit (see the following illustration) and using the entire top of the unit as heat sink. This specific brand also comes with two temperature gauges, one for the hard drive and the other for the chassis.

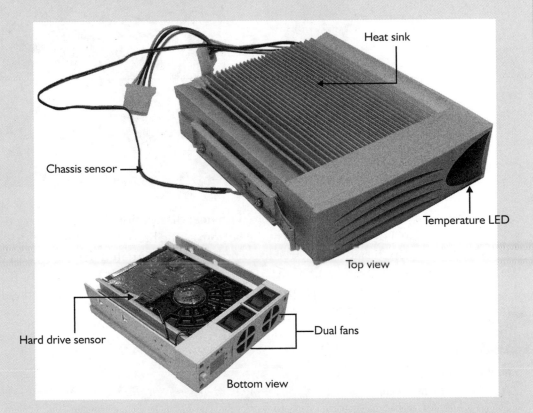

Heat sink

Chassis sensor

Temperature LED

Top view

Hard drive sensor

Dual fans

Bottom view

If you choose to use 80GB or greater hard drives rather than the twin 20GB hard drives I have suggested, keep this example in mind. It could save you time and possibly hardware (if you don't catch the problem in time).

Excessive heat will damage and/or reduce the life expectancy of the hard drive. My first step was to remove the middle of the three drives (the 120GB drive) and add a $20 hard drive cooler. I moved the hard drive with the hard drive cooler up to the 5¼-inch bays using an adapter, which provided more room for the heat to dissipate, and the hard drive cooler that added another half-inch to the overall height of the hard drive. If you run out of fan connections on the motherboard, there are adapters available to create a link between devices (see Figure 7-2).

Figure 7-2
Power cord adapter
for CPU, hard drive,
and system fans

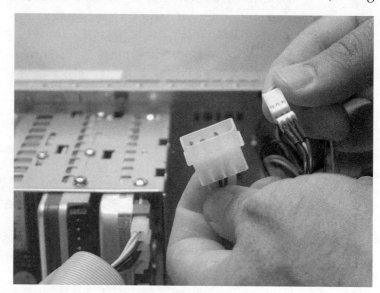

Hard drive coolers help with heat dissipation for today's larger (and hotter) hard drives. Attached at the bottom of the hard drive, the hard drive cooler fans keep the side holes free to secure into its designated drive bay, and not force you to purchase an adapter to move it to the 5¼-inch bays. Again, if you do have more than two hard drives, you will need to spread them out and will need to use a 5¼-inch drive bay.

Make Sure It's Right-Side Up

A common mistake people make when installing hard drives is to slip them in upside down, which forces the read/write heads to work twice as hard, thus decreasing the meantime between failure (MTBF).

Next, I placed a bay cooler that I picked up from NewEgg.com (see Figure 7-3) into the bay that originally housed the 120GB hard drive. This device can be used either parallel inside a 3½-inch bay or perpendicular within a 5¼-inch bay. This pulls heat away from the 80GB hard drive on top and blows a cooler version of the air onto the 60GB hard drive below. The entire system is now running much cooler.

Figure 7-3
A bay cooler, designed to be used in either the 3½-inch or 5¼-inch bays

The system's speaker is typically in the same location as the front exhaust fan (see Figure 7-4). This is important for diagnosing any problems with BIOS, RAM, or the video adapter with specific warning alarms unique to your version of BIOS. For example, during the POST, if your Award BIOS recognizes a problem with the memory, it'll set off an alarm of one long beep, then three consecutive beeps. Other alarms will warn you of CPU failure, video memory misreads, and so forth.

Figure 7-4
The location of the front case fan and system speaker

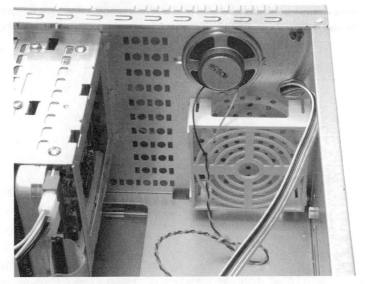

Beyond The Traditional Midtower Chassis

The traditional midtower chassis, like the one we're using here, limits the amount of drives you can use and cooling exhaust fans you can install. If you're planning to use more than three large hard drives for your server, you'll most likely be out of our $400 budget. Therefore, you shouldn't skimp on the chassis case to support and protect those drives. The following example uses the ANTEC Plus1000 small-office, home-office (SOHO) file server as an example of the additional features a larger file server chassis offers.

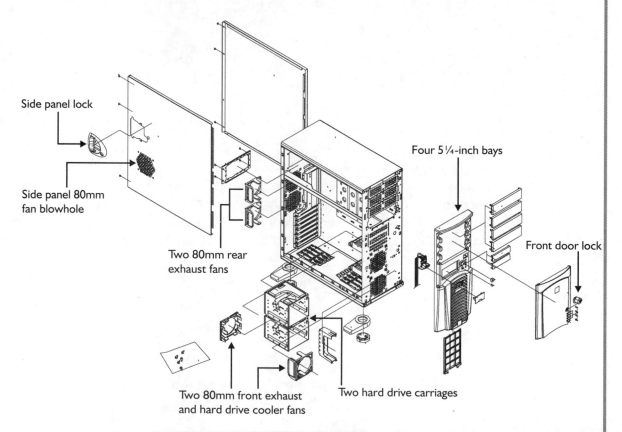

Side panel lock

Side panel 80mm fan blowhole

Two 80mm rear exhaust fans

Four 5¼-inch bays

Front door lock

Two 80mm front exhaust and hard drive cooler fans

Two hard drive carriages

The ANTEC Plus1080 comes with four chassis exhaust fans, with an additional fan blowhole on the side panel. In addition, the front two exhaust fans push the incoming air through any two hard drives installed in the lower hard drive carriage, eliminating the needed for a separate hard drive cooler. Other features include a chassis lock and key, and a front door lock that will protect the drives inserted in the 5¼-inch bays using slide rails (for easy maintainability).

Most computer chassis have a bracket frame at the front bottom of the case, designed to hold the typical 80mm case fan, shown next. This particular one didn't require a screwdriver to remove, as it's kept in place by hooks at the base of the outer frame.

Chassis fan connector

To insert the front case fan, pull out the frame holder from the case, as just shown, and place the 80mm case fan inside, with the direction of the airflow blowing inside the case. The airflow follows the label position on the fan itself.

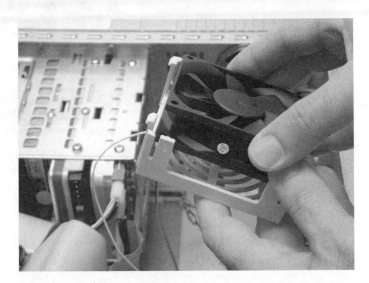

Next, snap the fan frame back into position, and secure the fan power cord by wrapping it around either the power and LED cables or the speaker cable. This will avoid the fan power cord snagging or becoming an obstruction.

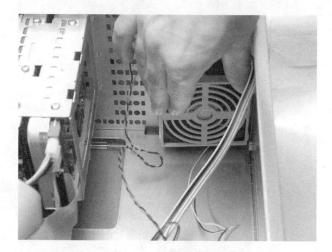

The second fan typically is positioned just below the power supply at the rear of the chassis. This fan blows the air outside, which keeps a constant cooling airflow traveling from the lower-front part of the chassis to the upper-rear part.

Case fans use a unique screw that actually screws into the plastic of the fan. If the fan you purchased didn't come with these screws, a small nut and bolt will also hold the fan in place.

In the event your chassis isn't equipped for an 80mm rear exhaust fan, the exhaust blower, which runs only a few dollars more, will also do the trick. However, these install in place of a PCI expansion card, so you will lose the use of a slot, shown next.

What a Tangled Web of Wires We Weave

Although today's faster CPUs require a larger, louder CPU fan, the extra noise could work to your advantage. If you boot up your server and don't hear that fan buzzing away, you better double-check to make sure it's working because, if it isn't, you'll burn up your CPU. Also, many BIOS systems now include an alarm that you can set that will warn you if your CPU fan isn't working for whatever reason.

Recently, I added another hard drive to an FTP server but, due to time constraints, neglected to secure the power cable. I booted up the system and noticed it was running a bit too quietly. I immediately shut it down and opened it up to discover that the cable I had just added was resting on top of the CPU fan, stopping it from working and potentially damaging the CPU (shown next). I untangled it and secured it, along with a few of the other cables, to the frame. Had I not realized this mistake, my CPU may have overheated and died. Quality assurance is very important at this stage, and I highly recommend that you create a checklist that should include some of the items I list later in this chapter.

You can easily prevent cables from becoming obstructions. The best way is simply to use either nylon or plastic lock ties to pull the jumble of cables away from the motherboard and CPU. You also can wrap the CPU fan cord around the bundle once you have it securely out of the way, as shown here:

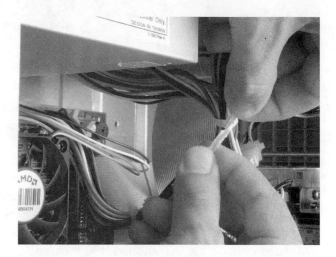

Wrap the CPU fan power cord around the nearest, secured bundle to avoid its becoming an obstruction within the fan itself.

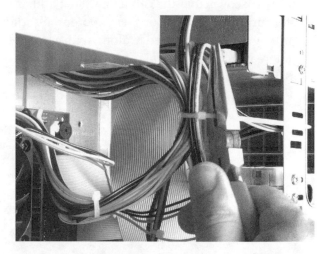

The device cables can also become cumbersome, making it difficult both for you to work and for air to flow freely. The best course of action is to fold and wrap any excess device cables with a rubber band or zip tie, as shown next.

The "Dark Side" of the Chassis

Once you have all the devices in place and have securely fastened any cabling, it's time to secure the "dark side" of the devices. Most of the time, you'll be working on one side of the chassis, the side that puts the motherboard flat and gives you access to all of its components. It's a good idea to install all the components first, and double-check them; and then, before booting up the system, secure the other side. The reason I recommend following this order is that it may potentially save you time—if you've unsuccessfully installed or configured a component (such as a hard drive) and have to pull it out to examine it, you'll have to unscrew only one side. Unscrewing both sides to remove a device can be quite tedious.

The two CD-ROM drives in the upper 5¼-inch bays require eight screws.

The floppy and two hard drives in the lower 3½-inch carriage require at least six screws.

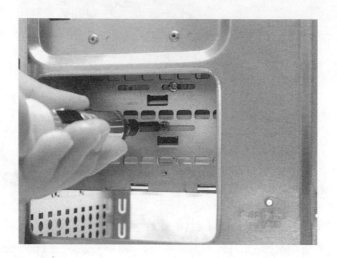

Secure Drive Devices on Both Sides of the Chassis

As I mentioned in Chapter 5, securing any drive devices on both sides of the chassis is important because a loosely fitted drive, especially any CD read/write drive, may cause misreads if it is not securely set into place.

The amount of time you'll spend on these steps depends largely on the condition of the interior of your server. Typically, assuming that you do have a fully compatible lot of components, you shouldn't have to take more than 30 minutes for a pre-operational check.

Pre-operational Check

Now that we've successfully put together the guts of a computer, it's time to perform an operational system check before we turn this machine into a server. Our first course of action is to see if it will at least boot up. You need to get into BIOS and then to the A:\ prompt; otherwise, you won't be able to use most of the diagnostic utilities if you need to troubleshoot a problem. If you purchased the same components that I recommended, there's a very good chance you'll have success because this configuration works for me—I've tested it.

A standard pre-operational check includes the following:

❏ Before touching any component, make sure you're properly grounded and free of electrostatic discharge (refer to Chapter 2 for more details).

❏ Make sure the CPU and the CPU heat sink and fan are securely in place. If you can wiggle the fan, it's either not on correctly or not the right size.

❏ Check that the motherboard is securely in place and that all the secure points are used, as shown next.

❏ Double-check that there are no cord, wire, or cable obstructions within the CPU fan, or within any hard drive cooler fan or case fan.

❏ Although this should've been checked and confirmed earlier, make sure the memory modules are the compatible speed for the motherboard and confirm proper insertion. Compatibility can be confirmed through the motherboard manual or (as I prefer) online at the manufacturer's web site, the latter of which should be more up to date and present any further incompatibilities discovered after the manual was printed.

❏ Check that the floppy drive is in its bay securely, and that both the power cord and data cable are correct.

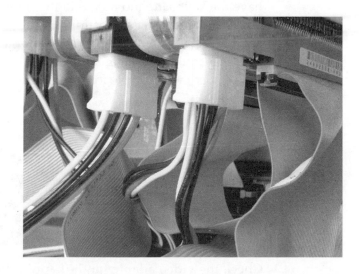

❑ Make sure the hard drive Molex power cables and IDE cables are snug within their appropriate controllers and that they are correctly configured as master and/or slave; if they are SCSI drives, double-check the ID assignments and for proper termination, as shown here:

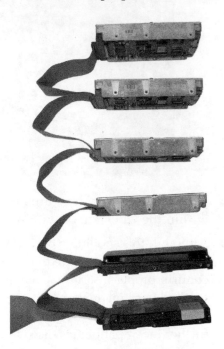

❑ Insert the keyboard cable and mouse cable into their DIN and/or mini-DIN connectors, and insert the power cord. Make sure that you have the keyboard and mouse in the right sockets; otherwise, you'll get a keyboard error message during the boot sequence. If you have the computer lying on its side, with the motherboard visible, the keyboard connects on the bottom and the mouse on the top. This is typically color-coded, with purple for the keyboard and green for the mouse.

❑ Check the video adapter and (if applicable) the sound card to ensure proper seating in their sockets. Then, plug the monitor into the VGA port of the video adapter.

❏ Make sure the motherboard is connected to the power supply using the standard ATX connector.

❏ Check for a power supply connection into an electrical outlet, and that the power supply switch (if applicable) is in the On position (typically the side of the switch marked with a line, as opposed to a circle for the Off position).

A Pre-operational Checklist

A short list of what to check before powering up your machine includes the following:

❏ CPU and the CPU heat sink and fan are securely in place.

❏ Motherboard is completely secured.

❏ Any cord, wire, or cable obstructions are cleared.

❏ Memory modules are compatible and properly inserted.

❏ Video adapter and (if applicable) sound card are seated properly.

❏ Motherboard is connected to the power supply.

❏ Power supply is plugged into an electrical outlet, and the power supply switch (if applicable) is in the On position (typically marked with a line).

❏ Floppy drive is correctly installed.

❏ Hard drives are properly installed and configured:

  ❏ Correct master and slave assignment.

  ❏ The red stripe on most cables for ATA devices points to pin 1; if there is no colored identifier, you can identify pin 1 by the notch on the cable connectors—if the notch is facing up, pin 1 is on the right side of the cable.

  ❏ If SCSI drives, double-check ID assignments and proper termination.

❏ Correctly inserted keyboard, mouse, and monitor cables.

❏ Power cords for the computer and monitor are plugged into electrical outlets.

❏ All appropriate devices are connected to the power supply, either using the four-pin Molex connector for your hard drives and CD/DVD-ROM drives or the four-pin AMP floppy power connector.

If you've purchased a new CPU, motherboard, and memory, there's an even better chance of success. In order to find out, first check the validity of all of your installed components. This will help reduce the number of possible variables involved in such a complex, independent system. You may have flipped on the power earlier to see if there's life in the motherboard (by watching the CPU fans start spinning), but now you need to see it come to life onscreen.

Supply Check

TIME CHECK

The amount of time for this step will vary widely. If you've assembled compatible components that are properly installed and configured, entering BIOS Setup to change the boot order of the drives and then rebooting would take no more than a minute or two. However, if you press the power switch and nothing happens, you'll need to step back and re-examine the components for any malfunction or incompatibility you may have overlooked. This has taken me anywhere from less than a minute (after discovering I didn't have the power cord plugged into the power supply outlet), to a few minutes, after reseating a memory module (remember to unplug the power supply when doing this procedure), to spending hours examining one component at a time, to finally discovering an incompatibility.

At this point, your system is a go, but a pre-operational check also includes gathering some tools and supplies. This includes a boot floppy disk or CD-ROM, which usually is or is part of your network operating system, or any operating system setup disk. You can easily create one using Windows 95 and 98 by inserting a blank floppy disk into the floppy disk drive, right-clicking the floppy drive icon in Windows, and simply choosing Format and then Copy System Files when formatting a disk. New hard drives, as well as many used or refurbished ones, are blank. If a boot disk was not included with your hard drive, you can download the manufacturer's hard disk preparation software (on its web site) and prepare a set of floppy setup disks on another computer. You must get to an A:\ prompt, since most diagnostics utilities from hard drive manufacturers and most flash BIOS utilities start there.

You also need to know how to get into the BIOS setup, which usually is accomplished by pressing DELETE, F2, or F1 once your BIOS has completed your RAM check. Typically, it will label how to enter BIOS at the bottom of the screen, such as "Press DEL to enter BIOS" (see Figure 7-5). Note that this information also is available in the motherboard manual, as it may scroll by too fast for you to read it (you could also press the PAUSE key to pause the screen, but you'll have to be quick). In any event, be prepared to press any one of those keys. This will get you into the BIOS setup screen.

If you're using a CD-ROM to boot up the system, then you'll most likely need to change the boot device order in BIOS (see Chapter 9). Typically, the initial boot process begins by looking for an operating system with the floppy disk drive, and if that is empty, moves to the first hard drive. If the hard drive is new and unformatted, BIOS will present a message indicating that no operating system was found.

All system BIOSs offer you the opportunity to change the boot disk order; this is one of two important steps once you enter into BIOS. The second step is to choose

Figure 7-5
A successful
installation begins
with the first boot
screen shown here.

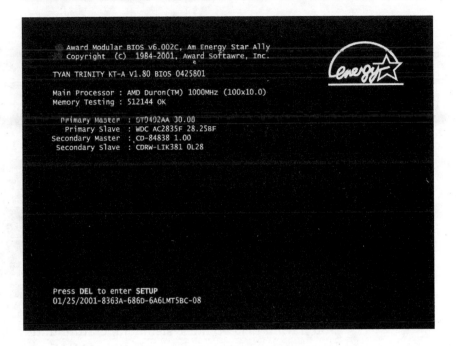

the "optimized" or "default" settings, and then save and exit. The system will then reboot with the new settings. If you're not familiar with BIOS, I recommend that you do not venture too deep into it and experiment, since you could stop the system from booting at all. If you stick to the boot order, and set the system defaults or optimal settings, you'll be fine. If you find that you've inadvertently changed something in BIOS, you can clear those changes by switching the CMOS jumper or removing the CMOS battery for about 60 seconds (refer to Chapter 3). This will bring your system back to the default settings.

Temperature Check

Many BIOSs provide a CPU and chassis-monitoring screen. The PC Health Status screen in the Award BIOS of the Tyan Trinity KT (see Figure 7-6) will give you the temperature of the CPU, the RPM of the CPU, and the RPM of one case fan, as well as the overall system temperature. If the BIOS on your motherboard doesn't offer this feature, you can download free utilities from Download.com, such as SpeedFan or System Monitor, that provide similar functionality.

Figure 7-6
The PC Health Status
screen in Award BIOS

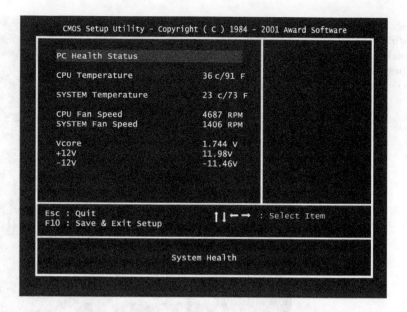

You'll want to keep the system temperature under 100 degrees at all times, and the CPU temperature (at least for this AMD Duron 1 GHz; your choice may vary) at between 90 and 110 degrees. If you wish, you can set a warning at a certain temperature, upward of 140 degrees. It's best to check your CPU documentation to see if it lists a preferable setting as a benchmark.

TESTING 1-2-3

❑ Use at least two chassis exhaust fans to create a constant airflow.

❑ Untangle the web of wires that may become obstructions to the system cooling fans and a blockage for proper airflow.

❑ Do not pack together hard drives of 60GB or more without additional cooling support, such as a hard drive cooler or hard drive cooling system, and/or separating them for better heat dissipation.

❑ When ready to boot up the system, make sure you have a startup floppy disk or CD-ROM.

Chapter 8

The Power of
the Network

Tools of the Trade

Precision screwdriver set

Needle-nose pliers

Anti-static sleeves

Electrostatic-free environment

Two PCI Ethernet network adapters

New Cat 5 network cables

Router

Hub or switch

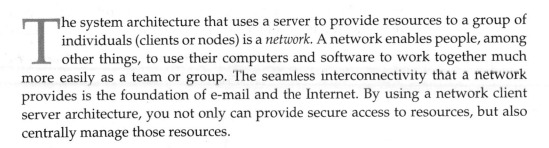

The system architecture that uses a server to provide resources to a group of individuals (clients or nodes) is a *network*. A network enables people, among other things, to use their computers and software to work together much more easily as a team or group. The seamless interconnectivity that a network provides is the foundation of e-mail and the Internet. By using a network client server architecture, you not only can provide secure access to resources, but also centrally manage those resources.

Ethernet and the Power Law

Robert M. Metcalfe, inventor of Ethernet, the most common technology for fast local area network (LAN) connectivity, believes that the network creates power, or energy, when interaction happens between the connected people and/or systems. In his attempt to explain this phenomenon, he describes it as the "Power Law." He claims that the power of any network goes as "2 to the nth," where n is the number of nodes (clients) of a network. Metcalfe's Law (as it has come to be known) explains that the power of the network increases exponentially by the number of computers connected to it, by both providing and using resources (see Figure 8-1).

Figure 8-1
Metcalfe's Law of the power of the network explains that the energy derived from the interaction within a network increases exponentially.

The power of a network creates monetary value through cost efficiencies. For example, the first "network" was the telephone system. The more people that joined the network, the more cost-efficient the network became. Its growth over time benefited all of its participants, as depicted in Table 8-1, which shows that the cost of a standard-rate, three-minute long distance call from New York to London in 1927 corresponded to 200 work hours compared to only a few minutes of one work hour today. The network also provides time savings and access to information that normally would have never been available to customers, associates, and partners, making it possible to do better business. The computer network, whether it's a LAN or the Internet itself, has taken this concept to a higher level, interconnecting people, places, and things asynchronously; there doesn't need to be anyone on the other line to complete the connection.

Year	Current Dollars	Hours of Work
1927	75.00	200
1928	45.00	120
1930	30.00	80
1936	21.00	56
1944	21.00	40
1945	12.00	20
1969	12.00	6
1970	9.60	5
1974	5.40	1.6
1980	4.80	0.9
1986	4.83	0.7
1991	3.32	0.3
1995	2.40	0.2
1999	0.30	0.02

Table 8-1
Cost and Corresponding Work Time for Three-Minute Telephone Call from New York to London

Andrew M. Odlyzko, Director and Assistant Vice President for Research at the University of Minnesota, has written over 150 technical papers regarding internetworking technologies, and doesn't believe in Metcalfe's Law, stating that "Not everyone on the network provides value, all the time." That's true, if we were looking at it from the perspective of each individual person, but a network is an ethereal collection of nodes that can take on a life of its own. In other words, the *entire* network, as an entity itself, holds the power and not the individual.

Networks or networking (to "network") materializes through communication: people using a variety of devices to connect. Any company is not one person. Sure, a visionary may exist, one who presses on through obstacles and carries the company to new heights, but that person has the support of other people. Capitalism is a team effort. I wrote this book, but editors, designers, artists, and others were also involved in making it happen. My point is that any capitalistic venture is only as good as its people and resources. One of the keys to success is to figure out a way to pull down those office or cubicle walls and make it as painless as possible for your most valuable assets to interact and collaborate, and bring out the best in everyone. The network can do that, bringing together people with the best tools, to accomplish the best work. Computer networks are capable of providing the following:

- ❏ E-mail
- ❏ File and print sharing
- ❏ Shared hardware resources (hard drives, CD-RWs, DVD-ROM, tape drives, and so on)
- ❏ Internet access
- ❏ Firewall
- ❏ Web server
- ❏ FTP server
- ❏ Remote access to applications
- ❏ Scalability
- ❏ Integration of different departments and systems
- ❏ Videoconferencing
- ❏ Chat
- ❏ Digital white-boarding for remote collaboration
- ❏ Global backup and recovery

Networks are also about *translation*—the translation of the value of multiple resources and different devices and thus transforming those resources and devices into something of a union. It's not about the football player, but the football team; not about the general, but the army. The server and network operating system combined become the translator. Oprah Winfrey once said that luck is "preparation meeting opportunity." How many opportunities were lost because someone in your company had no knowledge of the success, resource, or capability of another? Alternatively, having had the knowledge and then access to a complex plan or proposal that closed a deal, corrected a problem, or put out the fire on a burning platform? There are collaborative tools (many of which are built into Windows 2000 Server and Server 2003) that will bring cohesiveness to your company.

Getting Wired

The International Organization for Standardization Open Systems Interconnection (ISO/OSI) reference model, also called the *OSI reference model*, is a primary architectural model for communications between computer systems. Many of the components of the OSI reference model exist in all communications systems. This model separates the typical networking system architecture into seven layers: application, presentation, session, transport, network, data link, and physical (see Figure 8-2). Each layer has its own unique functions and protocols. A computer networking protocol is a set of standards and rules that hardware and software must follow in order to communicate with other computers.

As part of the Network and Transport layers of the OSI model, Transmission Control Protocol/Internet Protocol (TCP/IP) has become a standard for computer communications. Any device running TCP/IP can communicate with any other shared device, anywhere in the world, running any type of operating system, software, or network topology, such as Ethernet, as long as it, too, is running TCP/IP. The following are the four general layers that make up this "translator" TCP/IP technology:

❑ Application layer

❑ Transport layer

❑ Internet layer

❑ Interface or physical layer

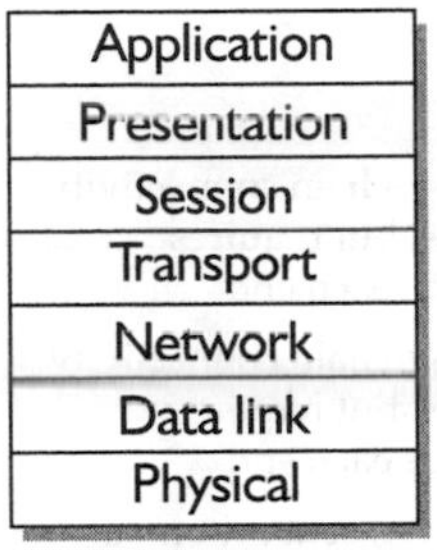

Figure 8-2
The Open Systems
Interconnection
reference model
is a standard
architectural model
for interconnectivity
between computer
systems.

| Application |
| Presentation |
| Session |
| Transport |
| Network |
| Data link |
| Physical |

The application layer holds the actual software and utilities that allow such networking functions as file and print sharing and authentication. The application layer passes the newly created data to the transport layer. This layer consists of the Transmission Control Protocol (TCP), a method of communication that confirms delivery of information, and the User Datagram Protocol (UDP), which just sends the information and hopes it gets there. This layer is all about traveling—moving data from one place to another.

The Internet layer includes the Internet Protocol (IP), Address Resolution Protocol (ARP), and Internet Control Message Protocol (ICMP). IP addressing standardizes how computers communicate with each other (see the section "IP Addresses"). This core scheme creates the ubiquitous communications between devices. The IP address typically consists of four octets of up to three digits (i.e. 192.168.0.1) as part of the Internet Protocol, while ARP is what translates those series of numbers to the physical Medium Access Control (MAC) address, which is the embedded hardware address. The Domain Name System (DNS), which is on the application layer, will resolve an IP address to a domain name, such as www.yourwebsite.com, while ARP resolves IP addresses to the device's physical address (more on this in Chapter 10).

The lowest layer (physical) is considered to be where the least amount of intelligence on the network is used. It simply deals with raw bits (0's and 1's) and frames. A frame is the logical grouping of information in a transmission, which is also referred to as the header and trailer. All data that is transport from one place to another retains a "header" and "footer" that serves as a label to explain its contents and for synchronization and error control. When you send a transmission, the physical layer handles putting the data on the wire in its rawest form (bits and bytes).

The next layer, the data-link layer, provides reliable transit of the data, or frames, across a physical link. The data-link layer is concerned with physical addressing, network topology, physical link management, error notification, ordered delivery of frames, and flow control. MAC addresses and switches (which use the MAC address to recognize each device on the network) work here as well. See Table 8-2 for a description of network design.

Topology	Ethernet	Description	Cable Type	Maximum Cable Length	Maximum Nodes	Data Rate
10Base5 bus (linear)	Yes	Straight daisy-chain connectivity with no hubs, but requires terminators at each end	RG 8 coaxial cable with BNC connectors and terminators	500 meters	30	10 Mbps
10Base2 bus (linear)	Yes	Straight daisy-chain connectivity with no hubs, but requires terminators at each end	RG 58 coaxial cable with BNC connectors and terminators	185 meters	30	10 Mbps
Token Ring	No	A token (frame) sent around a ring-based topology (logical ring) where the nodes do not look for a carrier on the line to transmit (collision detection), but avoid collisions completely	Category 2 or 4	45 meters	72	4 or 16 Mbps
10Base-T, 100Base-TX star	Yes	Multiple workstations connected to a hub or switch	Category 5 twisted-pair	100 meters	1024	10 or 100 Mbps

Table 8-2
Network Designs

The network interface card, sometimes referred to as a NIC (pronounced "nick") card or a network adapter, works at the data-link layer of the OSI reference model, or the network access layer of the older Department of Defense (DOD) model. The software driver allows the operating system to "drive" the hardware functions. The majority of this layer is invisible, which greatly reduces its complexity and thus increases its usability.

Peer-to-Peer and Client/Server

Peer-to-peer and client/server are two basic network types. A peer-to-peer network interconnects independent workstations to share files and printers (see Figure 8-3). Although installing this type of network is easy, it drains resources from each individual workstation, thereby slowing down its performance, and is less secure than a server-based network.

As the example in Figure 8-4 depicts, if you're using Windows 2000 Professional and/or Windows XP Professional as your workstation operating system, you can create a simple peer-to-peer (server-less) network simply by installing network adapters into a free PCI slot on each of two computers, and installing the appropriate software driver. The drivers usually come with the network adapter on a floppy disk or CD-ROM, and many of the drivers for the more popular devices are included within Windows 2000 Professional, Windows 2000 Server, Windows Server 2003, and Windows XP Professional. You can connect the two computers by plugging a Category 5 crossover cable into the outlet on each network adapter. A crossover cable is used to interconnect two computers by "crossing over" their respective pin

Figure 8-3
Small peer-to-peer
network

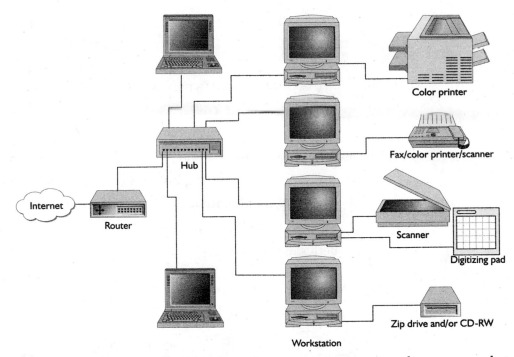

connectors. This is a simple way of creating a peer-to-peer network, as you need at least two or more machines (see Figure 8-4).

Figure 8-4
A simple peer-to-peer
network, created by
installing network
adapters in each
computer and
connecting them

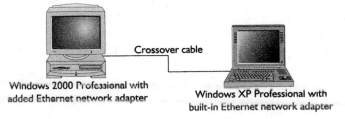

Once you've chosen two machines to network, you need to do the following steps:

1. Install a NIC in each machine.

2. Configure the proper driver on the NIC for the workstation's operating system.

3. Configure TCP/IP by assigning a unique IP address on each node with a common 24-bit subnet. For example, assign node 1 the IP address of 10.0.0.1, with a 24-bit mask of 255.255.255.0. Configure the other workstation as 10.0.0.2 with the same 24-bit mask. This will allow them to communicate via TCP/IP.

4. Connect both workstations via a hub or a crossover cable

5. Configure your Windows OS to be a client on a network: right-click My Computer, select Properties, and click the Network Identification tab.

Change both workgroups to be identical, or else they will not be able to share resources.

The client/server environment provides a multitude of advantages (many of which have been mentioned in previous chapters), including the following (see Figure 8-5):

- ❏ Better security
- ❏ Centralized administration
- ❏ Reduction of processing burdens on individual workstations
- ❏ Increased collaboration
- ❏ More extendibility
- ❏ Better maintainability

Figure 8-5
Converting peer-to-peer into a client/server network

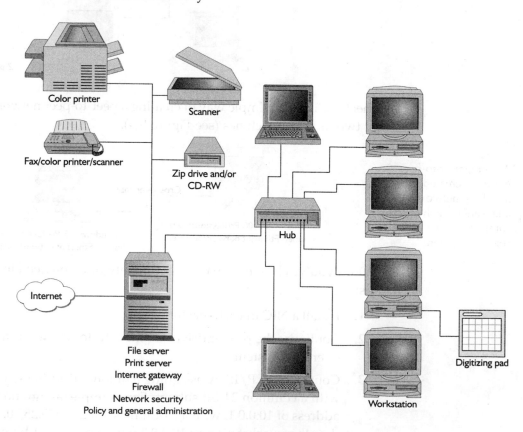

The first step in network design involves determining how you want to configure your network. This includes creating a *topology*, a pictorial description of how your network is set up, which is driven mostly by your office environment and locations. The following are the three basic types of topologies:

- ❏ **Bus**   A daisy-chain linkage with termination and ground required on both ends. Holds a maximum of 30 nodes.
- ❏ **Token Ring**   Incorporates nodes within a circular channel that's always "on" and looking for the right data. Holds a maximum of 72 nodes.
- ❏ **Star**   Gives you the option of linking up to 1024 nodes to one network and is the most popular topology.

Figure 8-3 depicts how a smaller company uses a peer-to-peer network to share access to the Internet through a hub or switch. A *hub* is an interconnected hardware device with a minimum of four Ethernet ports (shown next) that send signals (packets) of data from one port to all other ports, creating a continuous connection between devices.

The switch or switching hub (shown next) only targets the destination port, thus keeping bandwidth at a maximum. If you have a broadband connection to the Internet, either using a cable or DSL modem, or a T1 line, rather than plug the Internet connection into one workstation to take on the burden of Internet sharing, you can plug the connection into the uplink of a router, thus opening up the signal for use by all who are plugged in. The router accepts the dynamic address from the service provider and can generate its own series of addresses for the LAN using DHCP.

There are usually individuals within an organization who have special devices linked to their own computer, via either a parallel or USB port. A few of these items are available to the network through a hub, except for workstations that have different operating systems and lack cross-platform interoperability. For example, you can configure Windows 2000 Professional and XP Professional to provide file and print sharing services for Macintosh computers, but the CD-RW, Zip drive, and scanner may involve some interaction with the users.

Many of today's Ethernet hubs and switches work at dual speeds: the original 10Base-T (transmission speed of 10 Mbps), and 100Base-T, called *Fast Ethernet*, with speeds of up to 100 Mbps. ("Base" refers to an exclusive Ethernet baseband signal, and *T* designates the media that carries the signal—in this case, twisted-pair cable.) You should keep the speed in mind when purchasing a hub or switch. If you're used to a cable or DSL broadband connection, with speeds up to 1.5 Mbps, you may feel that 10 Mbps is a big enough jump until your server is up and running and you're sharing 50MB files with colleagues. There is a noticeable difference between data transferred on a LAN at 100 Mbps and at 10 Mbps. Table 8-3 shows the various types of network cable, their capacity, and use.

Category	Data Rate	Typical Application
Cat 1	Less than 1 Mbps	Analog voice—Plain Old Telephone Service (POTS) Doorbell Silver Satin–type RJ-11 cabling
Cat 2	4 Mbps	Mainly older Token Ring networks
Cat 3	16 Mbps	Voice and data on 10Base-T Ethernet
Cat 4	20 Mbps	Rarely used except for 16 Mbps Token Ring
Cat 5	100 Mbps, Gigabit Ethernet	100 Mbps (100Base-T) 155 Mbps ATM
Cat 5E/Cat 6 (fiber-optic and copper)	1000 Mbps (four pair)	Gigabit Ethernet

Table 8-3
Cable Types and Speeds

Setting Up a Star Network

The most important advantage to the Ethernet star topology is expandability. As long as a computer has an Ethernet network adapter, you can join up to 1024 nodes to a star network by plugging into an RJ-45 jack on a hub or switch, which may be uplinked from another hub or switch (see Figure 8-6). Some configuration is involved, but with the right OS and server configuration, it could be minimal. The requirements for an Ethernet network include compatible OSs, network adapters with appropriate drivers, a twisted-pair cable for each node, and enough hubs and/or switches to accommodate each connection. If you're planning to link a few dozen computers within the near future, segregate them by department or location.

Each group could have its own switch, which in turn could uplink to another switch, turning your star into a spanning-tree topology. This is by far the best course of action, as it gives you the flexibility to expand: more nodes, more stars.

Figure 8-6
Groupings in a peer-to-peer star topology network

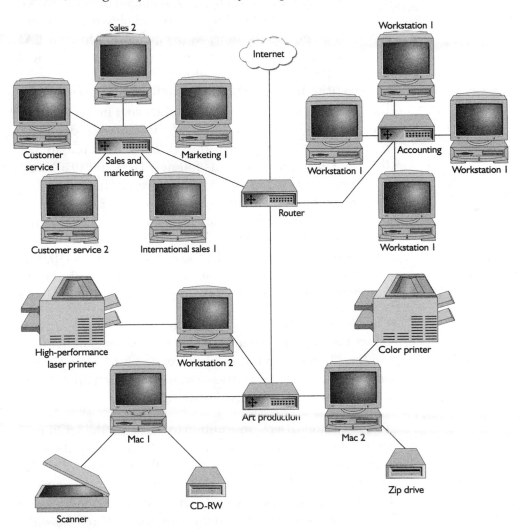

The last port of the eight-port hub, depicted in Figure 8-7, converts to an uplink port by pressing the button next to it. Most hubs label the uplink port, and most have an associated button to convert a traditional connection into an uplink connection. The uplink is a special port on a hub or switch that gives you the ability to connect more ports via additional hubs and switches.

Figure 8-7
The connections on a simple eight-port hub

IP Addresses

Now you'll begin to understand why you need all those PCI slots on the full-ATX motherboard, rather than the few available on a micro-ATX board. The server that provides Internet sharing needs two network adapters: one as the gateway to the Internet, and the other as the gateway into your LAN. Typically, using a public static IP address, from your Internet service provider (ISP) or telecom, and the IP addresses used within private LANs.

The IP address is a 32-bit number that becomes the address of the sender and receiver of information across the Ethernet network. Also referred to as a *dot address*, it includes four octets of three or less decimal digits separated by periods, as shown in this example: 192.168.100.100. In 32-bit binary language, the same example appears as follows: 11000000.10101000.1100100.1100100.

There are two parts of an IP address. The *network identifier* and the *host identifier* within that network. The preceding examples are the same IP address, with 192.168 being the network identifier and 100.100 being the host identifier. If you split the network into subnet groups, the network identifier stays the same, but the subnet is identified by the first 100 octet (or 1100100), and the last digits, or the second 100 octet, recognize the device. Both the subnet and the device numbers thus become the host identifiers (more on subnets in Chapter 10).

The Network Identifier   The Internet is made up of many individual networks. The Internet Protocol is how one network communicates with another. To have communications on the Internet, your host must have a valid and unique public IP address assigned through an ISP or numbering authority like Network Solutions (www.netsol.com).

The Host Identifier   In addition to the network identifier, the devices, such as a switch or host machine (a client or server computer), need identification as translator, sender, or receiver. Part of this host identifier signifies the *subnetwork* using a *subnet address*, which divides the physical networks into subcategories to handle many devices. The host identifier is the remaining numbers available after you subnet the IP address…if the network is 192.168.0.0 with a 24-bit subnet mask (255.255.255.0), then you can have up to 254 usable network host addresses.

When you click a hypertext link on a web page or send e-mail, the IP address becomes the address of the sender and receiver. When resolving to a domain, using Domain Name Service, these numeric addresses are resolved into a URL (Uniform Resource Locator), such as www.yahoo.com, which is easier to remember than a series of arbitrary numbers (more on IP addressing in Chapter 10).

IP Address Classes   There are four different address formats or *classes*, but only three are significant in a corporate setting. Each one provides for different amounts of networks (through changing subnets) and hosts available (using IP addresses). Anything outside of your internal LAN environment needs a formal application to the Internet Corporation for Assigned Names and Numbers (ICANN) (www.icann.org) for a network IP number. You can obtain your own series of global IP addresses through your Internet Service Provider (ISP).

- ❏ **Class A** Large networks with many devices
- ❏ **Class B** Medium-size networks
- ❏ **Class C** Small networks (less than 254 devices)

The first few bits of each IP address indicate from which address class it originates. The Class A network begins with 0. Any binary IP address beginning with 0 belongs to a Class A network. The Class B network begins with 10; Class C begins with 110. For example, the IP address 66.218.71.198 belongs to Yahoo.com. Its binary number is 1000010.11011010.1000111.11000110, which puts it into the Class B network category, since it starts with 10.

Decimal-to-Binary Conversion

To convert a decimal number to a binary number (or vice versa) in Windows 2000, XP, or 2003, select Start | Programs | Accessories | Calculator. After the Calculator opens, select View | Scientific. Your Calculator expands and gives you options to identify the numbers you enter as decimal (select the Dec radio button) or binary (select the Bin radio button). If you select the Dec radio button and then enter a number, say **192.168**, you can convert it to its binary equivalent either by pressing F8 or by selecting the Bin radio button. After clearing the Calculator, if you select the Bin radio button and then enter **1000010**, you can convert it to its decimal equivalent, 66, either by pressing F6 or by selecting the Dec radio button.

The explosive growth of the Internet is gobbling up the 32-bit IP addresses (four billion of them) because today's IP version 4 (IPv4) originated 20 years ago, and many people back then didn't imagine ever needing more than four billion addresses. It's been projected that we'll run out of addresses by 2005. The new IP version 6 (IPv6) will expand the size of the IP address to 128 bits, which will increase the number of available IP addresses to 340,232,366,920,938,463,463,374,607,431,768,211,456 (340 duodecillion, or 34 trillion trillion trillion, or 3.4×10 to the power of 38). That should cover us for a while.

We'll dig into more details about the relationship between the IP address and a physical machine in Chapter 10, when you configure your network operating system.

Cut My Wire

Wireless technology continues to proliferate, all the while speeding up from 1.6 Mbps, to 11 Mbps commercially, with 22 Mbps on the horizon. There's no doubt that eventually the speed of wireless technology will parallel the traditional landlines. The popularity of wireless technology has created a demand for faster speeds of over 11 Mbps, while dramatically reducing the prices of older 1.6 Mbps versions.

I've used the 1.6 Mbps Symphony Cordless HomeRF adapter, which uses the older ISA slot but is Plug and Play. I haven't experienced any compatibility problems when installing and configuring this device, once I have downloaded the latest drivers from Proxim.com. I picked up the Symphony Cordless HomeRF adapter for only $10, with an original price tag of $150, along with three Personal Computer Memory Card Industry Association (PCMCIA) cards at $10 each for three laptops (refer to Chapter 2). Fortunately, my Tyan Trinity KT motherboard has a single ISA slot (you won't find these on any newer motherboards), and the Internet connection I'm sharing is a cable modem, with not much more than a 300 Kbps download speed. The 1.6 Mbps Symphony Cordless HomeRF adapter may be inadequate for an internal LAN connection, at 100 Mbps, but to provide laptops with Internet access, without wires, it works like magic.

The wireless local area network (WLAN) uses the Ethernet protocol and path sharing and collision avoidance technology in three specifications, developed by the Institute of Electrical and Electronics Engineers (IEEE). The IEEE 802.11a, 802.11b, and 802.11g specifications define the standards for WLAN, at progressively faster speeds. The latest specification, 802.11g, offers 54 Mbps, compared to the 11 Mbps of the 802.11b standard, or *Wi-Fi*. Wi-Fi can become a valuable technology, with very little overhead and maintainability costs. For example, if your company employs traveling sales representatives who jump from one satellite office to another or telecommute occasionally, providing those individuals with wireless adapters for their laptops clears up any time lost in trying to find that extra Cat 5 cable, RJ-45 port with a free work area when they visit your office. They can boot up anywhere within range of the access point, or wireless router, and have instant access to the Internet, files, and printers.

There are a few advantages to using wireless over the traditional wired network connection. First, of course, there are no wires to run through the facility. This can be a big project, if you choose to keep the cables out of sight. Many companies will feed cable through the panels in the ceiling or along the walls. When you're talking about dozens or hundreds of clients and feet of cable, you're looking at a hefty added expense in time and money that wouldn't exist with a wireless solution.

The disadvantages include the limitation of 11 Mbps (although they've reached 44 Mbps for noncommercial use). The most significant disadvantage, however, is its lack of security. My Symphony network requires a "security code" to be a part of the network and access its resources, called a Service Set Identifier (SSID) in most wireless networks today. That's all anyone would ever need to gain access to my wireless network—as no one even needs a plug, they just need to be within range (up to 150 feet).

When a colleague of mine travels, which he does quite often, he prefers to stay at a Marriott Hotel, as most of them have broadband Internet connectivity. Assuming that all of them had broadband, he was greatly disappointed when he found one that didn't. The idea of connecting at 56 Kbps was enough to try something else entirely. He set up his wireless PCMCIA adapter to the default SSID setting of "default" and, being in a large city, hoped to link up to anyone's wireless network within range. Sure enough, he gained wireless access to the Internet at 11 Mbps, from an unknown wireless network, by simply rebooting the computer and letting the DHCP client inside Windows XP look for the network and login.

Wireless Access Points (WAPs) are devices that are inexpensive and readily available to allow you to extend and share an Internet connection wirelessly—as long as you have a wireless network adapter in each computer. It's very easy to simply take a laptop with a wireless PCMCIA network card (shown next) and use somebody else's wireless Internet access (referred to as "war driving") because the majority of people who set up wireless networks don't use the most basic security features. Many small company administrators and home users negate the use of a complex alphanumeric password to avoid, having to remember it and type it in when necessary.

The default configuration for many WAPs has Wired Equivalent Privacy (WEP) security turned off. WEP originated in the late 1990s when the 802.11 protocol was developed and is limited to only a 40-bit key (we're up to at least 128 bits now) because of the export laws at the time. This limited level of encryption is easy to compromise. WEPcrack, Ethereal, and Airsnort are just a few freeware applications available online that can easily crack the WEP 40-bit encryption.

I needed to know if this endeavor at the Marriott Hotel was simply an isolated incident. To my amazement, an attempt to duplicate the same scenario in my own office building accomplished the same thing: free wireless Internet access from the ether.

In Chapter 11, I'll show you how to set up your Windows 2000 or Server 2003 to act as a Wireless Access Point, only with far greater security capabilities.

The Importance of That Password

The default installation on any software application doesn't provide real-world security protection. Take the time to create solid choices for workgroup names, passwords, and security codes. All a hacker needs, once inside your wireless LAN (WLAN), is a choice of free sniffer software downloads from the Internet, and they will be able to extract names, addresses, account numbers, passwords, e-mail—anything accessible to your administrator.

Network Adapters Installation

In order for your server to communicate with more than one type of network, especially if you plan to offer Internet connectivity (one network) to your LAN (another network), you need dedicated hardware for each assigned IP address. For example, the network adapter that is connected to your broadband connection will have an IP address associated with a Class B network, or something like 66.100.12.121. The network adapter linked to your internal LAN will be assigned another, Class C address, or the typical 192.168.$x.x$, where x is the designated host number (anywhere from 1 to 254). This is how you create a clear path for data to move from one place to another, from the Internet to your internal network and back out to the Internet. IP addresses are a lot like street addresses: it's hard to deliver the goods if you don't know the correct address of the house.

In order to prepare your server for centralization, you'll need to install at least two network adapters. For proper installation, follow these suggested steps:

1. Ground yourself free of ESD (electrostatic discharge). I've seen expansion cards that were bent still work, but one fatal electrostatic discharge will destroy the card instantly (see Chapter 4).

TIPS OF THE TRADE

2. Clear a path for the installation of the network adapters (shown next) onto the expansion slots on your motherboard. I've chosen two standard Ethernet cards and one wireless adapter, so we can provide Internet access to any laptops with a compatible wireless PCMCIA card. I've also picked one network adapter with a Wake-on-LAN (WOL) connection. This links the adapter to a special connection on the motherboard that will allow incoming data on that adapter to bring the server out of standby mode or hibernation, to save power.

The single ISA slot for the wireless adapter   The two PCI slots for the two NIC cards

The WOL socket on the motherboard

TIPS OF THE TRADE

Once you've opened up two PCI slots, identify the availability of a WOL socket (not all motherboards have them), as shown next.

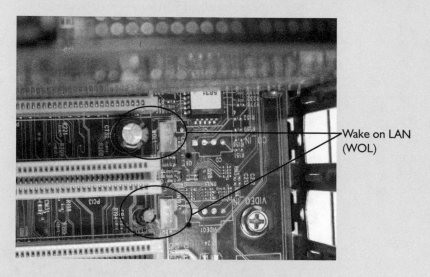

Wake on LAN (WOL)

3. As always, before you insert or pull out any computer component, make sure to turn off the power, and unplug the power cord from the system.

4. Insert the WOL cable into the socket on the motherboard using a pair of needle-nose pliers, shown here:

TIPS OF THE TRADE

5. Once that's securely in place, insert the network adapter (with the WOL cable already attached) into the PCI slot. This is a Belkin 10/100 adapter:

You may wish to hold off securing it into place with the one screw until you have all the adapters in place. The second network adapter is a Kingston Technology 10/100 KNC111, and I already know that there are no drivers for it incorporated into the Windows 2000 Server library. This is why it's important to hang on to the drivers on floppy disk or CD-ROM that come with the adapter. If no drivers were included, you can download them from the manufacturer's web site.

6. Once you feel confident you have the first adapter properly seated, insert the second network adapter into a neighboring PCI slot.

Properly inserting a network adapter works the same way as with the video adapter. You should apply even pressure, pushing it into its slot. The PCI cards are usually easier to insert than the older ISA cards, which tend to need more pressure.

TIPS OF THE TRADE

7. Once you've inserted both of your network adapters, secure them tightly in place with a screw. An improperly inserted adapter card will slip out of its expansion slot when tightening the screw to secure it in place.

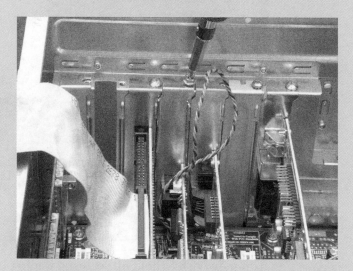

8. If you've decided to add the third wireless network adapter, you need to open up another adapter port by using needle-nose pliers to pull off the port cover, as shown next.

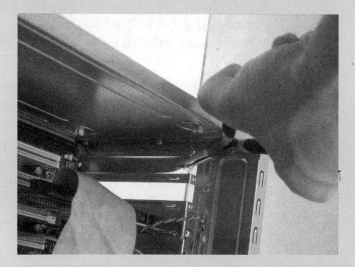

Most cases have the port covers embedded into the chassis, but I've seen a few that have screwed-in cover plates instead.

9. Insert the wireless adapter into the appropriate slot, and secure it into place with a screw. This procedure is not much different than a typical network adapter, with the exception that there is no socket for a cable connector, but instead an antenna of some kind.

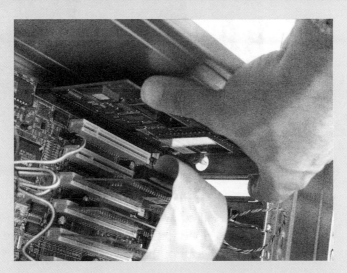

10. Check to make sure all three adapters are firmly seated within both channels of their slots, and then add the extension antenna to the wireless adapter, as shown next.

TIPS OF THE TRADE

11. Seal up any unused, opened ports with a cover plate, as shown next.

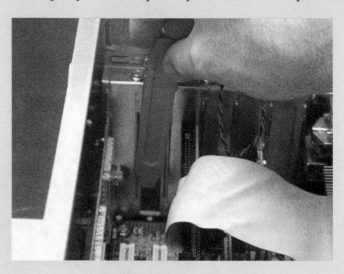

You can purchase expansion slot plates for about a quarter at your local computer store. This ensures proper heat dissipation (as described in Chapter 7) and keeps any foreign objects, dust, and bugs out of the server.

TIME CHECK

The installation of network adapters is a relatively simple procedure and shouldn't take you more than 30 minutes. However, if you find that the expansion cards are not staying properly seated when you're attempting to secure them into place with the screw, revisit Chapter 4 and the installation of the motherboard. You may have used the wrong standoffs to secure the motherboard into the chassis. Typically, there are only two sizes, and you need to make sure you use the right one that comes specifically with the motherboard.

Expansion Card Summary

To summarize our collection of expansion cards, shown from left to right in Figure 8-8, the leftmost is the wireless network adapter that you just installed. You'll use this to provide mobile laptops with wireless sharing of the Internet, files, and printers. Next to the wireless adapter (on this motherboard; the location of yours may vary) are two empty slots for future use. The IDE host adapter (to the right of the two empty slots) enables us to have up to four more devices (although we only have room for two more in this chassis), one of which could be a tape backup unit and the other a third hard drive.

Figure 8-8
The expansion card
line up

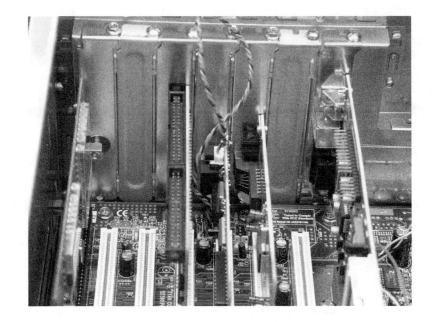

To the right of the host adapter are the two network adapters—one is a gateway to the Internet, and the other gives all LAN users access to the gateway plus all other resources on this server. This configuration will establish your server as a pseudo-wireless "access point" for the LAN. At the far right is our AGP video adapter.

We've completed building the hardware for your server. Beginning in the next chapter, we'll focus on the software that makes it work for you.

TESTING 1-2-3

Keep this in mind when finishing assembly of your server:

❑ The network provides seamless communication between individuals and their attributes and resources.

❑ Expansion cards are especially vulnerable to ESD.

❑ Client/server networking provides centralization of resources and administration over peer-to-peer networking.

❑ You need at least two different Ethernet adapters.

Part III

Network Operating System Installation, Configuration, and Troubleshooting

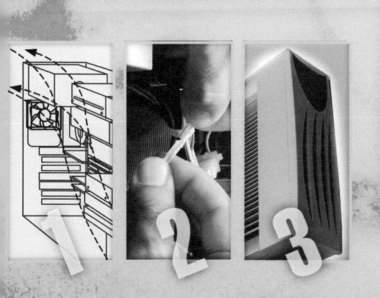

Chapter 9

Installation, Setup, and Configuration

Tools of the Trade

Network operating system installation disks and CD-ROMs
Hard drive setup utility (FDISK, Max Plus II, EZdrive, etc.)
Motherboard setup CD-ROM
Video adapter driver (if applicable)
Sound card driver (if applicable)
One to four floppy diskettes
Third-party SCSI drivers (if applicable)

This chapter covers systematic procedures for the installation of a dual-boot Windows 2000 Server and Server 2003 system. It assumes that your hard drives are unformatted and your server is still without an operating system. The following topics are covered:

- ❑ Preparation
- ❑ Dual booting
- ❑ Hard drive partitioning
- ❑ File system formatting
- ❑ Installation process for Windows 2000 Server and for Windows Server 2003
- ❑ Service packs, updates, and patches
- ❑ Startup and recovery

Installing Your NOS

This chapter shows you how to install both Windows 2000 Server and Server 2003 from a CD-ROM; so before you begin your installation, you need to check and make sure you meet the following requirements:

❏ You have a bootable Windows 2000 Server CD-ROM and a bootable Windows Server 2003 CD-ROM.

❏ The boot sequence in your BIOS is configured to boot from the floppy drive and CD-ROM first.

❏ All the hardware within your server is compatible with your choice of network operating system. Take special care in choosing video adapters for Server 2003. If you've come across a component that's not compatible, you'll have made the decision whether you can live without it until a driver is available (if ever). For example, can you live if your server didn't have sound or only 256 colors for video? Remember that Microsoft provides you with a Hardware Compatibility List on the actual installation CD-ROM (with Server 2003 giving you an option to scan the system automatically for potential compatibility issues).

BIOS Boot Setup

To set up your system to boot from the CD-ROM drive first, you need to press the appropriate key to enter your BIOS Setup utility. Many systems use either the DELETE key or the F1 key, but check your motherboard documentation to verify the correct procedure.

Once you've entered BIOS, choose Advanced BIOS Features or Advanced from the menu. This takes you to a screen similar to the one shown in Figure 9-1. Typically, you press either the plus or minus key to change the value. Make sure that the CD-ROM drive is set up to boot first. If you have the floppy disk drive set up to boot first and the CD-ROM second, make sure that there are no disks inside the floppy disk drive when you're booting up. Once you've made the appropriate change, press F10 to save and exit, and press Y (for yes) when you are prompted for confirmation. The system will then reboot with the new settings.

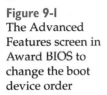

Figure 9-1
The Advanced
Features screen in
Award BIOS to
change the boot
device order

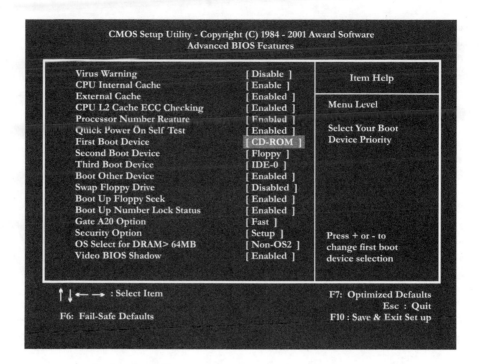

Dual-Boot System

I'm an advocate for a dual-boot system, in which you have two *separate* operating systems sitting on two *separate partitions*, using two separate sets of system files, although they share the same boot file–based environment. Do not install two operating systems on a single partition. It may cause instabilities and file corruption.

In a dual-boot environment, you have a choice of operating systems through the NT Loader (NTLDR) when you boot up the computer, as shown in Figure 9-2. The NT Loader is a program that loads the core Windows 2000 Server and/or Windows Server 2003 into memory.

There are numerous advantages to a dual-boot system, depending largely on your needs, but usually they include the following:

❏ One computer costs less and takes up less space.

❏ If the computer crashes, you can boot up quickly from the other OS, which can be a duplicate of your primary system.

❏ You have flexibility with regard to hardware compatibility issues.

Figure 9-2
The dual-boot options
screen for the NT
loader

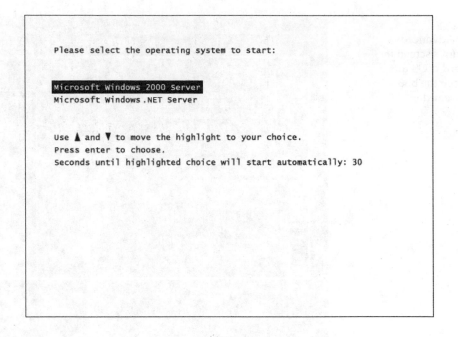

```
Please select the operating system to start:


Microsoft Windows 2000 Server
Microsoft Windows .NET Server



Use ▲ and ▼ to move the highlight to your choice.
Press enter to choose.
Seconds until highlighted choice will start automatically: 30
```

Recently, I was working on two separate projects requiring two very different flavors of technology. As part of one team, I was assigned to analyze a possible electronic document management system (EDMS) solution for a primarily Windows environment. We decided that a Microsoft SharePoint Portal Server prototype, on a Windows 2000 Server, would give us some hands-on experimentation for an electronic documentation management system (EDMS). This would allow us to share various types of electronic files, keeping track of versioning, position, authors, editors, etc.

The other project involved web site analysis and development, hosted on a UNIX/Apache system, so I also needed a UNIX/Apache server for web development and testing. In this case, the dual-boot environment saved me time and resources (monetary or otherwise) by turning a single server into a multi-dimensional tool; essentially, I turned one computer into a Windows 2000 Server and a Red Hat Linux development server, thus providing the environment to install two sets of different tools, exclusive to two different operating systems—one at a time.

More important, if you find yourself with limited resources, such as awaiting approval to purchase a second server to implement a redundancy strategy, a dual-boot system becomes an insurance policy. A few of my colleagues call allocating a separate partition for a second backup NOS space lost, but the time and money saved by having this option will outweigh the loss of the few gigabytes. You'll need a bare minimum of about 1.5GB for the NOS itself, plus whatever necessary space requirements for your server applications. Keep in mind that duplicating the configuration of your server on this second NOS partition will save you loads of time in the event of disaster. All you'll need to do is boot up the untainted NOS, run your Windows Update (more on this in the section "Part 9: Service Packs and Automatic Updates"), and duplicate the parameters to run the same applications. You can keep this second NOS lean and mean, like a miniature spare tire that keeps the car running long enough to get the other fixed.

How the Windows Boot Loader Works

The Master Boot Record (MBR) of any PC usually resides within the first partition (the C drive in DOS; hda in Linux). The Windows MBR includes a file called boot.ini, which resides in the system root. If you can't see it (on the C drive on most PCs), you need to change your folder options. Start Windows Explorer, select Tools | Folder Options, and click the View tab. Select Show Hidden Files And Folders, and clear Hide File Extensions For Known File Types. Close the windows and move to the root directory of the boot volume of your computer. Right-click the boot.ini file, select Properties, clear the Read-Only attribute, then click OK. Now, when you double-click the file icon, it will open in Notepad. If you are using the command prompt, use the following commands instead:

```
cd \
attrib -s -h -r boot.ini
notepad boot.ini
```

If done correctly, each command will return you to the command prompt until the last, **notepad boot.ini**, which will launch the boot.ini file in Notepad.

A typical multiboot, boot.ini file may look like this:

```
[boot loader]
timeout=30
default=multi(0)disk(0)rdisk(0)partition(1)\WINNT
[operating systems]
multi(0)disk(0)rdisk(0)partition(1)\WINNT="Microsoft Windows 2000 Server"
/fastdetect
multi(0)disk(0)rdisk(0)partition(3)\WINXP="Microsoft Windows Server 2003"
```

The various OS options are under the section marked [operating systems]. They're identified by partition number in DOS, or by the friendly name that appears within the quotation marks during the boot process. This would look something like Figure 9-2. If you don't choose an option within an allocated time, a default OS is selected. This would follow default= and is highlighted in the list. The time limit (in seconds) is assigned after timeout=. The default OS does not need to be the first one on the list or on the first partition. The boot process looks for the first line that matches within the [operating systems] section.

Under the [operating systems] section is the ARC path to the OSs. This includes the device, hard disk, and partition and system directory. It would look something like this:

```
\Device\Harddisk0\partition1\WINNT
```

These paths are on the Emergency Repair Disk (ERD), which is discussed later in this chapter in the "Emergency Repair Disk" section.

Clearly, there are advantages to a dual-boot system, such as maximization of resources within a development environment and added security, maintainability, flexibility, and compatibility. Setting up a dual-boot system involves extra time and effort, but it is well worth it in the long run.

Two Stages in Eleven Parts

The Windows 2000 and Server 2003 installation has two stages. The first occurs in a DOS-like environment. The installer prompts you with a few questions about your preferred partition and file system. This is when you can set up partitions and format the hard disk. The second stage of the installation is within Windows. This part of the installation installs hardware and software used within Windows 2000 Server. In addition, the installer will be able to select protocols for networking and set up services for the server to use once the Windows Setup program is complete.

Part 1: Basic Installation

Insert the Windows 2000 or Server 2003 CD-ROM into the CD-ROM drive and power up the computer. It does not matter which one of the two OSs you choose, unless you are using Windows 9x as a second OS, which I do not recommend, or Linux, which is a completely different scenario. Windows 2000 and Server 2003 (and Windows 2000 and XP Professional) give you the option of choosing your installation partition. If you do decide to install an older version of Windows, or even MS-DOS, the best way is to install the oldest OS first and the newest OS last—that is, MS-DOS, Windows 95, or Windows 98, and then Windows NT,

Windows 2000 Professional or Server, Windows XP, or Windows Server 2003. The reasoning behind this suggestion is quite simple: Windows NT, 2000, XP, and 2003 provide advanced installation customization, while previous versions do not. This offers the option of changing the partition, drive, and/or system folder location of the OS directory. They update the MBR, adding the installed OS to a list created within the boot.ini file. However, the OS is a separate entity. Incidentally, the advanced options also offer the opportunity to copy the I386 file folder to the hard drive. This eliminates the need for the Windows 2000 CD-ROM when adding new hardware, so I highly suggest making the room.

During setup, all the installation files required for setup must reside on the hard drive to continue.

This is where you may encounter your first trouble. Windows 2000 and Server 2003 both require Setup files to be copied to the hard drive. If the hard drive has no partition and is unformatted, it will display the message "Could not find a place for a swap file," as shown in Figure 9-3. This is when you need the software that came with the hard drive to do an initial installation of the hard drive, preparing it for the NOS installation.

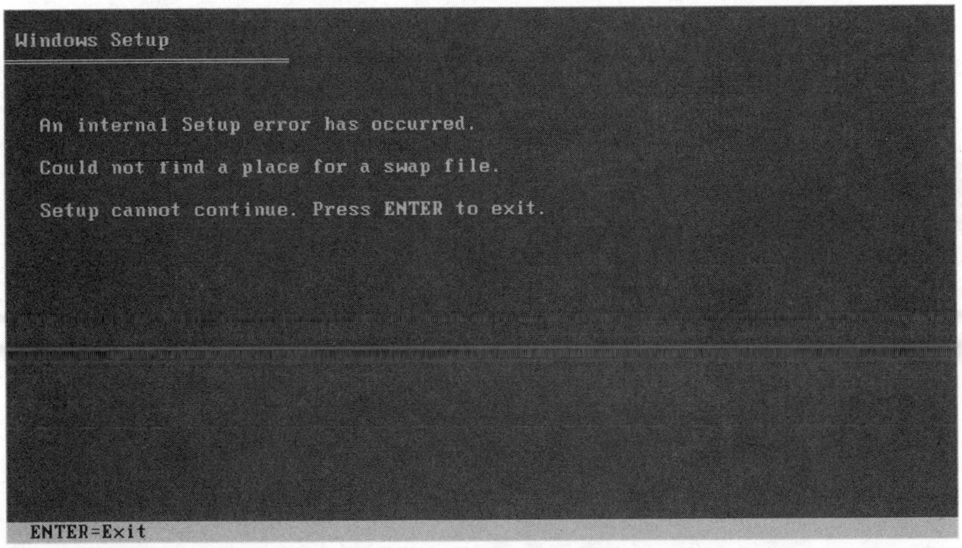

Figure 9-3
If there is no hard drive partition, you will receive this swap file error when attempting to install.

```
Windows Setup

An internal Setup error has occurred.

Could not find a place for a swap file.

Setup cannot continue. Press ENTER to exit.




ENTER=Exit
```

You can also use a Windows boot disk, with FDISK (see Figure 9-4), to create an initial partition for those Setup files. Once all the Setup files are on the hard drive, the installation can proceed.

Figure 9-4
FDISK usually comes with most hard drive applications and is available on MS-DOS and most Windows boot disks.

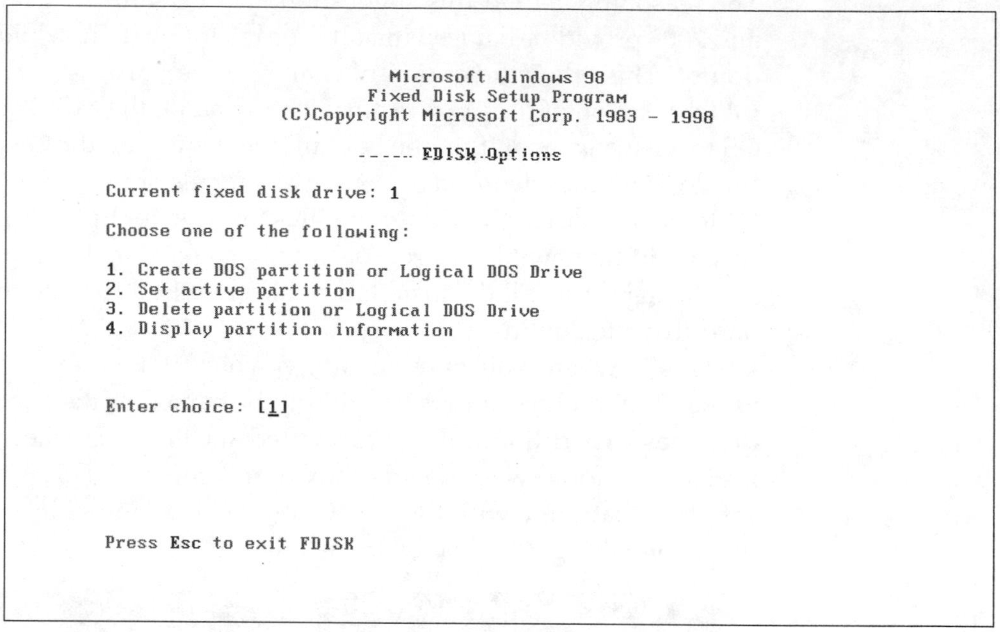

```
                    Microsoft Windows 98
                    Fixed Disk Setup Program
                 (C)Copyright Microsoft Corp. 1983 - 1998

                    ------ FDISK Options

      Current fixed disk drive: 1

      Choose one of the following:

      1. Create DOS partition or Logical DOS Drive
      2. Set active partition
      3. Delete partition or Logical DOS Drive
      4. Display partition information



      Enter choice: [1]




      Press Esc to exit FDISK
```

TIPS OF THE TRADE

Partitioning and File System Formatting

A new hard drive, or one you'd like to bring back to its original state for a "clean" install, is unformatted and has no capabilities to read and write files. System formatting is used to prepare your hard drive to understand the forthcoming data.

A computer-related partition is a logical division of a hard disk. Initially, file system formatting was limited in its capabilities, and partitioning provided a means of utilizing larger hard drives by splitting them up and giving them the appearance of multiple hard drives. Partitions are also created for multiboot environments, where you'd install a separate OS an each partition, represented as a hard drive volume. This can protect system files and critical data. In the Windows environment, a partition gives you a separate data "hard drive" in the event the system crashes on the first partition (or hard drive), leaving the critical data untouched. You create partitions during the initial formatting of the hard

TIPS OF THE TRADE

drive, at which point, in a Windows environment, they are assigned drive letters. Although applications are available that enable you to split up empty space on an active hard drive, if you damage the partition table, you've lost everything on that physical hard drive.

The critical partition table information and boot data reside on the first sector of your hard disk, typically drive C. This information includes the size and format definitions for all the partitions, how many partitions exist, and the address for each partition. This sector also includes the MBR for all the OSs on the server. If you damage the first sector of the hard disk, even if the last OS rests on the very last partition, you will lose that as well. This is the time to use the ERD and the Recovery Console (more on this later, in the section "Part 11: Startup & Recovery").

The best way I've found to install a NOS on a hard drive is to use FDISK (or the application provided by the hard disk manufacturer) to create an initial partition on the hard drive for the OS, leaving the rest unallocated. Once you've finished with the installation of Windows 2000 or Server 2003, you can manage the remaining space much easier within Computer Management, a choice within the Administrative Tools menu and part of the default Microsoft Management Console (MMC).

When the basic Windows 2000 and Server 2003 Setup begins, you're given two choices: press E NTER to continue with the installation process, or press F3 to quit Setup. A third option appears if you already have a Windows 2000 Server installation, giving you the choice of repairing the existing installation (see Figure 9-5)

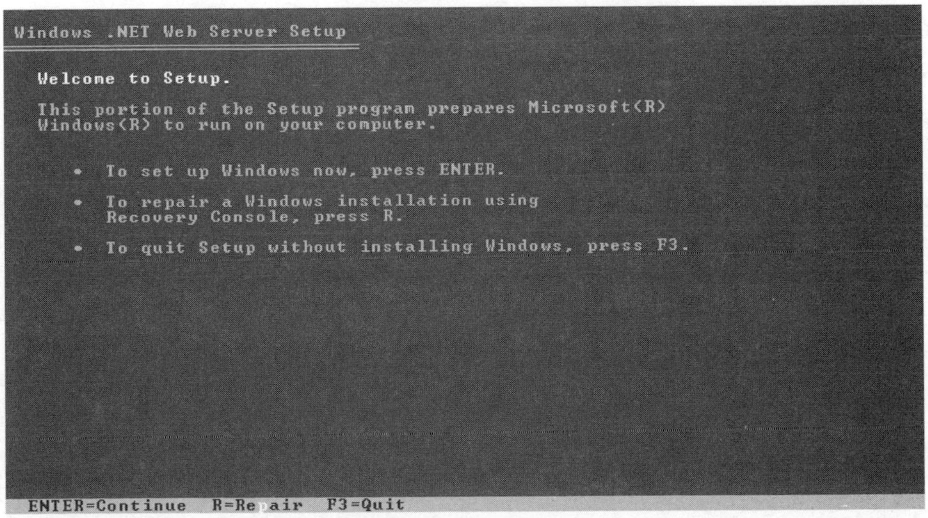

Figure 9-5
The first screen in the installation process

```
Windows .NET Web Server Setup

  Welcome to Setup.

  This portion of the Setup program prepares Microsoft(R)
  Windows(R) to run on your computer.

      •  To set up Windows now, press ENTER.

      •  To repair a Windows installation using
         Recovery Console, press R.

      •  To quit Setup without installing Windows, press F3.



  ENTER=Continue   R=Repair   F3=Quit
```

Part 2: Partitioning and File Formats

The next portion of this stage of the installation involves choosing the partition for the OS (see Figure 9-6). This is where you can choose a different partition for the second OS as well.

Figure 9-6
Choosing the
partition for the NOS

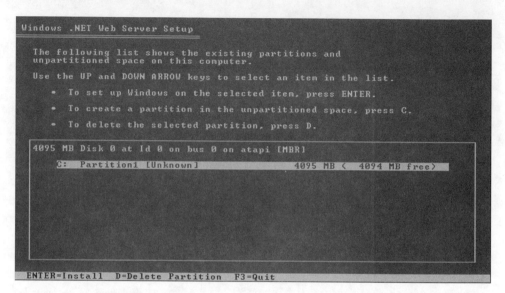

```
Windows .NET Web Server Setup

    The following list shows the existing partitions and
    unpartitioned space on this computer.

    Use the UP and DOWN ARROW keys to select an item in the list.

       •  To set up Windows on the selected item, press ENTER.

       •  To create a partition in the unpartitioned space, press C.

       •  To delete the selected partition, press D.

    ┌────────────────────────────────────────────────────────────────┐
    │ 4095 MB Disk 0 at Id 0 on bus 0 on atapi [MBR]                   │
    │   C:   Partition1 [Unknown]                  4095 MB (  4094 MB free) │
    │                                                                  │
    │                                                                  │
    │                                                                  │
    └────────────────────────────────────────────────────────────────┘

    ENTER=Install   D=Delete Partition   F3=Quit
```

Your next choice is the file system format. There are some issues to consider when picking file system formats. The different Windows file systems, briefly discussed in Chapter 6, are FAT (file allocation table), FAT32, and NTFS (NT file system). These formats are how your hard drives maintain data: a database of sorts. FAT is the oldest version, and thus is compatible with all flavors of Windows. However, FAT does not recognize any of the advanced security available in Windows 2000 or Server 2003, and does not recognize an NTFS partition or drive at all. The other drawback to the FAT partition is its 2GB file size limit, which becomes a serious problem when working with expanding databases or large media files, such as video captures. FAT32 extended support for larger hard drives, up to terabyte sizes, but it only increased file size support to 4GB. If you need larger than 4GB file sizes, NTFS is the way to go.

NTFS is my recommendation for your server. You may wish to add a smaller FAT32 partition to support legacy systems, but the NOS should reside on an NTFS partition, if only for the added security benefits. NTFS is also required if you intend to make use of file-level permissions and Active Directory Services. NTFS is also another reason Windows 2000 and Server 2003 are much more stable than previous versions of Windows—simply because they do not "sit" on top of MS-DOS, as do previous versions of Windows. The command-line prompt you see in Windows 2000 Server and Server 2003 is an MS DOS–emulated environment specifically created for backward compatibility. After you choose the file format (again, NTFS is recommended for servers), the Windows installation program will format your entire partition (see Figure 9-7).

Figure 9-7
Formatting the partition during the installation process

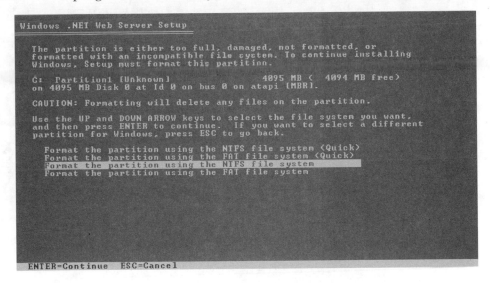

If you plan to include Windows NT into a mix of servers and workstations, you need to be sure to bring Windows NT 4.0 up to date with at least Service Pack 5 or, preferably, the latest, SP 6a; otherwise, even the Windows NT version of NTFS will not read the NTFS version 5.0 of Windows 2000 and Server 2003.

Once you have created and formatted your partitions, the system will copy all the installation folders to the hard drive (see Figure 9-8). It will then reboot and bring you into the next part of the installation. I'd like to reiterate, before moving on to this next stage, that when you partition or format a hard drive, you erase everything that is on that disk.

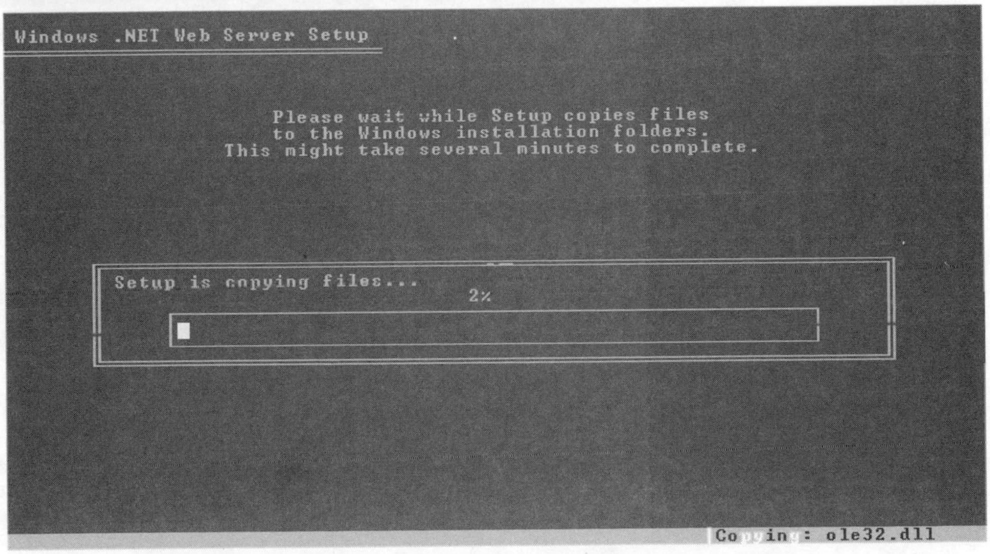

Figure 9-8
The Setup program copies all the installation files to the hard drive.

If you have any third-party RAID or SCSI controllers, keep a close eye on the initial screens just after the formatting process or you may miss the message at the bottom of the screen that instructs you to press F6 (see Figure 9-9).

Figure 9-9
Press F6 to add third-party RAID or SCSI controllers.

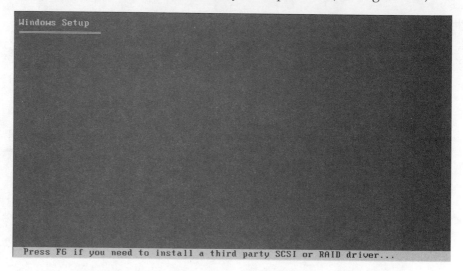

Part 3: Into Windows and the Setup Wizard

Once the server reboots, the Windows portion of the installation begins (see Figure 9-10), and the Windows 2000 or Server 2003 Setup Wizard prompts you to continue by clicking Next.

Figure 9-10
Stage two brings you into the Windows portion of the installation.

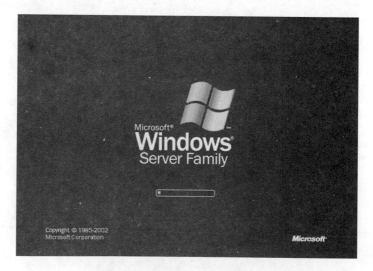

The first part of the Windows portion of Setup installs all the Plug-and-Play (PnP) hardware and non-PnP hardware required to run the server (see Figure 9-11). This could be a lengthy installation, depending on how much hardware is in the system.

Figure 9-11
The Windows-based
installation screen for
Server 2003

Part 4: Regional Settings

After the hardware detection, the Regional And Language Options window appears (see Figure 9-12). Here you'll have the choice to set your clock and calendar, based on your specific time zone. You can also choose different languages. The next wizard page, shown in Figure 9-13, prompts you to type your full name and a company or organization (the Organization field is optional).

Figure 9-12
Requesting regional
information

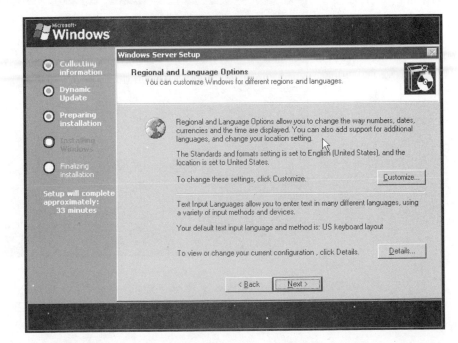

Figure 9-13
Windows 2000 Server
and Server 2003
(pictured) give
you the option to
personalize your
system.

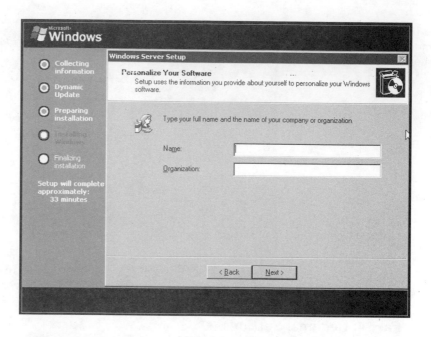

Click Next, and you are prompted to enter your product key (see Figure 9-14). You must enter the product key to continue.

Figure 9-14
Product key
request screen

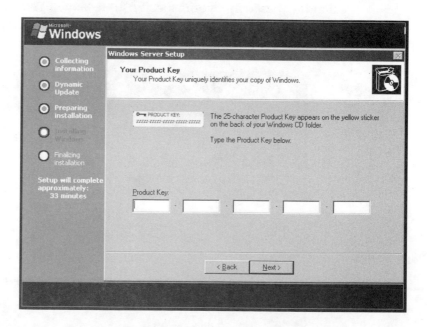

Once you have filled in the product key, click Next to move to the Licensing Mode dialog box. You have two choices of licensing for both Windows 2000 and Server 2003:

❏ **Per Server license**   Requires that, in a client/server environment, each concurrent connection to the server have its own client access license (CAL).

❏ **Per Seat license**   Requires that each individual *seat* or client have its own CAL.

If you don't understand the difference between a connection and a seat, consider a mobile user, who may *connect* to the server from a desktop at the office, a PC at home, and a laptop on the road. A seat license only gives that single seat access privileges. This distinction becomes crucial when we discuss Terminal Server in Chapter 14.

Part 5: User and License

The next page of the Windows 2000 or Server 2003 Setup Wizard asks for your choice of a computer name. This is how the server appears throughout the network, so you should choose something simple for easy recognition and configuration (see Figure 9-15).

Figure 9-15
Name your computer for easy recognition on the network, rather than using the system default.

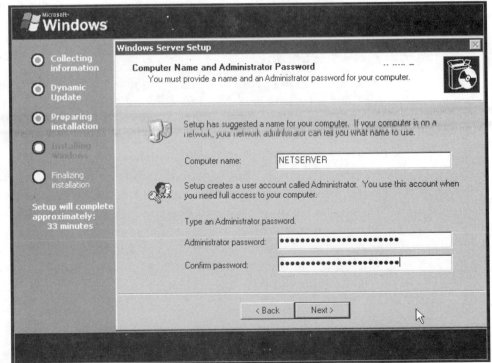

The installation wizard provides an alphanumeric suggestion by default. Besides the computer name, this dialog box also requests an administrator password. Unlike the name of the computer, the administrator password should not be "password" or any other obvious name or number. To establish a level of security necessary to protect your systems on your LAN from internal and external threats, the password should be a lengthy, alphanumeric code. (Chapter 14 discusses security in greater detail.) If you choose a simple (or no) password right now, to make the installation less painful (during reboots), you can change this password later by pressing CTRL-ALT-DEL once you've successfully launched Windows. Click Next to move to the next screen.

Part 6: Choosing Components and Time

The next screen is the Windows 2000 Components menu. This is where you select your initial list of services, applications, utilities, and tools. You can choose the default (which I recommend for now) or customize your own selection, but you can always access this menu (from the Add/Remove Programs option in the Control Panel), so you do not need to get it all done at this time.

The next screen gives you the option to adjust the date, time, and time zone. You can do this later by double-clicking the time on the rightmost side of the System Tray within the Taskbar. By using a drop-down menu, you simply select the date, time, and time zone, adjusting the system to reconfigure itself for daylight saving time.

Part 7: Network Settings

The Networking Settings window, shown in Figure 9-16, gives you two initial options—Typical Settings and Custom Settings. Choosing Typical Settings creates network connections using Client for Microsoft Networks; File and Print Sharing for Microsoft Networks; and the TCP/IP protocol with Dynamic Host Configuration Protocol (DHCP), which is dynamic IP addressing (with minimal additional configuration required). Windows attempts to detect and install all of your network components: drivers for your NIC cards and the required protocols. If you're using an obscure NIC card, you may need to update the drivers later, but most of the common brands and models are automatically installed, since Windows 2000 Server and Server 2003 include an impressive library of third-party drivers. Once you've chosen your option (Typical is recommended at this stage), click Next.

Figure 9-16
The Network Settings
page for both
Windows 2000 and
Server 2003

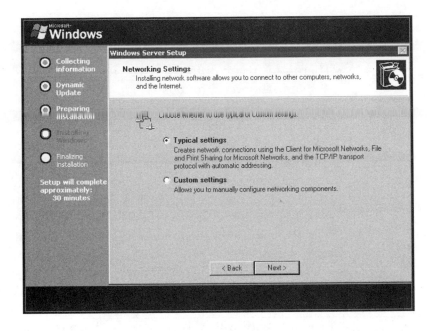

The second half of the network configuration involves choosing whether the server will be part of a workgroup or domain (see Figure 9-17). Choose the option of "No, this computer is not part of a network, or is part of a network without a domain," and then type in the member name of the workgroup. You must provide a workgroup name before you can proceed.

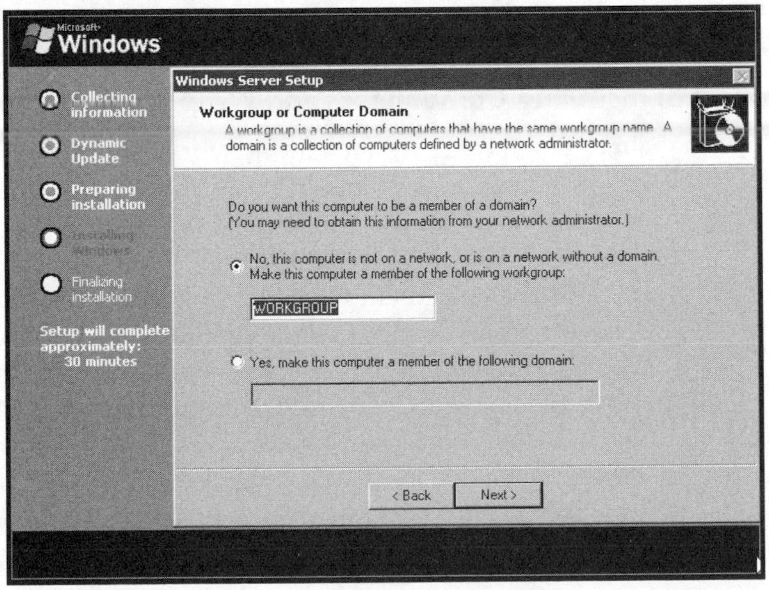

Figure 9-17
Choosing between a
workgroup and
domain

Workgroup vs. Domain

There are major differences between your choice of workgroup and domain. The workgroup is Windows default choice for networking and only requires a computer running Client for Microsoft Networks; TCP/IP; and, if you're planning to share resources, File and Print Sharing for Microsoft Networks. By choosing Typical Settings for your network configuration on more than one machine, you can link them together, as part of a peer-to-peer network called a workgroup. You need nothing else to set up a workgroup, using Windows. You can transform the peer-to-peer network into a client/server environment by adding a server that also runs with the same configuration, plus the added benefits of a centralized server.

The domain, on the other hand, requires at least one domain controller, which is set up in Windows 2000 Server and Server 2003 using Active Directory. The domain includes the advantages of a workgroup, but also provides a directory of groups and users managed centrally by an administrator, and the added security of segregated domains with crossovers only allowed with a "trusted relationship" between the domain controllers. The domain concept uses the same methodology as the Internet, using DNS to resolve IP addresses into domain names, such as myintranet.com.

Part 8: Installing Components and Wrap-Up

Once you have completed the network configuration and have chosen the name of the workgroup or domain to use, the Setup Wizard installs those components you chose earlier. This process could take a while, depending on how many components you chose to install.

This is the segment where I encountered the most problems, most of which were the result of neglecting to check the HCL on the Windows CD-ROM or the Microsoft web site. So, to reiterate, it's very important to do some research on the components before you install the NOS because, if the component you plan on using is not supported by all the NOS you're planning on installing, that component will not be recognized by that particular NOS and thus will not function. If you do encounter a problem, it may get to this point and then suddenly crash. You'll then need to start all over again.

After the Setup Wizard adds the Start menu items and registers the components, it saves all the settings. It then removes all the temporary files used during the installation process. This portion of the installation (along with the installation file copying stage, in the DOS-like environment), are the two longest stretches in the installation process overall.

Once completed, the server will shut down and restart. Upon booting up your new NOS, eventually, the Welcome To Windows screen appears, shown next. Press CTRL-ALT-DEL to bring up the login screen. Enter the Administrator password, press ENTER, and you'll enter the operating system for the first time.

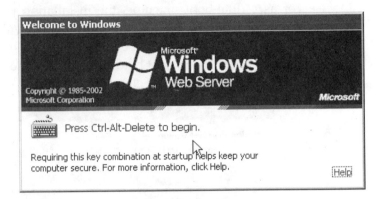

Part 9: Service Packs and Automatic Updates

If you don't have a copy of the latest Windows 2000 or Server 2003 service packs, you can easily obtain a copy by accessing the built-in Windows Automatic Update utility, which is standard in Server 2003 but a downloadable update for Windows 2000 Server. You must bring your NOS up to date before bringing it live, as many of these updates and patches resolve critical security issues. You can also download the entire service pack, usually over 100MB, from the Microsoft.com web site.

To connect to the Internet, Windows provides you with another wizard to help you. Simply double-click the Internet Explorer icon on the desktop or the System Tray, or, if you're using Windows Server 2003, you can access it from the Start | All Programs | Internet Explorer. Once you launch the web browser for the first time, it immediately takes you to the wizard. Windows Server 2003 will also automatically configure web browser settings to access the Internet immediately without any required wizard.

You can find the Automatic Update utility in the Control Panel. I highly recommend configuring this to keep your server updated with the most recent patches and service packs. I've scheduled my servers to retrieve any possible updates and then install them automatically at 3:00 A.M. Better yet, if you have the time, set it up to simply download and require your review, prior to installation. You need not worry if no one is locally logged in, since most of the applications you'll run are services, and they are active even before someone logs in locally. I'll get into more details about this in the next chapter, when we configure your server with Terminal Services, giving you remote access from anywhere.

Part 10: The Second Operating System

Once you have your first NOS set up and updated, if you decide to establish the server as a dual-boot machine, the installation process is the same, with the exception of a couple of procedures. You will be able to begin in the Windows environment first and then reboot, leaving Windows for the DOS-environment stage of the installation. Just before leaving Windows for the DOS environment, you'll be prompted with the Select Special Options window, shown in Figure 9-18.

Figure 9-18
Select Special Options window

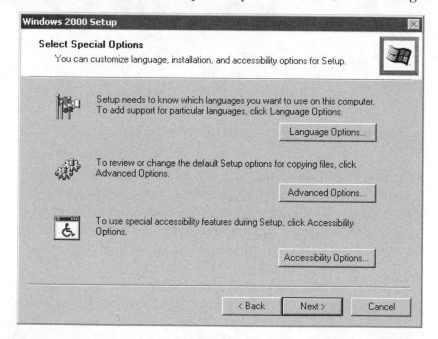

This window gives you three choices: Language Options, Advanced Options, and Accessibility Options. Click the Advanced Options button to open the Advanced Options dialog box, shown in Figure 9-19. You'll be required to supply the location of the Windows 2000 files for installation and the name of the system folder (WINNT is the default). I recommend changing the name of the second OS default installation directory, so you can clearly distinguish between the two later.

Figure 9-19
Advanced Options
dialog box

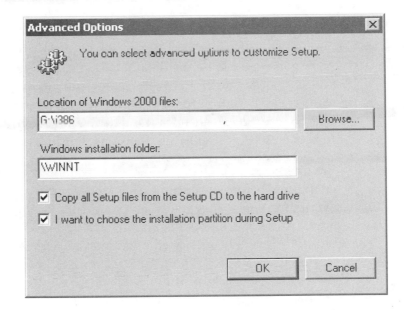

The first of the two check boxes at the bottom of the Advanced Options dialog box gives you the option to copy Setup files from the Setup CD-ROM to the hard drive (see Figure 9-19). This puts a copy of the I386 folder onto the related OS partition. This comes in handy when you install a new piece of hardware and Windows prompts you to insert the Windows CD-ROM to obtain the necessary drivers. This way, instead of having to dig for the CD-ROM, you can just click Browse and point it to the appropriate I386 folder. You may wish to do the same for the first operating system and partition.

Figure 9-20
Installing a second
NOS will still take
you into a DOS-like
environment, even
if you started in
Windows.

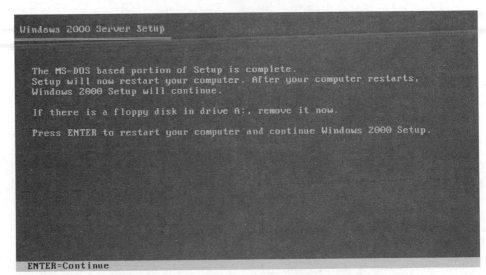

Part 11: Startup & Recovery

Once you have completed the installation of both OSs, you can choose which NOS you prefer to be the default by using the Startup & Recovery option. To access the Startup & Recovery dialog box, in Windows 2000 Server, simply right-click My Computer, select Properties to open the System Properties dialog box, choose the Advanced tab, and then select Startup & Recovery at the bottom. In Server 2003, it's relatively the same, but the design has changed.

Emergency Repair Disk   You need to wait until you have the core of each NOS configured before you create the ERD for each one. The ERD must also be updated every time you change the system state, such as add new applications, uninstall applications or components, and so forth. The ERD may take some time to create, but in the event of a disaster, it will make up for it, tenfold.

To create an ERD, from the Start menu, choose Programs | Accessories | System Tools | Backup. The wizard will take you through the process of making the ERD.

Recovery Console   The last part of setting up your NOS is to install the Recovery Console so that you have it as an option in the boot.ini file. With the Recovery Console on the local hard disk, it's accessible from the Windows 2000 startup boot screen. However, with a damaged boot sector, you'll need to start the computer using either the Windows 2000 Server Setup floppy disks or the Windows 2000 Setup CD-ROM.

To add the Recovery Console to the startup screen, from within Windows 2000 or Server 2003, place the Setup CD-ROM into the CD-ROM drive, click the Start menu, choose Run, and then type the following command: **F:\I386\Winnt32.exe /cmdcons** (where *F* represents the CD-ROM drive).

Creating a Windows 2000 Server and Server 2003 Boot Disk

I've found that a system boot disk is one of the most important tools you can have when troubleshooting any Windows-or Linux-based computer (server or workstation). I'm not talking about the four floppy disks you'd need to make to get into repair mode (if your CD-ROM malfunctions) with Windows 2000 Server or Server 2003, but rather a single floppy disk that will jumpstart the boot process in the event your MBR is corrupted.

To create a single boot disk, you need to find a few system files that are typically located on the C drive. To see system files, on the C drive, choose the Tools | Folder Options | View (see Figure 9-21). Select the Show Hidden And System Files radio button and then, just below that, uncheck Hide Protected Operating System Files (Recommended). Several additional files should appear, including boot.ini, NTLDR, and ntdetect.com.

Figure 9-21
Finding the hidden
system files

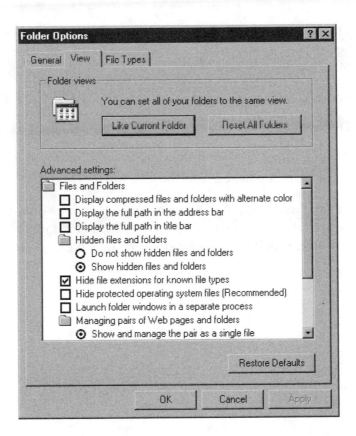

Place a blank floppy disk in drive A and format the disk using Windows NT or later. Copy the previously listed files to the floppy disk and then restore the hidden and read-only attributes to the files on your hard disk. If you also find either the bootsect.dos or the ntbootdd.sys file residing there, copy it to the floppy disk as well. You now have a floppy disk that will boot up your system and, if you have a dual-boot system, give you a choice of NOS.

Chapter 10 provides detailed information about setting up your network configuration, step by step.

Some things to keep in mind when installing your NOS:

❑ Make sure your BIOS is updated and your boot order includes your setup disk media.

❑ A dual-boot system is a great way of creating a failsafe backup.

❑ There are two primary stages to the installation process for Windows 2000 Server and Windows Server 2003: one in a DOS-like environment and the other through Windows.

❑ The NTFS file system is the best way to go for a server.

❑ The workgroup is an easier setup than the domain.

❑ Always update the NOS with the latest critical security service packs, updates, and patches.

❑ As long as the second operating system in your dual-boot server is comparable or a newer version, you'll be able to import original resources, such as web sites, into the new NOS.

Chapter 10

Network Configuration

Tools of the Trade

Network operating system installation disks and CD-ROMS
Floppy or CD-ROM with third-party drivers for network adapters and printers
A calculator that can convert decimal numbers to binary numbers

This chapter explains how to set up your server to provide several functions that are beneficial within a diverse network environment. The focus of the discussion will be on network configuration of both Microsoft Windows 2000 Server and Windows Server 2003. Although their system interfaces are functionally alike, the overall design and enhancements added to Windows Server 2003 (the latest generation) actually add a few valuable components.

You can configure these capabilities, and more, on other NOS, including the various flavors of Linux, Apple, and Novell, but this chapter focuses on the specific steps for the Windows NOS environment.

Microsoft Windows Networking: Built for Simplicity

Windows 2000 Server and Windows Server 2003 include added networking functionality to take advantage of the Windows automated peer-to-peer and Dynamic Host Configuration Protocol (DHCP) network setup. Any Microsoft OS from Windows 98 to the most recent Windows versions will set up a LAN connection automatically after the proper installation of a network adapter. If you've installed a network adapter, and the driver is part of the Windows library, then when you boot up the system, Windows will set up a default client configuration for you. The plug-and-Play functionality built into Windows will find the new piece of hardware, install the driver, and set up a network connection using Client for Microsoft Networks as the client software, File and Print Sharing for Microsoft Networks as a sharing service, and the built-in TCP/IP protocol.

Even if Windows cannot find a DHCP server to dynamically deliver an IP address, Windows 2000 Server and Windows Server 2003 have built-in Automatic Private IP Addressing (APIPA), a unique default feature that *serves* dynamic IP addresses when no DHCP server is available (because it either is temporarily down or does not exist). Windows 2000 Server and Windows Server 2003 assign an IP address in the range 169.254.0.1 to 169.254.255.254, which is reserved by the Internet Assigned Numbers Authority (IANA) exclusively for Windows. Thus, APIPA provides a failsafe mechanism in the event a DHCP server is down. The client uses the Address Resolution Protocol (ARP) to ensure an exclusive IP address on the network.

The default for the TCP/IP protocol is to obtain an IP address automatically, so that when you plug a Cat 5 cable into the adapter, the adapter begins looking for an address assigned by a DHCP server. DHCP allocates a "scope" or range of public or private IP addresses (depending on the size and location of the network), and dynamically assigns them to DHCP clients. Therefore, theoretically, if you install a network adapter (and its driver) into a Windows workstation and then plug it into the DHCP network, you're connected, automatically. Most of the time, this works, but I'll show you why it may not, in the next chapter about network troubleshooting.

Your guide during the configuration process is the Windows 2000 Configure Your Server Wizard or the Windows Server 2003 Manage Your Server Wizard; but before we begin the wizard, we need to confirm the proper installation of our network adapter drivers. Once all the devices are properly installed and recognized by the NOS, we'll move into file and print sharing, static IP addressing, and then dynamic IP addressing using DHCP, which will offer quick network accessibility, from any linked location.

Naming Conventions

To convert your isolated workstations and peer-to-peer networks into a client/server environment, the client workstation will relinquish some of their individual control. You need a naming convention that makes each server, and workgroup, easily recognizable by the individual nodes. Those names need to be consistent in order to create a sharing environment controlled by a server. Providing a consistent naming scheme for your workgroup, computer, and each individual network adapter will help you and others maintain the network and its assets. All too often I see networks in small - and medium- sized companies that have no centralized control and not only do you have to uncover the name of a target computer, but also the name of the personalized workgroup.

If everyone has an individual workgroup, you need to unify them all into one group, or group them by department or some other naming convention that makes sense for your organization. For security reasons, you should not use the default name "workgroup"; make the names unique to your company (see Figure 10-1).

Figure 10-1
Avoid the obvious
default when naming
your workgroup.

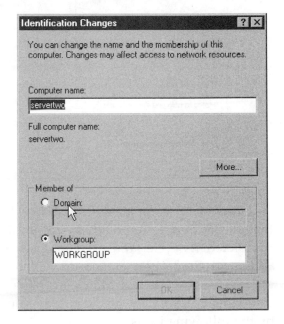

Your company policy dictates the naming convention for your computers. Windows 2000 Server and Windows Server 2003 provide the capability to stop individuals from installing any unauthorized software applications or making any administrative-level changes to the workstations. These safeguards make it difficult for users to manipulate any system files and easier for you to diagnose any problems that may arise later.

Network Adapters Driver Installation

For easier administration, I recommend naming the three adapters inside your server based on their function, as shown in the example in Figure 10-2. The first adapter, named Internet, is the adapter linked to your ISP-supplied device and should be configured with the static IP address that the ISP has supplied you for Internet access. The second adapter, renamed LAN, links to a router, hub, or switch, depending on how you configure your server. The last adapter is the optional wireless adapter, which is renamed Wireless. Simple and easy to recognize names will come in handy later when you're configuring Internet sharing and other routing preferences.

Figure 10-2
Changing the name of each adapter for easier administration

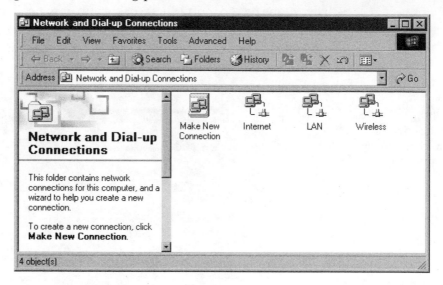

Once you've completed the NOS installation process, you shouldn't assume that all the devices are ready to go simply because the hardware wizard has completed its cycle. You need to check the Device Manager (select Start | Settings | Control Panel, and then choose Administrative Tools | Computer Management | Device Manager). This gives you a clear view of all the components of your server and informs you of any problems, which are indicated by the following icons:

❏ **Red X**   Indicates that the device has been disabled or is not functioning properly.

❏ **Yellow question mark**   Indicates that the operating system hasn't fully recognized the device and, consequently, the device is not functioning (see Figure 10-3). This usually means that you need a third-party driver or need to try to manually install that driver.

❏ **Yellow exclamation mark**   Indicates that there's a problem with the installed device and/or device driver.

Figure 10-3 illustrates a problem I've encountered when installing two network adapters. If Windows doesn't recognize either adapter, the Device Manager displays "Ethernet Controller" twice, with a yellow question mark next to each and no sign of which adapter is which and what driver disk to use.

Figure 10-3
The sign of needed attention

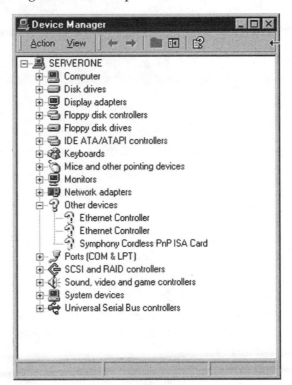

If both adapters are the same, you won't have a problem installing them, but you may encounter administrative problems later when you're trying to decipher which is which yourself. I've found that the quickest course of action is to try both and see which one is accepted. Even if you attempt to uncover more details through their individual properties, you'll still be presented with little details (see Figure 10-4).

Figure I0-4
Properties for the
unknown Ethernet
controller

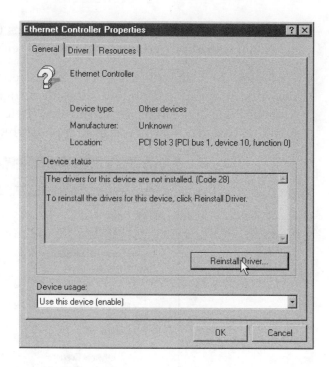

To clear the symbolic alarms, you'll need to install the third-party drivers using the Device Manager. Again, you can access the Device Manager from Start | Control Panel | Administrative Tools | Computer Management | Device Manager. Right-click on the first Ethernet Controller icon and choose Properties. In the Properties dialog box, choose the Driver tab and then click the Upgrade Driver button in the lower-right corner. This opens the Upgrade Device Driver Wizard (see Figure 10-5).

Figure I0-5
The Upgrade Device
Driver Wizard

When you click Next, Windows asks if you'd like to automatically search for the driver. There are two ways of doing this procedure—the easy way and the hard way. Of course, you want to try it the easy way, first. Insert into the appropriate drive the floppy disk or CD-ROM that came with your adapter and click Next. The Windows Hardware Wizard will search through the floppy disk or CD-ROM and find the right driver for the device. It will then inform you that it did indeed find the right driver and ask you whether you want to proceed with the installation. Click Next and Windows will install the device driver. You'll then see in the Device Manager which device it is, since Windows now recognizes it.

TIPS OF THE TRADE

The Handy Taskbar

When you open the Properties dialog box of a network adapter from within the Device Manager, you have an option of showing the connectivity status in the taskbar. This comes in very handy when you're troubleshooting and checking the traffic on any given network.

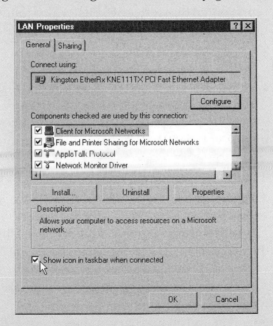

If your network connection is live, the network icon will change screen colors to indicate active communications. If the network is down, which could mean an unplugged cable, disconnected hub, or disconnected switch, or your ISP is down (to name a few possibilities), then you will see a red X over the icon. Moving your mouse pointer over the icon will also inform you that the connection is unplugged.

Subnets

The following table outlines the classification system of IP addressing (explained in Chapter 9), wherein a specific class is assigned to a network based on its size and function. Each of these classes has a unique subnet mask address (much like the IP address) that corresponds to the network ID. Short for "subnetwork," the subnet is a network identifier, separating IP segments by geographic location, or local area network (LAN).

Address Class	Bit Address for Subnet Mask	Subnet Mask
Class A	11111111 00000000 00000000 00000000	255.0.0.0
Class B	11111111 11111111 00000000 00000000	255.255.0.0
Class C	11111111 11111111 11111111 00000000	255.255.255.0

Subnet masks in their decimal numeric form don't really make much sense; but if you convert them into their binary form, you can see how subnetting works. People tend to make binary numbering more complex than it really is—simple 1's and 0's. As mentioned in Chapter 7, each octet in an IP address is represented by a series of 8 bits, which totals 32 bits for four octets. The following table outlines binary numbering and its decimal numeric counterpart:

Binary	1	1	1	1	1	1	1	1	= 8 bits
Decimal	128	64	32	16	8	4	2	1	= 255 (highest possible 8-bit binary number)

So, for example, if you wanted to know the decimal numeric value of the binary value 00110011, you could determine it as follows:

Binary	0	0	1	1	0	0	1	1	
Decimal	0	0	32	16	0	0	2	1	= 51

As this example demonstrates, first list the binary value. For each 0, insert a 0 for the decimal value; and for each 1, insert the corresponding number for the decimal value. The sum of the remaining numbers in the decimal value is your answer: 51.

To convert a decimal number to a binary value, reading from left to right, you would delete each number in the decimal row in the second table that would take you over and above that numbered value. For example, if you wished to find the binary value of 90, that would be as such: 0+64+0+16+8+0+2+0 = 90. Keeping in mind that binary numbers are made up of only 1's and 0's, then you could chart out your answer as follows:

Binary	0	1	0	1	1	0	1	0	
Decimal	0	64	0	16	8	0	2	0	= 90

This is how you would create subnetworks from specific IP address ranges. Each IP address class has its own unique subnet identifier, which also enables you to create other subnets of that specific IP address range. This is how you would get 1024 nodes on an Ethernet network that appears to have only 254 IP addresses, such as 192.168.0.1 through 192.168.0.254. Subnetting is the process of taking large, cumbersome networks and shrinking them down into smaller ones that are more manageable. To understand how this is done, there is another method of addressing classification called *classless interdomain routing (CIDR)*, where addresses are not segregated into a class, but are "classless addressing." This is a newer method of assigning IP addresses, which attempts to take the original convoluted address and make it more readable.

Classless addressing looks at the IP address and its subnet mask to distinguish between different networks, instead of just an assigned class. For example, your ISP may provide your company with the address 63.14.38.0/20, which is its CIDR notation. The network ID is 63.14.38.0, which is typically the IP address that ends with 0. The subnet mask uses 20 bits, or 255.255.240.0. The /20 in decimal numeric form equals 255.255.240.0, displayed in the typical four octets of IP addressing, but its binary value represents the *first 20 bits in the subnet mask,* or 11111111 11111111 11110000 00000000. The binary 11111111 is equal to 255, so the first two octets represent 255.255. The binary 11110000 of the third octet represents 240, and the last is 0. This means that your company owns the range of IP addresses beginning at 63.14.38.1 (63.14.38.0 is the network identifier) and extending to 63.14.38.254 (63.14.38.255 is the broadcaster).

There are a total of 256 host addresses for each Class C network (without subnetting), but you always subtract two: one for the network identifier and the other as broadcaster. Therefore, there are only 254 host addresses. You'll find that even when subnetting host addresses, you need to subtract these two addresses—the first, which is all 0's (the network identifier), and the last, which is all 1's (the broadcaster).

You can validate subnets and their host addresses by converting the subnet into binary. For example, if the IP address is 192.168.0.1 and the subnet mask is /24 or 255.255.255.0, you can't really read anything in decimal; so converting it into binary, the mask value is 11111111 11111111 11111111 00000000.

The first 24 bits represent the network and the last 8 bits (32 bits minus 24 bits equals 8 bits) represent the host on the network. You can then determine how many hosts are allowed on the network by taking 2 to the power of 8, or 256. You must subtract the first address (192.168.0.0), as this is the network identifier, and the last address (192.168.0.255), as this is the broadcaster. That leaves you with 254.

To determine the valid host addresses for subnet masks, you need to *AND* it. This is a method of calculating binary numbers. When calculating AND values, a 0 will zero out any bit, so while 1 AND 1 = 1, 1 AND 0 = 0 and 0 AND 0 = 0.

Now, going back to our IP address 63.14.38.0/20, in binary, the IP address is 00111111.00001110.00100110.00000000, and the subnet mask is 11111111.11111111. 11110000.00000000.

```
IP:    00111111 00001110 00100110 00000000
SM:    11111111 11111111 11110000 00000000
AND:   00111111 00001110 00100000 00000000
```

To decipher the AND number, follow the AND calculations. Once completed, we take the sum and convert it back to decimal, and we get 63.14.64.0. This is the network ID for a new subnet from the first valid host at 63.14.64.1 to the last valid host at 63.14.64.254.

Private and Public IP Addresses

As discussed briefly in Chapter 7, Class C networks use a range of IP addresses that have been reserved for internal usage on private networks and are not routable onto the Internet, except through a router or server. The following are the private ranges of IP addresses, which can be used by anyone within a closed environment (one that is not routed through the Internet):

10.0.0.0/8 (hosts from 10.0.0.1 to 10.255.255.254)
172.16.0.0/12 (hosts from 172.16.0.1 to 172.31.255.254)
192.168.0.0/16 (hosts from 192.168.0.1 to 192.168.255.254)

Windows 2000 and Server 2003 also use another range, 169.254.0.0/16, for APIPA. This is used when you configure Internet sharing through Network Address Translation (NAT) and have the server assign dynamic IP addresses to the clients sharing the Internet connection. Again, a standard default installation of a properly installed network adapter could then plug into this network and immediately connect to the Internet with no further configuration required on the client side.

Relationship of the IP Address to the Physical Address

The machine or physical address used may be different than the Internet's IP address. Therefore, TCP/IP includes ARP, which lets the administrator create a table (the *ARP cache*) that maps IP addresses to physical addresses (also known as the Media Access Control, or MAC, addresses). The MAC address is your computer's unique hardware number, typically found on the computer's network adapters. Most network devices, such as routers, cable modems, and wireless access points, include a physical MAC address.

The ARP cache resides on a server in volatile memory to help each network computer recognize the others. You can view the ARP cache through the command-line prompt (select Start | Run, type **CMD** in the Run dialog box, then click OK). At the command prompt, type **arp -a**, and it will show you the IP address and physical (MAC) address, and how the IP address was generated. ARP resolves the IP address into the MAC address as a physical recognition of the computer.

The MAC address is usually hard-coded onto the network adapter. This means that there is no way possible to change the number, which is a series of alphanumeric numbers, such as 00-50-118-02-56-ce. If you know the IP address of a device and wish to learn its MAC address, type **arp -a** at the command prompt, and it will display a list of IP addresses and their associated MAC addresses.

Static vs. Dynamic IP Addresses

The difference between a static IP address and a dynamic IP address is how the network adapter receives the assignment. Figure 10-6 shows the dialog box in which you can deselect the Obtain An IP Address Automatically radio button and input a specific IP address, its subnet mask, the default gateway (typically either the router or your Internet sharing server), and a set of DNS servers. Which IP address you should enter depends on what the computer is for, the subnet, and how it will access the Internet.

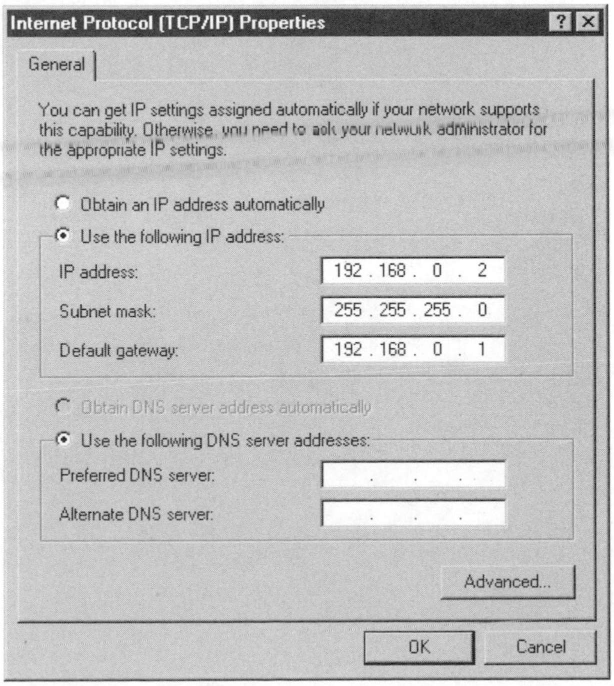

Figure 10-6
Adding static IP addresses to your network configuration

If you plan to use your server as a gateway to the Internet, to provide Internet sharing for your organization, then you will have at least one static IP address provided to you by your ISP. You need to have IP addresses configured statically on devices that will not change, and should not change. In other words, a web server on the Internet that resolves to a DNS name needs a fixed IP address. Network clients need not use static IP addresses, but instead can use dynamically assigned addresses. This way, as I've mentioned before, you're not assigning a fixed numbered resource onto a computer that may not be used on a LAN, and you can use any one of the addresses available. Do you need static IP addresses for Internet sharing? No. If you're using a DSL or cable-modem line in a home office, then you can set up your server as a router that will accept a dynamic public address to one network adapter and deliver a dynamic private address to the clients in your LAN.

Dynamic addresses come from a pool, assigned to a DHCP server by an administrator (more details on this are provided in the next chapter). This not only makes Plug-and-Play networking easier, because Windows defaults to dynamic IP addressing (see Figure 10-7), but also reduces the number of allocated IP addresses. For example, America Online changes a user's IP address from one logon session to another because AOL uses a smaller pool than its total base of subscribers.

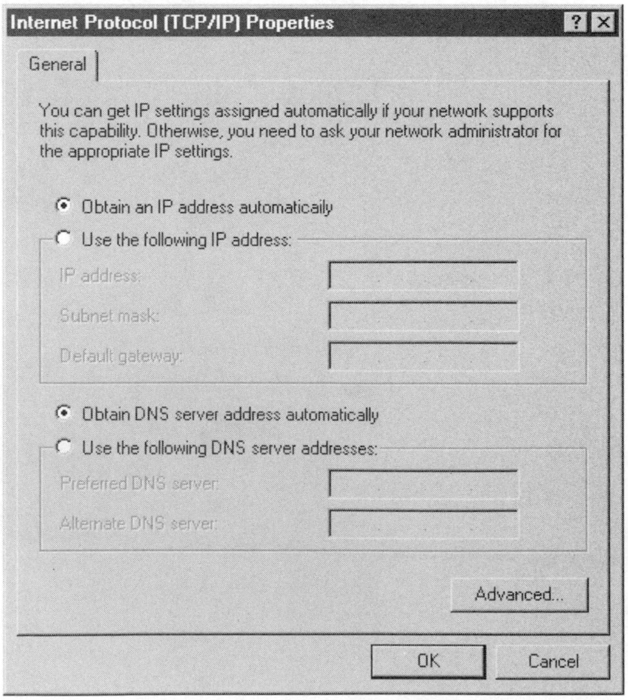

Figure 10-7
The Windows default prepares the client for DHCP.

Configuring a Static IP Address   Suppose you've just installed and configured three workstations and your new server and you'd like for all of them to communicate as quickly as possible. Follow these steps:

1. Open the Properties dialog box of your network adapter named LAN (see Figure 10-8) by right-clicking the My Network Places icon on your desktop and choosing Properties, or from the Start menu, and choose Properties.

Figure 10-8

The LAN network adapter Properties dialog box

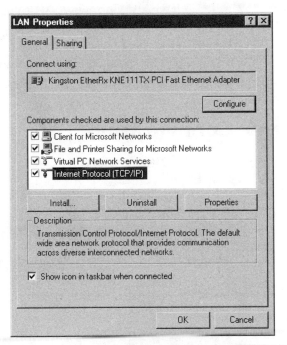

2. Highlight Internet Protocol (TCP/IP) in the center window and click Properties. The IP Addressing dialog box opens. If you've just finished a default installation, then you should see Obtain An IP Address Automatically selected and Obtain A DNS Server IP Address Automatically selected.

3. Click the Use The Following IP Address radio button to make available the data entry fields for IP address and DNS servers.

4. For the IP Address field, enter **192.168.0.1**. Click the Subnet Mask field and 255.255.255.0 should automatically appear. Since we're just setting up an initial peer-to-peer network, skip the Default Gateway field and the DNS Servers IP Addresses for now, and click OK.

5. Open the same window in Workstation #1 and add the number **192.168.0.2** and then **192.168.0.3** for the next one and **192.168.0.4** for the last one.

6. Make sure that all four computers are on the same workgroup. In Windows 2000 (both Professional and Server), right-click the My Computer icon and choose Network Identification. In Windows Server 2003 or Windows XP, select the Computer Name tab.

7. If you have all Windows 2000 Professional or Windows XP workstations, you may not need to reboot (unless you needed to change the workgroup name); but if the OS prompts you to do so, then reboot. Upon rebooting the system, double-click My Network Places, and you should see a list of icons, each representing one of the computers on your network.

File Server Configuration

To set up a file server, you need to create some file folders that are accessible on the network. You can do this by using the Server Configuration Wizards (see Figure 10-9) available with Windows 2000 or Windows Server 2003 .

Figure 10-9
Windows 2000 Server
Configuration Wizard

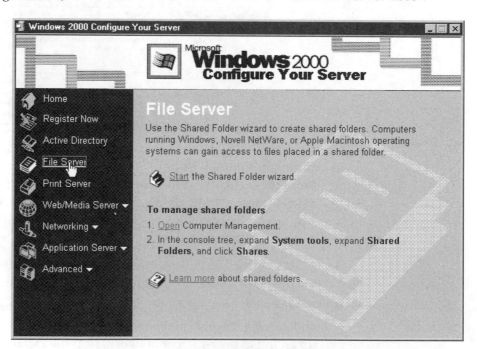

In Windows 2003 Server, upon making your choice from the Manage Your Server Wizard (see Figure 10-10), you're then asked if you'd like to assign disk quotas, limiting the amount of room on the hard drives that can be used for corporate files. Both Windows 2000 Server and Windows Server 2003 enable you to be far more granular with respect to personal limitations (we'll get into that more in Chapter 12).

Figure 10-10
Windows 2003
Server's new Manage
Your Server Wizard

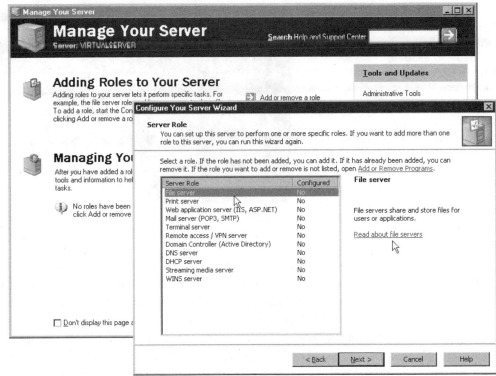

After assigning disk quotas, you also have the option to create a new shared folder (rather than use an existing one). Figure 10-11 demonstrates how you can create a new folder during the configuration to a file server process.

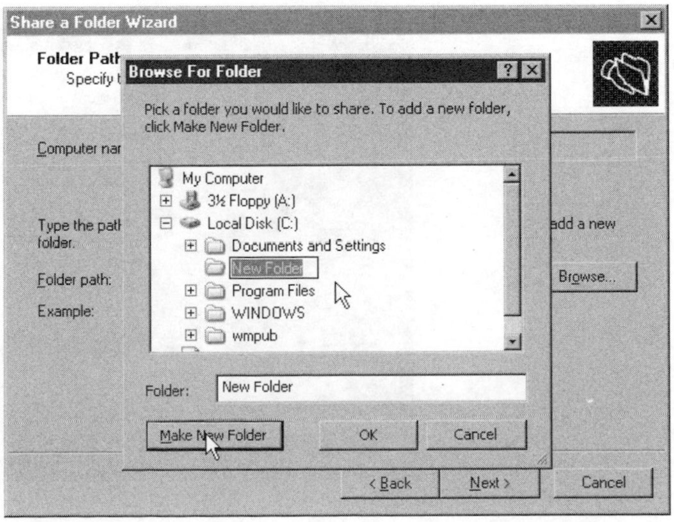

Figure 10-11
Creating a new
network share

If you installed the File and Print Sharing Protocol for AppleTalk Networks, you'll have the option here to choose if you wish to give Apple Computers access to the file server as well (see Figure 10-12).

Figure 10-12
Choosing a share name and whether you'd like to include Apple and Novell Computers

Once you've completed creating the share, Windows 2000 and Server 2003 both provide you with a few quick choices for access control. The first choice, displayed in Figure 10-13, is All Users Have Full Access. I'll explain this more in Chapter 12, but "all users" really means all users. If someone hacks into your system, you've given him or her full control of those assets. The second choice is more conservative, giving only administrators full control and other users only read access. The third choice is even stricter, giving everyone other than administrators no access at all. This choice becomes a problem if you'd like to give users some permission to write and save files to the disk. This is when you choose the Customize Share And Folder Permissions where you can distinguish between the varying authority in your organization.

Figure 10-13
Permissions set up for shared access to the file server

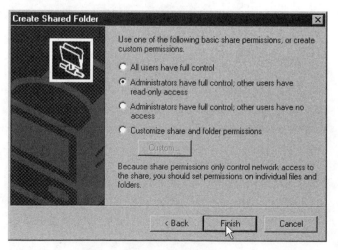

The reason I suggested using the Windows NTFS file system for your hard drive is its multilayered security features. While FAT and FAT32 file systems offer access control as share permissions, Windows 2000 Server and Windows Server 2003 include file-level permissions, web permissions, and even file-level encryption, beyond the typical shared access control. I'll get into more details about this in Chapter 13.

Print Server Configuration

You can also add the role of print server to your machine, again by following the Windows 2000 Server or Windows Server 2003 Configure Your Server Wizard. In Windows 2000 Server, follow these steps:

1. Click Start | Programs | Administrative Tools | Configure Your Server.

2. Choose the Print Server link on the left side of the dialog box, and then click Next to launch the Add Printer Wizard. On the Welcome page, click Next.

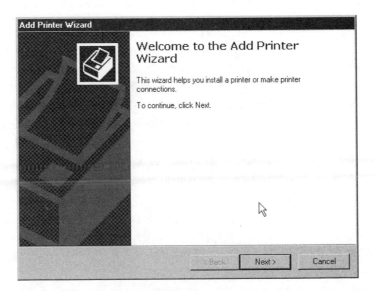

3. Select the Local Printer radio button and then click Next. You can also allow the NOS to automatically search for the printer and install the printer driver (if that printer's driver is in the Windows library), or you can clear that check box, select printer port, and then click Next. Windows then lists a huge library of the makes and models of numerous printers,

so make sure you know the exact model number of the printer you plan to use.

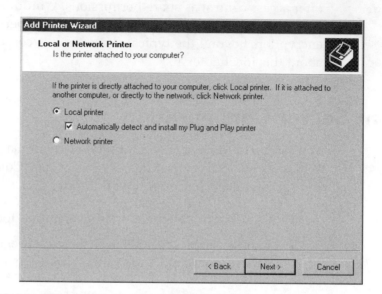

4. Select the printer make and model from the list. If you don't see it on the list, you need to pull out your printer manufacturer's driver disk, and then click Next. You can use the default name for the printer, but picking something a bit more specific and recognizable is useful. This is especially important if you have more than one of the same make and model. For example, instead of choosing HPLaser1, HPLaser2, HPLaser3, you can help users know which is which by adding something unique, like the location, such as HPSouth, HPNorth, and HPWest. You can also add a description.

5. Once the wizard has taken you through the installation process, click the Print A Test Page button, click Next, and then click Finish to close the Add Printer Wizard. To confirm that you've successfully installed the printer, you should see an icon for the printer displayed in the Printers folder.

Shared Security

In Windows 2000 and Server 2003 , your hard drive is automatically a shared resource using an invisible naming method, recognizable from the Computer Management component of the MMC. Choose Start | All Programs | Administrative Tools | Computer Management. Access the Shared Folders directory, and then Shares. Highlight Shares in the left window, and you'll expose the invisible shares, named with the drive letter and then the dollar sign (such as C$ or D$).

Everyone Means Everyone

The Everyone group in Windows 2000 or Server 2003 means everyone. Anyone who gains access to the server will be a part of this group and given whatever privileges are assigned to this group. This can also be the culprit in access and security problems by creating conflicting permissions. Delete the group from any share and keep access user specific!

When you create a new share, Windows adds a hand icon to the bottom of the directory folder to inform you of this shared directory. However, these shares are invisible from remote users and are used only for administrative purposes.

Windows 2000 and Server 2003 can assign printing privileges to six groups of users (who gain access through these invisible shares): Administrators, Creator Owner, Everyone, Power Users, Print Operators, and Server Operators. There are three set permissions for shared printing: Print, Manage Documents, and Manage Printers. A combination of the printer permissions are default, with only Administrators and Power Users given full privileges, and Creator Owner and Everyone allowed only printing privileges. The Print Operators and Server Operators groups are included when Windows 2000 Server becomes an Active Directory domain controller.

Incidentally, just because those administrative shares are invisible to the outside world doesn't mean that no one can gain access over the network or the Internet. All anyone needs is your computer name and the username and password of someone who's a member of the Administrators, Backup Operators, or Server Operators group. Anyone who gains access to the server can then view all folders and files on that drive, even Administrators, Backup Operators, or Server Operators group, who are seemingly protected with NTFS permissions (more on security in Chapter 13).

In the next chapter, we move into network troubleshooting, an Active Directory primer, Domain Name System (DNS), and Terminal Services. Setting up your own Web/Media Server will be covered in Chapter 12.

Chapter 11

Network Troubleshooting

Tools of the Trade

Crossover cable
New Cat 5 network cable
Network operating system Setup CD-ROM
Antistatic pouches/bags
Cat 5 cable tester (optional)
A good network adapter
Router hub or switch

Before you venture into the depths of more sophisticated network configuration in the upcoming chapters, this chapter provides an overview of how to troubleshoot your network. Understanding how to troubleshoot your network is vitally important because problems may be masked or hidden in a network's layers of complexity. Troubleshooting a server system constitutes working knowledge of computer hardware components, networking technologies, and the diagnostic tools available within Windows 2000 Server and Windows Server 2003. Any previous network experience you have will help you diagnose and troubleshoot potential problems, but you may not know where to start when a problem arises. This chapter will help you determine where to start troubleshooting and how to proceed from there.

If you've set up a Windows peer-to-peer network, with new network adapters, TCP/IP, static IP addresses, and a single subnet, you shouldn't have any problems. The Windows architecture is built on simple and straightforward network configuration. This makes any connectivity problem even more frustrating.

However, there are built-in utilities that can help you quickly diagnose any trouble, from clear network path to faulty hardware.

Windows 2000 Server and Windows Server 2003 TCP/IP Utilities

Windows 2000 and Server 2003 offer a suite of utilities for managing, configuring, and troubleshooting networking using TCP/IP. This section describes several of these utilities including administrative devices such as PING, NETSTAT, and TRACERT.

PING

Using the built-in Windows PING utility to diagnose a network connection is a popular technique because of its simplicity. PING is a simple method of validating communications, through a network or modem, via a ricocheted message. As mentioned earlier in this chapter, each computer (server or workstation) using TCP/IP has assigned IP addresses, whether they apply statically, or are generated dynamically. The IP address, as described in Chapter 9, is a set of four octets, separated by a period or "dot." The PING utility sends a small 32-byte message from your IP address to another IP address. If communication is clear, the other computer returns the 32-byte message back to your computer, without any loss.

To PING another computer on the network, open your command-line prompt by clicking Start | Run As. Type **CMD** into the field and press ENTER. At the C prompt, type the following:

```
C:\>ping 66.218.71.198
```

Then press ENTER. If you're on the Internet right now, this is an example of a successful reply:

```
Pinging 66.218.71.198 with 32 bytes of data:
Reply from 66.218.71.198: bytes=32 time=70ms TTL=241
Reply from 66.218.71.198: bytes=32 time=70ms TTL=241
Reply from 66.218.71.198: bytes=32 time=70ms TTL=241
Reply from 66.218.71.198: bytes=32 time=70ms TTL=241
Ping statistics for 66.218.71.198:
Packets: Sent = 4, Received = 4, Lost = 0 (0% loss)
Approximate round trip times in milliseconds:
Minimum = 60ms, Maximum = 70ms, Average = 65ms
C :\>
```

The message indicates that four packets traveled through the Internet, and four returned, all in an average of about 65 milliseconds. You don't need to uncover any specific IP address of the destination computer; all you need is any computer off which to bounce the test. The preceding example is the IP address for Yahoo.com, which is usable for this exercise. However, you can also use PING to test the availability of another computer on the network.

If the network is down, there will be no reply, with a message signaling "Request Timed Out." If the power connections are all secure and the cabling is correct, but a PING returns a "Request Timed Out" message, does not return all the data, or takes excessively longer than normal for operation, then try the same IP address on another, nearby computer. This will verify the validity of the destination computer, just in case that one is down. However, if you do not receive a reply, try another outside IP address, because some destinations (such as www.msn.com) may drop Internet Control Message Protocol (ICMP) traffic to protect against ICMP-based attacks. PING uses ICMP to communicate between hosts on the Internet.

PATHPING

PATHPING is an advanced version of the PING utility that provides statistics on packet loss at intermediary routers and shows you what path your ping takes to arrive at its destination. This is a very useful utility if you're trying to diagnose an Internet sharing problem with your LAN, since it will tell you how it reaches out to the network. Therefore, if you've been having problems connecting, it will stop at the device creating the blockage. PATHPING will give you the IP addresses of every router, DNS server, and computer as it ricochets to your destination IP address and back again.

The following is a quick example of PATHPING, using the www.buildyourownserver.com server. Obviously, because the server is only a few feet away, there isn't much of a path (compared to the upcoming TRACERT example).

```
C:/>pathping www.buildyourownserver.com
Tracing route to www.buildyourownserver.com [12.213.197.81] over a maximum of
30 hops:
0       p4hp [10.1.1.131]
1       12-213-197-81.client.attbi.com [12.213.197.81]
Computing statistics for 25 seconds...
Hop     RTT     Lost/sent =Pct          Lost/Sent =Pct          Address
0                                                               p4hp [10.1.1.131]
1       0ms     0/100=0%        0/100=0%        12-213-197-81.client.attbi.com
[12.213.197.81]
Trace complete.
C:/>
```

ARP

The Address Resolution Protocol (ARP) utility will resolve an IP address to the physical MAC address of the computer. It will also allow you to modify the ARP cache, which stores your LAN IP to MAC address mappings. To uncover the IP address and MAC address of a device, you would type the following at the command-line prompt:

```
C:/> arp -a
```

The response would be something like this:

```
C:\>arp -a
Interface: 10.1.1.131 on Interface 0x60000004
Internet address    Physical address    Type
10.1.1.3            00-50-19-03-56-ce   Dynamic
```

The IP address 10.1.1.131 is for my laptop network adapter, as is the physical MAC address of 0x60000004. The Internet gateway is my router, which has a static IP address of 10.1.1.3, a physical address of 00-50-19-03-56-ce, and, using DHCP (more on this in Chapter 12), generated my 10.1.1.131 IP address dynamically.

TRACERT

The TRACERT utility will trace the route that a packet takes to reach the domain name or IP address you specify. You receive in return not only the IP address of a specific domain, but also the route the packet takes to reach the destination. This works exceptionally well to trace any network obstructions. The following is an example of TRACERT in action, using the McGraw-Hill/Osborne web site:

```
C:/>tracert www.osborne.com
Tracing route to www.osborne.com [198.45.24.162]
Over a maximum of 30 hops:
1     <10 ms     10 ms      <10 ms      10.1.1.3
2     10 ms      10 ms      10 ms       10.163.216.1
3     40 ms      20 ms      10 ms       12.244.106.129
4     20 ms      10 ms      10 ms       12.244.68.26
5     10 ms      50 ms      10 ms       12.244.68.30
6     40 ms      10 ms      10 ms       12.244.72.242
7     10 ms      20 ms      20 ms        gbr1-p50.cgcil.ip.att.net
[12.123.5.74]
8     20 ms    10 ms         10 ms          gbr1-p70.cgcil.ip.att.net
[12.122.5.218]
9      40 ms        20 ms     10 ms          gbr1-p00.cgcil.ip.att.net
[12.122.5.13]
10     10 ms        20 ms        10 ms        graywhale.netexpress.net
[64.22.197.23]
11     20 ms        10 ms        20 ms        64.22.197.50
```

```
12     10 ms      30 ms      20 ms      64.22.208.90
13     10 ms      20 ms      30 ms      198.45.24.244
14     40 ms      10 ms      30 ms      198.45.24.162
Trace complete
```

NSLOOKUP

Using NSLOOKUP will resolve the domain and name server for the domain (DNS server). For example, if you wanted to know the specific domain and name server for visualstorytelling.com, you would type the following at the command-line prompt:

```
C:/> nslookup www.visualstorytelling.com
Server: ns6.attbi.com
Address: 63.240.76.4
Name: www.visualstorytelling.com
Address: 12.129.206.111
C:/>
```

Task Manager

The Windows 2000 Server and Windows Server 2003 Task Manager (see Figure 11-1) can verify responsiveness of processes and running applications. It can also display CPU utilization and memory usage by process. To access Windows Task Manager, press CTRL-ALT-DEL and then choose Task Manager.

Spyware

A recent problem I've encountered with connectivity and even overall network performance is that "spyware" can clog bandwidth and resources. Spyware is a small, inconspicuous software application that sits in the background and gives you personalized advertisements when surfing the Internet. Spyware also tracks your habits, steals information, and hogs bandwidth. You should never install anything on your server that is not in the service of the server-specific function.

Windows 2000 Server and Windows Server 2003 enable you to establish a global security policy that will prohibit users from installing any new software without authorization. This will help control the flurry of traffic from these types of applications.

Obviously, as a server, you shouldn't install any applications not specifically used for server functions; but if you find the server suddenly sluggish, research the names of any new services that may appear within the processes window of the Task Manager.

Figure 11-1
The Windows Task
Manager screen

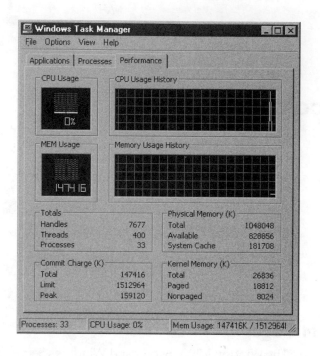

NETSTAT

NETSTAT will display information about current TCP/IP sessions on connected
hosts and the port numbers that are being used by those sessions. This is one of my
personal favorites because it can provide valuable information about who has
access to your server and which port they're using. NETSTAT on its own will give
you the protocol, local address, foreign address, and state in which that
connection resides. By adding **-a** at the end of the NETSTAT command, as follows,

```
C:/>netstat -a
Proto          Local Address      Foreign Address        State        PID
TCP            0.0.0.0:0000       0.0.0.0                Listening    233
```

you'll get a display of all connections and state. The state of the protocol and port
number can be "established," meaning that there's connectivity, or "listening,"
which are ports assigned to specific processes or applications on your system,
and the port is waiting for its unique connection. Port 3386 is assigned to
Terminal Services, and sits and waits, listening for a Terminal Server Client to call
upon the server.

You can use Task Manager to match the PID (process identifier) that is using
a listening port to a specific process name and program. Ports assigned to a
process/program cannot be used elsewhere. If you wish to match the PID to
a program, you first need to access Task Manager (press CTRL-ALT-DEL, then

click Task Manager). Choose the Processes tab; if you do not see a PID column, click View | Select Columns | PID. Choose the column header labeled PID to sort by PIDs, and then you'll find the process ID/program match listed in Task Manager.

The following are some other switches that you can add to the end of NETSTAT:

❏ **-e** Gives you specific Ethernet information, such as how many packets have been received and sent

❏ **-n** Gives you the addresses and port numbers in numerical form, without any name resolution

❏ **-s** Displays information by protocol

❏ **-p** *protocol* Displays protocol-specific information (where *protocol* is a specific protocol, such as TCP or ICMP)

IPCONFIG

IPCONFIG will become very useful later when you configure the server for DHCP. If you type **IPCONFIG /ALL** at the command prompt, you see the current TCP/IP configuration of the machine, including the IP address, subnet mask, default gateway, DNS servers, and domain suffix (such as yahoo.com). It will also let you know this information for every network adapter by name and whether the adapter is configured for DHCP (and the DHCP server) or has a static IP address.

Here's an example of using IPCONFIG with the /ALL switch:

```
C:/>ipconfig/all
Windows 2000 IP configuration
Host Name                           p4hp
Primary DNS Suffix
Connection-Specific DNS Suffix      attbi.com
Description                         National Semiconductor Corp. 10/100 PCI
Adapter
Physical Address                    00-23-9F-0F-65-9E
DHCP Enabled                        Yes
Autoconfiguration Enabled           Yes
IP Address                          10.1.1.131
Subnet Mask                         255.255.255.0
Default Gateway                     10.1.1.3
DHCP Server                         10.1.1.3
DNS Servers                         63.241.76.6
                                    204.128.198.6
Lease Obtained                      Wednesday, December 11, 2002 5:34.5 PM
Lease Expires                       Wednesday, January 22, 2003 5:34.5 PM
C:/>
```

IPCONFIG comes with a few other helpful switches, which can be used by adding the specific command after the initial IPCONFIG at the command prompt. For example, if you type the following at the command prompt and press ENTER, the lease of the IP address will be released from all DHCP-configured network adapters on a system:

```
C:/>IPCONFIG/RELEASE
```

To obtain a new IP address lease, you need to type the following command and then press ENTER:

```
C:/>IPCONFIG/RENEW
```

The following is a summary of a few IPCONFIG switches that are available to you:

❑ **/release**   Releases a DHCP-obtained IP address

❑ **/renew**   Obtains a new DHCP IP address

❑ **/all**   Displays all TCP/IP configuration information

❑ **/flushdns**   Purges the local DNS resolver cache

❑ **/regsiterdns**   Refreshes DHCP leases and re-registers with DNS

❑ **/displaydns**   Shows the contents of the DNS resolver cache

Troubleshooting Hardware

There is a multitude of possible culprits when troubleshooting a network, and hardware is not immune to malfunction or misconfiguration. There are a few failed hardware components that are more obvious than others, but I've found these initial steps—from checking power to all devices, including hubs, routers, and switches (as well as the computer) to swapping devices to determine the failed component—to be important.

1. Check connectivity by device activity lighting.
2. Check cabling.
3. Make sure the network adapter is enabled.
4. Swap suspect component/equipment with a known-good replacement.

Many times, if a network system is not functioning properly, the cause may be a hardware failure. Check the activity lighting on the network adapter . . . and on any routers, hubs, or switches. Hardware failure can also be due to electrostatic discharge (ESD), so have some static-free pouches handy when handling any network adapters.

Overheating of the system as a whole can be another culprit, if the computer or server is located in direct sunlight, next to a heat duct, or in a warm environment, or if the chassis is improperly ventilated. The symptoms may include hardware failure, grinding noises, or constant NOS hangs and freezes.

If communications with the server are down, the culprit may be network-related hardware such as an Ethernet router, hub, or switch. I've learned from experience that you should assume nothing and check everything. You may need to experiment with a specific device to uncover the problem. For example, if a single workstation is not connecting to a dynamic IP addressing network, grab an extra hub and one other workstation, and configure the two workstations as a small peer-to-peer network by using static IP addressing through the hub. If the two systems communicate successfully, then you know to move beyond the network adapters, operating systems, and the cabling.

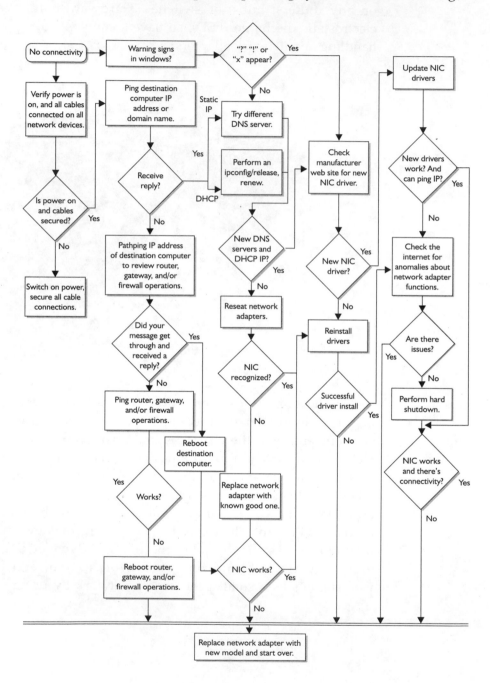

You may wish to follow the troubleshooting options shown next, as I've discovered these are the path of least resistance. After confirming connectivity using the PING utility, the next-immediate step is permissions and access rights. Does this user have adequate permissions to access the network resources? Did he change his password and the server is looking for the old password? It pays to start with the most obvious possibilities.

1. Check permissions and access rights.

2. Rewire the connections, swapping ports, and hub connections.

3. Pull out the hub and try connecting the computers together using a crossover cable.

4. If you have more than one network adapter running on the system, disable all but one, and try the connection with that single one.

5. Check that all devices have power. Many times a power cord is inadvertently unplugged or damaged. This includes the power cord for the server or any workstation computer, routers, hubs, or switches.

6. Reboot. More times than not, rebooting the system will clear any anomalies.

The first step I take is to check whether I disabled the network adapter through Windows or if the NIC driver has become corrupted by a recent software install. You can check the status of the network adapter in either of two ways: through the Device Manager, as shown in Figure 11-2 (right-click My Computer and choose Properties | Hardware), or by choosing Start | Settings | Network And Dial-Up Connections (in Windows 2000 Server) or Start | Control Panel | Network Connections (in Windows Server 2003).

If your adapter is disconnected or disabled, for whatever reason (manually or otherwise), a red X appears over the listing of the network adapter in Device Manager. A red X over the network connection icon (in Network & Dial-Up Connections) usually means that there's a connectivity problem. A device driver problem typically is indicated by a yellow exclamation point over the device icon in Device Manager (see Figure 11-3).

Upon checking the status of your network adapter, if you see a red X over its icon, do the following:

1. Double-check that your network cable is securely in place at both ends.

2. Replace the cable with a known-good one to check the validity of the cable.

Figure 11-2
Device Manager clear
of any warnings is a
sign of good health.

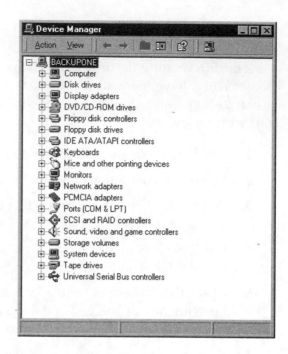

3. Open the chassis and check whether the device is securely seated.

4. If you see a yellow exclamation mark over the network adapter's icon:

Figure 11-3
Device Manager will
warn you if there's
a problem with your
network adapters.

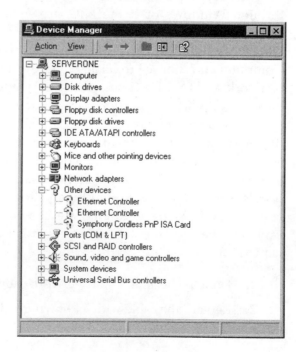

5. Reinstall the driver.

6. Update the driver.

7. If you see a yellow question mark over the network adapter's icon:

8. The server no longer recognizes the device: reinstall the driver.

9. Open the chassis and check whether the device is securely seated.

Cabling

Technically, this topic may belong under hardware, but it deserves its own section. I've learned from experience to have a good Cat 5 cable with me when troubleshooting network connectivity, especially if I'm unfamiliar with the cable history. You can buy a cable tester, but I've found an extra Cat 5 cable works better; if you find that the cable is bad, you have an immediate (at least temporary) replacement.

The RJ-45 connectors on a Cat 5 cable are susceptible to damage. The locking pin can easily be broken off if not protected by a guard (see Figure 11-4). Unfortunately, an RJ-45 connector without a locking pin may appear inserted when in fact it's not, which can make detection difficult. This is why I highly recommend replacing the cable (or the RJ-45 connector, if you're so inclined). The cost is nominal. I just purchased some 10-foot Cat 5 cables from Computer Surplus Outlet (www.computersurplusoutlet.com) for 99 cents apiece and a 50-foot cable for under $5.

Figure 11-4
Cat 5 cable connector
with locking pin

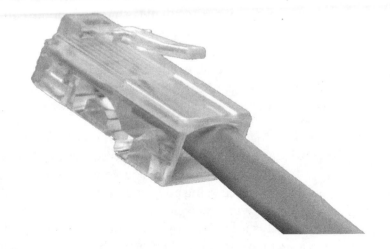

Do Not Use a Broken Locking Pin

You should not use a Cat 5 cable with a broken locking pin. You may forget about its defect months later when troubleshooting the network, only to rediscover the defect after spending an hour trying to troubleshoot software-related connectivity.

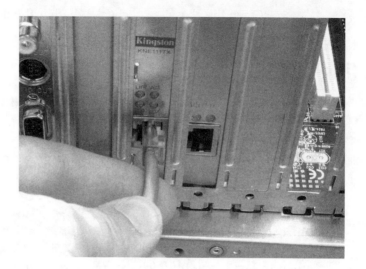

Networking Configuration

How you configure the network can also play a part in network problems. If you have a single client disconnected from an Ethernet network, then it's relatively easy to troubleshoot the problem because it's focused on one machine. However, if an entire network of clients is having trouble connecting to a file server or to one another, the list of possible problems is much longer.

Assuming that you've checked the hardware (routers, network adapters, and so on) and cabling (Cat 5 cables and power cords), the process of elimination moves next to the software configuration. Follow these steps when troubleshooting the configuration of a TCP/IP Ethernet network:

1. Check for improperly configured firewall software. Even home applications such as Black Ice and Zone Alarm are fantastic at keeping intruders from accessing your machine, but they can also keep you from accessing anything outside your hard drive. Check whether the software's access filters are properly configured. The best way to do this is to shut down the software (making the system wide open) and then check whether the problem goes away.

2. Check the Internet TCP/IP properties of each network adapter and confirm proper configuration. This includes checking for correct IP addresses, subnet mask, default gateway (more on this in Chapter 12), and the proper DNS server IP addresses from your ISP (if applicable).

3. In a peer-to-peer network, there's no need to concern yourself about access permissions because each client can access any other client, with the proper credentials (i.e., ID and password). However, with a client/server environment set up, improperly configured permissions play a big role in networking problems (more on permissions and security in Chapter 14).

4. Make sure that each client has a unique IP address, DNS (domain name), and/or NetBIOS computer name. Each client must be *uniquely identifiable*; otherwise, confusion and conflicts will disrupt connectivity.

Keep Names and Addresses Separate

You cannot have two computers or servers using the same IP address. The system will hang and an "IP address conflict" warning message will appear. A similar message will appear if you have two computers with the same name.

Permissions

Improper access permissions are another common culprit in network connectivity problems. For example, a user who attempts to print on a network printer but does not have the appropriate print permissions or is assigned as a member of the wrong group won't be able to print. You should also avoid any permission conflicts by having one user assigned to multiple groups, each with unique permissions. Each group you use or create should have specific permissions assigned, and the right users need assignment to a specific group. Although this important topic is covered in depth in Chapter 13, it should be included in your list of variables when troubleshooting a network.

Recent Software Installation

If your network connectivity goes down shortly after installing new software, you should try using the built-in troubleshooting utilities (refer to "Windows 2000 Server and Windows Server 2003 TCP/IP Utilities," earlier in the chapter) before uninstalling the software and trying again. New software also includes any update patches and service packs for the operating system, antivirus software, or other typical applications. Many service packs cannot be uninstalled, so, if you are asked whether you wish to archive the service pack so, that you can later uninstall it, I would highly recommend that you choose to do so.

TESTING 1-2-3

❏ Network troubleshooting includes evaluation of hardware (network adapters, routers, and hubs), software (add-ons and device drivers), and the NOS (configuration and permissions).

❏ Always begin troubleshooting a network by evaluating the most likely problems, so you don't waste time when the problem is nothing but a bad cable, for example.

❏ Learn to use all the built-in utilities and diagnostic programs available within the NOS.

❏ Use a symptoms approach to troubleshooting, and the process of elimination.

Chapter 12

Beyond File and Print Sharing

Tools of the Trade

Network operating system setup CD-ROM
Router
Hub or switch
New Cat 5 network cables

Now that you understand how to troubleshoot the network, you're ready to take the next step beyond file and print sharing. This includes how to configure a DHCP server to automatically assign IP addresses for instant network access; configure a DNS server to resolve IP addresses into user friendly domain names; configure ICS or NAT to share Internet connections; and learn about AD, Microsoft's advanced networking solution.

Configuring a DHCP Server

DHCP "leases" an IP address, dynamically, for a specific amount of time for a target computer. By using very short leases, DHCP can reconfigure networks on-the-fly and stretch out a limited number of IP addresses to the clients that need them. If a DHCP client is down for a week, and the lease is valid only for a few days, once that lease expires, that IP address is then assigned to another computer. When the original computer comes back online, the DHCP server assigns that computer a new lease on another IP address. This process is invisible to the client users (see Figure 12-1).

DHCP is an alternative to the Bootstrap Protocol (BOOTP), which is another network IP management protocol (although DHCP is more advanced). The procedures for installing a DHCP server on Windows 2000 Server and on Windows Server 2003 are relatively the same; only the GUI is different, as shown in Figure 12-2 (Windows Server 2003) and Figure 12-3 (Windows 2000 Server). You have to specify certain parameters (including a static IP address) to make your DHCP server function properly. For example, unless you're an ISP, the scope of your IP addresses will be private.

The server configuration wizards are the Configure Your Server Wizard in Windows 2000 Server, and Windows Server 2003 has both a Configure Your Server Wizard and a new Manage Your Server Wizard. In Windows 2000 Server, making a choice from the menu at the left (see Figure 12-3) will launch the Add Windows Components Wizard from the Control Panel, to install new components. You can add the DHCP module (if you haven't already done so) by launching the Configure Your Server Wizard by clicking on Start | Programs | Administrative Tools | Configure Your Server Wizard. Choose the DHCP Server under the Networking menu in the left column of the wizard.

After the DHCP module is installed, your next step is to create a new *scope*, which is a range of IP addresses from which the DHCP server will choose when assigning the leases to the client computers. You use the New Scope Wizard,

Figure 12-1
DHCP uses dynamic
IP addressing.

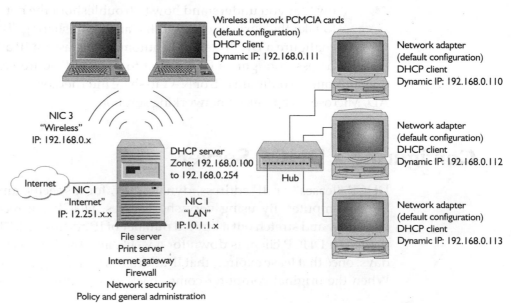

Figure 12-2
The installation of
a new server role as
DHCP in Windows
Server 2003

shown in Figure 12-4, to create a new scope. This is accessed by choosing Action |
New Scope from the top menu of the DHCP manager.

Figure 12-3
Configuring DHCP in
Windows 2000 Server

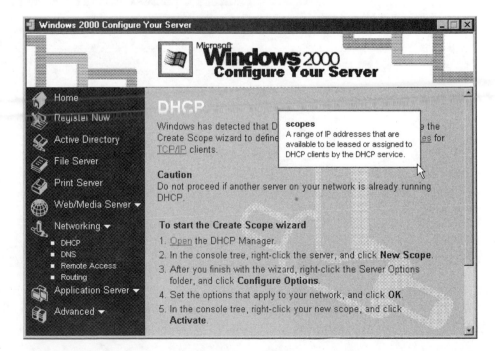

Figure 12-4
Creating a new
scope using the
New Scope Wizard

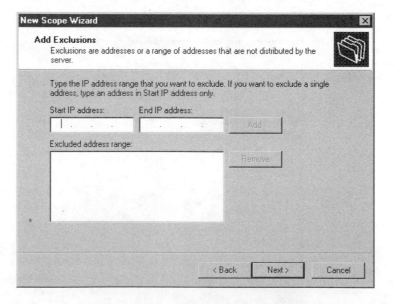

In addition to establishing a range of IP addresses to use, you can also add a range of IP addresses within that range not to use, unique to specific computers or devices.

The next step in the process is to specify the length of the lease—the amount of time the specific IP address belongs to the destination client computer. You can designate this value in days, hours, and even down to the minutes. One of the benefits of using only short leases is increased security by way of making a computer a "moving target." No static IP address will make it more difficult for anyone to find the system. Although DHCP is used primarily to increase the number of available IP addresses (and for its simplicity), it can also ensure that a host will get the same IP address over and over again. By releasing the same number to a specific host, it keeps the DNS and WINS databases current.

The configuration of the most common options, including a router address, DNS server, and subnet, is necessary before client computers will be able to plug into the network. It is important to establish these attributes with the server so that the client computers will not need to be concerned with anything but making sure they have network connectivity—the DHCP server takes care of the rest.

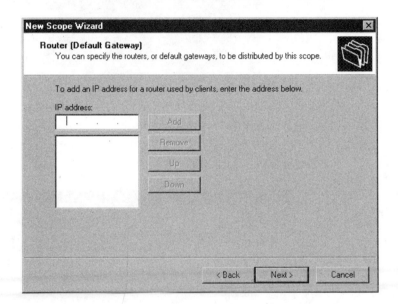

After you've established the router and gateway for the network, you need to fill in the computer name and resolve the IP address (see Figure 12-5) with the primary domain name. The router, domain name, and DNS server are all components that are necessary give your client computers shared Internet access, dynamically.

The next step involves configuring the Windows Internet Naming Service (WINS) server. The WINS server (also built into Windows 2000 and Server 2003s) maps the computer's NetBIOS names to their IP addresses. A WINS server automatically creates a mapping table that lists all the computers and their current associated IP address and automatically updates that table when the information changes. WINS complements the DHCP service by monitoring each computer. The WINS server manages a database of mappings of NetBIOS names to IP addresses, so

Figure 12-5
Although DHCP provides dynamic connectivity for clients, the server needs to know where to route them.

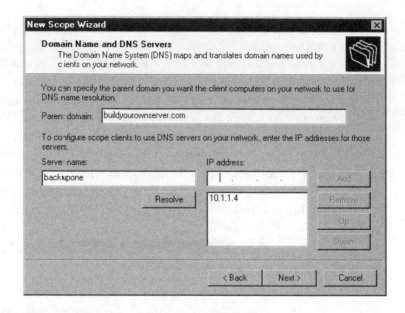

that continuous broadcasts are not excessive. You can also replicate WINS databases across WAN links on timed intervals to keep bandwidth consumption to a minimum. If you add the server name in the appropriate field, Windows will resolve the IP address for you (see Figure 12-6).

Figure 12-6
Setting up the WINS server will help map computer names to IP addresses.

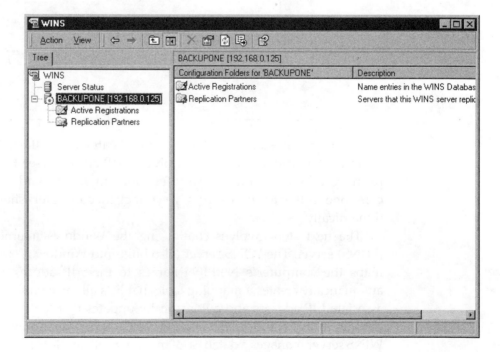

Figure 12-7
Active DHCP
server with assigned
address pool

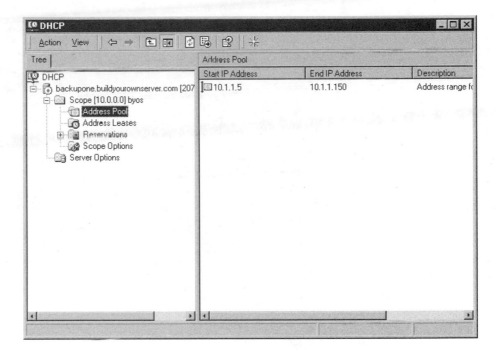

Your last step activates the new scope on the network; and if you choose to authorize the DHCP server, the machine will only communicate with other authorized servers in the designated network group and will add more security and management functions.

When you restart the DHCP server (highlight the computer name in the left pane and choose Action | All Tasks | Restart), you should see a green arrow over the server name icon in the left pane (see Figure 12-7). As the next section describes, you can further configure your DHCP server to dictate how DHCP interacts with DNS, thus making the DNS entries also dynamic.

Configuring DNS

To install the DNS server component of Windows 2000 Server and Windows Server 2003, launch the Configure Your Server Wizard once more, but this time choose to install DNS. The server configuration wizards will again launch the Windows Components Wizard in Windows 2000 Server and the Manage Your Server Wizard in Windows Server 2003 to install the DNS module (if you haven't already done so). If you have already installed it, launch the Configure Your Server Wizard from the Administrative Tools folder (see Figure 12-8), extend the Networking menu once again, and choose DNS from the drop-down menu.

Figure 12-8
Choose the Configure
The Server option in
the DNS module

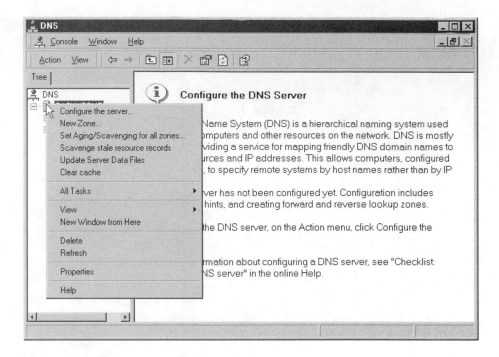

This launches the DNS Configuration Wizard. When you click Next, the installer searches the server to compile configuration data and then launches the Root Server dialog box. Choose the default, This Is The First DNS Server On This Network, and then click Next. Your next step is to create a forward lookup zone, which will resolve domain names to specific IP addresses (for example, it will resolve yahoo.com to 64.58.76.177).

Choose Yes and then click Next. This will take you to a choice of zone types (see Figure 12-9). Choose Active Directory-Integrated if you've installed Active Directory. Choose Standard Primary if this is the first DNS server on your network. Choose Standard Secondary if this is another DNS server on your network.

After you choose, click Next, type in a zone name, then click Next again. You'll be prompted to create a reverse lookup zone. This database will translate IP addresses to domain names. Click Yes, then click Next to continue. You'll be asked once again which zone type you prefer; choose Forward or Reverse, and then click Next. Figure 12-10 shows the New Zone Wizard's Reverse Lookup Zone page, in which you can either add the network ID (the first three octets of the IP address) or the reverse lookup zone name.

Figure 12-9
If you've installed
Active Directory, you
need DNS to resolve
the domain name.

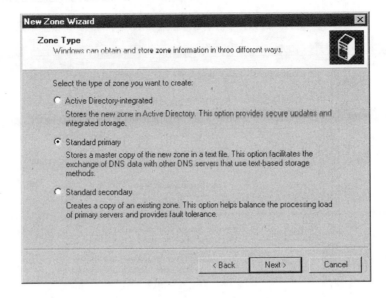

Once you've completed the reverse lookup configuration, click Finish and the DNS management console appears. You've now set up your DNS server. As shown in Figure 12-11, the server named backup.buildyourownserver.com has become the name server for the domain named zone.buildyourownserver.com.

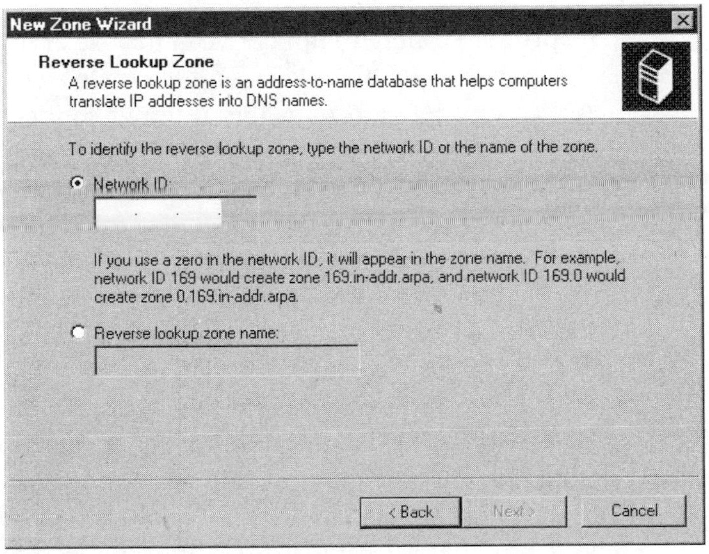

Figure 12-10
Reverse lookup
zone configuration

Figure 12-11
The server is now
a name server
for the domain
zone.buildyourown
server.com.

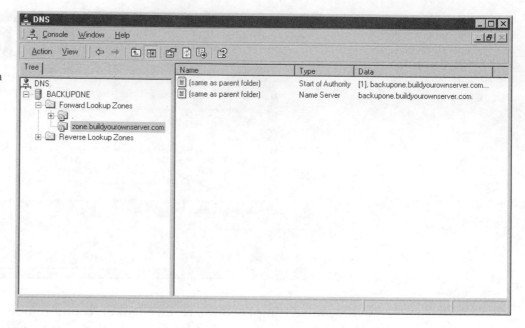

Configuring Internet Connection Sharing with Network Access Translation

The primary differentiator between the use of Internet Connection Sharing and NAT is that while ICS allows you to create a bridge of sorts between your one LAN connection and your one Internet connection, NAT will also share that Internet connection with multiple adapters and multiple networks.

The first step in configuring your server as an Internet share is to determine which network adapter is connected to the Internet and which network adapter is connected to the computers that wish to access the Internet. If you've followed my recommendations about naming conventions, and have named each network adapter relative to its function, you should be able to identify your Internet connection easily.

The ICS component of Windows is very simple and may be sufficient for your purposes if you have only one LAN that needs connectivity. Open the Properties dialog box for your network adapter connected directly to the Internet (this is typically the one with a static IP address). Choose the Sharing tab. Select the check box that activates ICS for this connection, then choose the network to which you wish to give access. You only have one choice, but I have two, as shown in Figure 12-12: the traditional LAN, with 100 Mbps, and the 1.6 Mbps Wireless network. The Proxim Symphony units I'm using only function up to 1.6 Mbps, but you can go up to 11 Mbps or more.

Because I needed to provide network sharing to both networks, I needed to configure NAT. This is done by launching the Routing And Remote Access Server

Figure 12-12
ICS in Windows
2000 Server

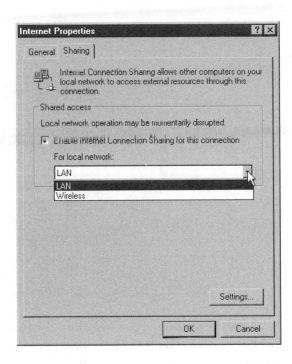

Setup Wizard from the Administrative Tools folder. As shown in Figure 12-13, this wizard offers you five choices of configuration. Choose the first option, Internet Connection Server, and click Next.

You are given the choice of either ICS or NAT. Choose NAT and click Next. The next wizard page, shown in Figure 12-14, lists your network adapters and requests that you choose the one that has the Internet connection.

Figure 12-13
Routing And Remote
Access Server Setup
Wizard options

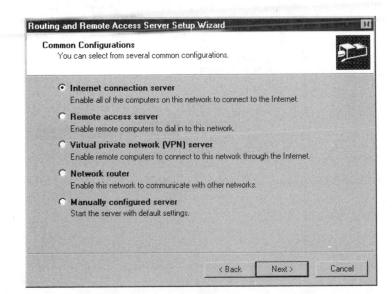

Figure 12-14
Picking the
Internet share for
the other networks

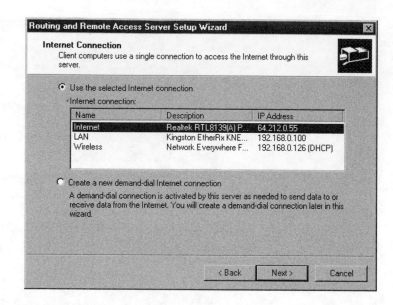

After you make your selection and click Next, the wizard automatically configures the server to provide Internet access from the one Internet connection you indicated to the other networks linked to your server. You can also add additional network interfaces by opening the Routing And Remote Access window and choosing NAT under the IP Routing icon in the left pane (see Figure 12-15).

You've now configured Internet sharing for your internal networks and, at the same time, increased security through Windows.

Figure 12-15
Adding new
interfaces to the
Internet share

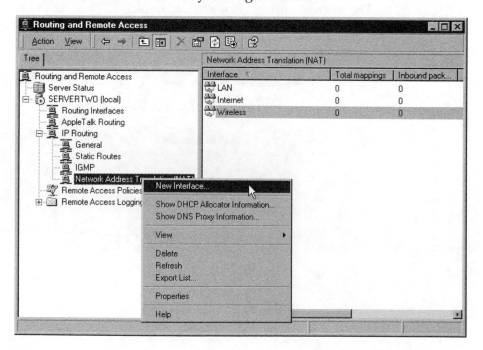

Active Directory

Microsoft's Active Directory (AD) is a complex yet wonderful object-oriented directory service designed for distributed computing environments. In an object-oriented directory service, an *object* is something (anything) that represents a network resource. Typical AD objects are users, groups, sites, computers, and printers. Every object has a number of attributes; for example, a user has a password, name, password length, and e-mail address. AD allows centralization of all network resources and users, and the central security authority through a domain infrastructure. One of the major benefits of a domain is its security boundary, which prevents security policies and settings from crossing over domains. AD can set up a "trust relationship" between domains so that they can work together, but otherwise they are isolated.

In Figure 12-16, the namespace of the tree is buildyourownserver.com, and that of the single domain on the right is builditagain.com, or it can be based on location rather than namespace. These are two distinct namespaces, but AD can join them together into a *forest*. A typical scenario for the use of a forest domain is in a company merger, or partnership, in which the forest consists of different domains of separate divisions, companies, or partners (see the example domain-based enterprise in Table 12-1). Each has its own administration and functions, but is part of a larger organization, and you can create virtual groups, with members from different domains.

Everything in the AD network is a specific object within the network, making it possible to make location, model, and even size irrelevant. For example, a network share of a folder named mydocs becomes a virtual drive share of mydocs, without any idea of location. I've known many network administrators and engineers who inherited AD networks and were lost. This becomes a very serious problem without the benefit of Implementation and infrastructure notes by the predecessor. A few administrators took months to find the specific location of servers throughout the enterprise, and then decipher where the shared folders were located.

Figure 12-16
Tree and forest domains in Active Directory

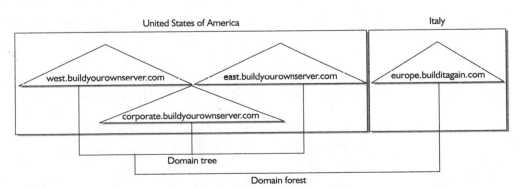

Office Location	Internal DNS Domain Name
My Company, Inc., Headquarters	.sanjose.mycompanyinc.com
Chicago	chicago.mycompanyinc.com
Boston	boston.mycompanyinc.com
New York	newyork.mycompanyinc.com
Rome	rome.mycompanyinc.com
Hong Kong	hongkong.mycompanyinc.com

Table 12-1
An Example of a Domain-Based Enterprise

When you implement AD, the entire network will change, but mostly behind the scenes for the users. The users will suddenly notice a seamless internetworking between offices, locations, and cities. This is accomplished by integrating the entire corporate network into AD.

Installing Active Directory

I wish I could tell you that the installation of AD is as simple as setting up a workgroup network, but it's not. This process involves changing the default on every computer on your network in order for them to join the domain. To install AD, you must either have an existing AD domain controller on the network or plan to convert this server into a domain controller. There is no domain without the domain controller. Fortunately, both Windows 2000 Server and Windows Server 2003 have Active Directory included within the Configure Your Server Wizards (see Figure 12-17), making the conversion process a bit less painful.

Before you jump into an AD environment, you must take several preliminary steps. You need to decide how to structure the domain, plan to migrate to a domain directory structure, and decide how to handle a deployment with the least amount of disruption to day-to-day operations. This is not something that can be done in an afternoon; although the initial installation and configuration is straightforward, you'll still have sites, users, groups, and group policies to set up. This step-by-step configuration of AD assumes that you do not have AD or a Windows NT domain active within your network.

When you continue with the configuration process, the AD wizard will scan the system components and hardware and then present you with a choice of domain controller type (see Figure 12-18). The domain controller is a role assigned to the server to manage the network resources and accumulate the data in a database that can be shared with other trusted domain controllers.

Figure 12-17
The Active Directory
Installation Wizard

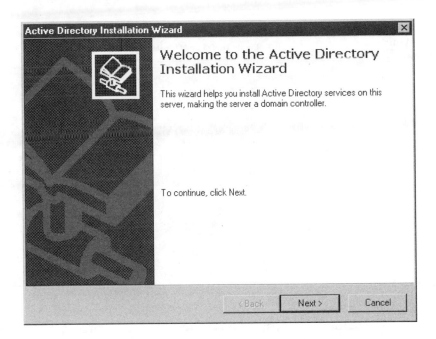

Your next step is to create the first tree domain, or a child domain within an existing tree domain (see Figure 12-19). Choose Create A New Tree Domain and then click Next.

Once you've chosen to create your new tree domain, you'll be prompted to either choose a new forest of tree domains or place this domain within another

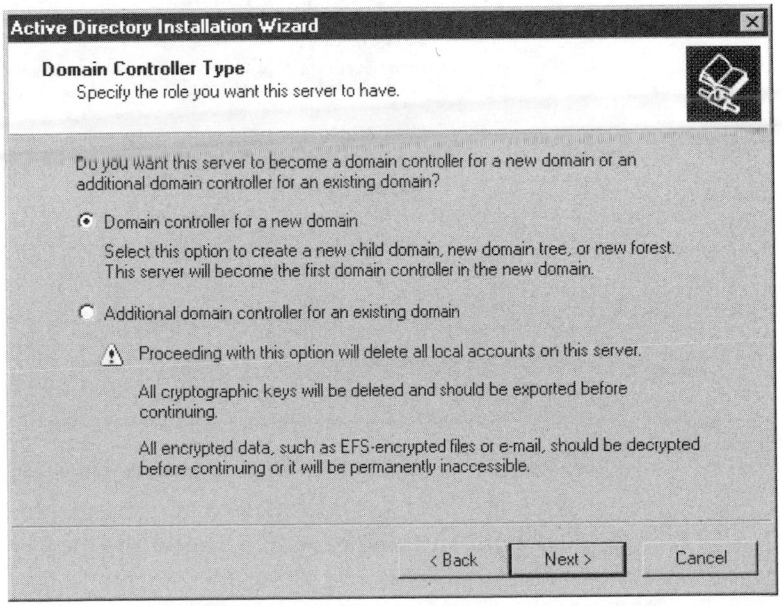

Figure 12-18
Choosing the
appropriate domain
controller type

Figure 12-19
Setting up your
tree domain

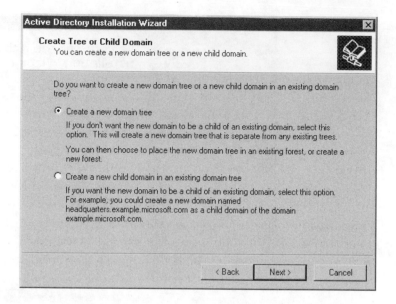

domain forest. Choose Create A New Forest Of Domain Trees and click Next, after which you'll be asked to name your domain.

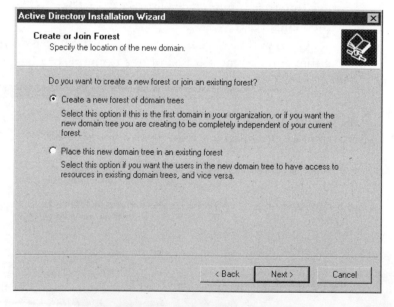

You can use an isolated internal namespace for a domain, but if you plan to host your own web-based server, you need a legitimate domain name (see Figure 12-20), registered with an Internet naming authority. A few sources I'd recommend for domain name registration are Register.com, Inc. (www.register.com), which charges $24.95 per year, per domain name, and Active Domain, LLC (www .active-domain.com), which charges only $9.95 per year, per domain name.

Figure 12-20
You need a legitimate domain name, registered with an Internet naming authority, if you plan to host your own web site.

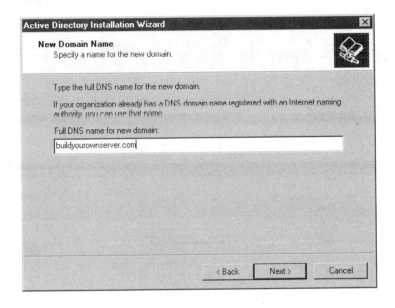

Once you've added the domain name, AD will request the NetBIOS name, which anything before Windows 2000 must use. The default is an abbreviated version of the domain. After you've completed your domain naming, AD will ask you where you'd like to store the AD database (the default is c:\winnt\ntds) and the AD log. Microsoft recommends having each on a separate hard drive to help with performance (see Figure 12-21). I left the database on the C drive, and moved the log to the F drive (my second hard drive).

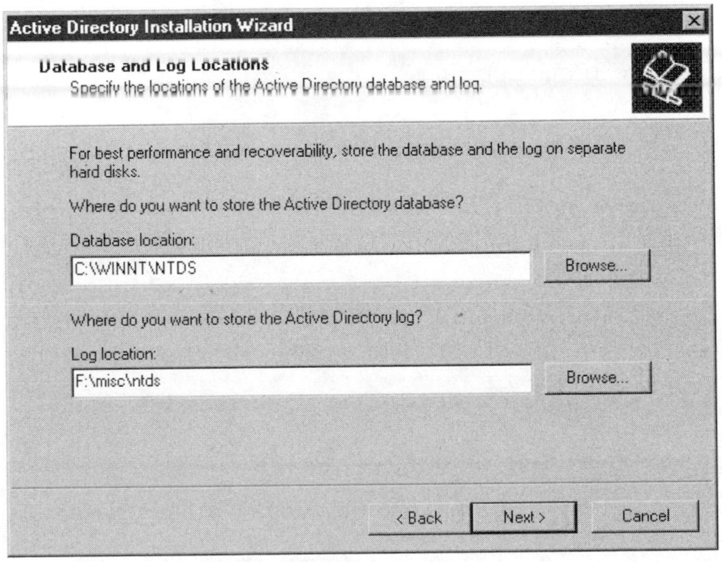

Figure 12-21
Placement for the database and log files should be on separate hard drives.

The final choice offered is to assign the permissions, compatible with either pre–Windows 2000 servers (if you have any Windows NT servers) or Windows 2000 Server and Windows Server 2003.

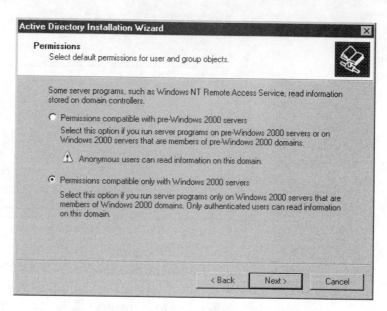

Click Next, and a summary of your choices will appear in a message window. Once you've carefully reviewed them, click Next. You've now installed and configured Active Directory onto your server. Table 12-2 provides some requirements and suggested choices during the installation process.

When Prompted For	Use
Format partitions	NTFS (you cannot install AD on any other file format).
Computer name	Add the computer name of the first forest domain controller.
IP address	Add a fixed IP address that you assign to the first domain controller; this must be a static IP address, either private or public.
Administrator password	Strong alphanumeric passwords (do not leave this blank or use the word "password").
Required networking components	DNS and Internet Protocol (TCP/IP).

Table 12-2
Overview of Choices to Make During AD Installation

When Prompted For	Use
Primary & secondary WINS server	Add the IP address of the existing primary WINS servers (for NetBIOS name resolution for older versions of Windows) or leave blank if there is no existing WINS infrastructure; this can also work to benefit DHCP components.
Preferred DNS server	Add the IP address of an existing DNS server or leave blank if there is no existing DNS infrastructure.

Table 12-2
Overview of Choices to Make During AD Installation *(continued)*

I found that attending one of Microsoft's Active Directory training classes or seminars helped me understand this new methodology, as well as reading a few reference books I purchased. The key is the "object-oriented" frame of mind. Although many Microsoft representatives negate that AD is truly object oriented, it helps to think along that path. I really do not recommend attempting to convert your entire network to AD unless you're very comfortable about how it's going to change everything. In addition, your organization needs to be large enough and spread throughout many locations before you can really see the benefit from this new framework.

The following is a summary of the points of this chapter:

❏ DHCP will provide dynamically assigned IP addresses that will connect a default Windows 95 or later system.

❏ You can configure your server to resolve domain names to IP addresses by installing and configuring DNS.

❏ Active Directory is a network resource management system that uses domains and an "object-oriented" framework for better security and centralized administration.

❏ You should become very familiar with the Active Directory methodology and how it may greatly change your network, before jumping in.

Chapter 13

Web and FTP Server Configuration

Tools of the Trade

Network operating system setup CD-ROM

Prior to the commercialization of the Internet in 1991, it was essentially a text-driven medium, used mostly by universities, scientists, and the military for transferring files, exchanging e-mail messages, and posting messages to newsgroups.

Although many people mistakenly believe that the Internet is synonymous with the World Wide Web, the Internet actually incorporates far more than just web servers and hypertext documents. The Internet includes FTP, IRC, POP3, and all the computers on its various networks and all the systems used to exchange information between those computers.

Why Use the Web?

The Internet functions through numerous protocols and standards, created to describe the composition of documents, specify links, and deliver files over computer networks. Built on the client/server architecture, today's Internet emerged between the late 1970s and early 1980s with the development and adoption of TCP/IP, which was developed by a team (led by Bob Kahn and Vint Cerf) at the U.S. government's Defense Advanced Research Projects Agency (DARPA).

TCP/IP is a standard "suite" of internetworking protocols that allows all applications and computers on any network to link with one another. With the development of TCP/IP, suddenly everything could "talk" with everything else, and the network soon grew even larger. The TCP/IP protocol suite includes not only TCP and IP, but also (among many others) the User Datagram Protocol (UDP), the Web's Hypertext Transfer Protocol (HTTP), the Simple Mail Transfer Protocol (SMTP), and even applications such as Telnet and FTP. Computer users who use dial-up telephone lines connect to the Internet through either the Serial Line Internet Protocol (SLIP) or the newer Point-to-Point Protocol (PPP). As DARPA became the catalyst for the Internet, the Internet became the framework upon which the World Wide Web developed.

Intuitive Simplicity

The Web is a hypertext page system, connected across the Internet, that allows users to view information from thousands of sources through primarily text and pictures—using audio and video, too. Hypertext Markup Language (HTML) documents are plaintext or ASCII (American Standard Code for Information Interchange) documents that, with the addition of simple markup tags, convert to a more attractive formatted document or web page.

A "universal text document" or ASCII (pronounced "as-KEE") file is compatible with a multitude of programs and computer platforms. ASCII is text without formatting and independent of any type font. It actually began as a data code but evolved into a universal standard for application communication by any computing device. ASCII text includes only 128 possible character combinations, which include the upper- and lowercase letters of the traditional Roman alphabet, the numerals 0 through 9, the space character, and the various punctuation marks. Other elements of ASCII are a few nonalphanumeric characters found on a standard keyboard, plus several "control codes" that denote invisible characters like the carriage return and tab.

You can get the same ASCII formatting effect as with HTML and a web browser with a word processing or desktop publishing application, because we sure like our fancy type fonts. However, the most important differentiator between how word processing applications format text documents is that HTML is simple and universally compatible; all you need is the web browser. It's a multiplatform technology that works on any computer, with any modem, anywhere. The simplicity of the tags used in HTML enables you to update information on-the-fly, create a more fluid presentation, and get information out on the Web almost instantly.

The Anatomy of the Online Image

The Web, with the use of a web browser, also provides a graphical user interface (GUI) with pictures, audio, and video possibilities. The unique hyperlink functionality supports interactive participation for entertainment, training, and information dissemination. The hyperlink provides content publishers with remote control of content that may be in front of their customer at that very moment. This content may be stored on a single server, with the user only viewing the content through their browser.

You can control access to sensitive files, confirm, and authenticate a user, and then create statistics and reports on traffic behavior—all of which is far less costly than traditional programming options or a focus group. In addition, whether you like it or not, you are instantly a global presence, and now open 24 hours a day, seven days a week, 365 days a year.

The Web originated in 1990, with a Swiss organization called CERN (the acronym for the Swiss name, which translates into English as the European Laboratory for Particle Physics). The HTML document type designed by Tim Berners-Lee at CERN was part of the 1990 World Wide Web project. Two years later, while at CERN, Dan Connolly wrote the HTML document type definition (DTD) and a brief HTML specification. You can visit the World Wide Web Consortium at www.w3.org for more information on the continued evolution of the Web.

This hypertext-based language originally was intended for electronic distribution of scientific documents on high-energy physics to researchers—internationally and at low cost. It's perfect in its simplicity. By creating computer linkages between users, they could navigate through literature located in different locations online. This was possible by simply following the designated *hyperlinks*, text highlighted a different color and/or underlined that a user can click to move to another document.

The same hyperlink is on the Web today and is one of the most attractive elements of the Web. The simplicity of ASCII and the markup tags of HTML make it possible for anyone to publish their own content; produce and distribute their own music or movie; and connect to friends, family, and businesses for promotion. Most people can learn basic HTML in a few hours, and hundreds of pages of free guidance are available on the Web. The emergence of this technology makes everyone a potential publisher/producer, dropping to zero the barrier to information dissemination—with nothing but the computer and modem.

The addition of inline images (thanks to the NCSA Mosaic browser) boosted the Web's popularity beyond the previously text-only Internet and online services such as America Online, CompuServe, and Prodigy. (Yes, that's right—AOL didn't have graphics in the old days.)

The standard image formats each have unique compression algorithms that shrink down the images to their smallest possible size to guarantee a speedy delivery time through the Internet. What makes it possible to quickly see those images is the maximum 72 dots per inch (dpi) for any image displayed on any computer screen. Commercial printing is far more demanding with the minimum required for the best high-resolution reproduction being 300 dpi.

Web Imagery

When web designers use the same images from their web sites for commercial printing, they appear as distorted, pixilated images in print. While they may appear great online, the computer screen (for the Web or multimedia) has a maximum capacity of 72 dots per inch (dpi), while commercial printing requires a minimum of 300 dpi for the best high-resolution reproduction. There's just not enough data in a web image for commercial printing.

The size of the graphics files are sometimes more dramatic than the actual quality of the finished compressed image. However, since it's difficult for me to reproduce how web compression algorithms behave in print, I've created a single page to present these figures on the Web at www.buildyourownserver .com/figures.html.

The first popular image format was the GIF (pronounced "JIF"), an acronym for Graphic Interchange Format, which was developed by CompuServe. Although the GIF file shown in Web Figure 13-1 is of acceptable quality, it's almost double the size of the high-quality JPEG (Joint Photographic Experts Group) shown in Web Figure 13-2. The JPEG (pronounced "JAY-peg") is part of the MPEG family of algorithms (MPEG3 for online music and MPEG2 for DVD), but is specific to static images.

The reason for the large size of Web Figure 13-1 is that the GIF compression algorithm is *lossless*, which means all data remains during the compression and decompression. The GIF compression can only take the file down to 24KB, whereas the JPEG compression shrank it to about 5 percent of the original file size because it "dumps" repetitive data. Using these examples, the JPEG file was able to discard much of the black background and hair and skin colors (reusing certain bits) and focus on the detail. It still is not as sharp, but it's usable in certain situations—and the smaller your page size, the quicker the download time.

Setting Up Internet Information Services

Your first step in setting up your server as a web server, if you haven't already done so during the initial installation, is to install Internet Information Services (IIS). This is Microsoft's web server and includes application server functionality that enables you to dynamically generate HTML pages as Active Server Pages (ASP). An application server gives you more accessibility and database options.

Both Windows 2000 Server and Windows Server 2003 come with IIS, which includes an HTTP web server, FTP server, SMTP mail server, and Network News Transfer Protocol (NNTP) server. To install IIS, access the Control Panel through the Start menu; open the Add/Remove Programs utility. The dialog box has two panes, much like Windows Explorer. The right pane lists all installed programs. The left pane has three icons: Change Or Remove Programs (top), Add New Programs (middle), and Add/Remove Windows Components (bottom). Click Add/Remove Windows Components (see Figure 13-1).

When the Windows Components Wizard opens, select the Internet Information Services (IIS) check box, and then click Next. If you haven't copied the I386 folder from Windows 2000 Server or Windows Server 2003 to the hard drive, you need to place your setup CD-ROM into the CD-ROM drive when requested. Once the installation is completed, you're ready to use IIS. However, if Windows prompts you to restart your computer, you should comply.

Configuring Your Web Server

Actually, upon installing IIS onto your server, you already have a web server up and running. The default virtual web directory is /inetpub/wwwroot on your system drive. Internet Services Manager now appears in your MMC in your Administrative Tools folder. Open it, highlight Default Web Site, right-click, and

Figure 13-1
Adding or removing components from the Windows NOS

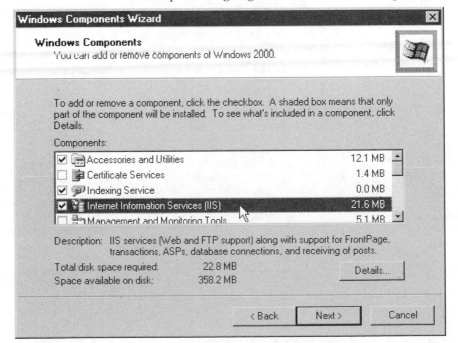

choose Browse (see Figure 13-2). Internet Explorer will launch an IIS Help page, informing you that you do not have a default web page and explaining how to continue. This confirms that you're up and running.

IIS is the most popular web server today because it's simple to use, flexible, and has the Microsoft support community behind it. However, its popularity also makes it vulnerable to hackers, who also find IIS assets attractive. Therefore, before adding web pages, you need to install a couple of tools that you can download for installation to guarantee that your web server is secure from intrusion. To test whether your web server is operational, open your web browser and type **http://localhost/localhost.asp**. If you've installed IIS successfully, you'll get a default "under construction" page.

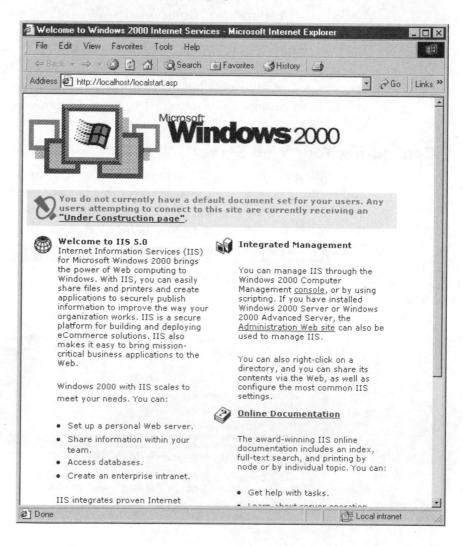

Figure 13-2
To test your web server, right-click the web site icon in IIS and choose Browse.

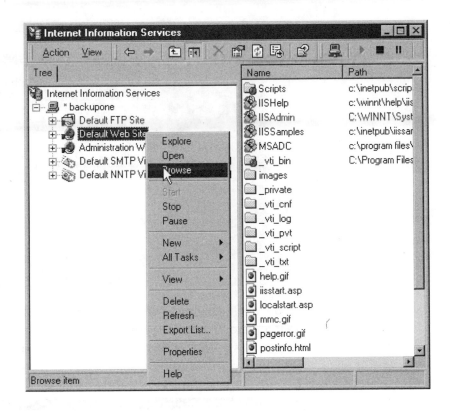

IIS Lockdown

Microsoft offers a utility called IIS Lockdown that will help you tighten up the security on IIS in Windows 2000 Server by turning off various features and services that you won't need. This utility is necessary immediately after you complete the installation of IIS because it doesn't take long for the automated web bots roaming the Internet to find default installations of IIS to encroach.

1. Download the IIS Lockdown utility free from www.microsoft.com/technet/treeview/default.asp?url=/technet/security/tools/lockdown.asp.

2. After you download the utility and begin the installation process, the IIS Lockdown Wizard appears, which will help you "lock down" your web server. This is accomplished by turning off services that may provide a back door for hackers to enter.

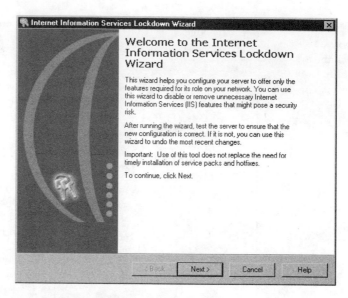

3. Choose a role your web server will play from a list of server roles. Choose the template that best describes your server. If you want to see the template's specific settings, check the View Template Settings box below the menu window. Click Next.

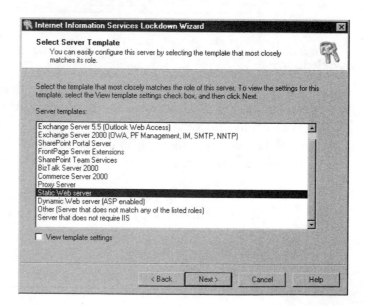

4. IIS Lockdown will now ask if you want to install the URLScan, which will improve the security of your web server. Whatever template you

choose, if you do decide to move forward with the URLScan, Microsoft recommends that you check the URLScan document to become familiar with the customization process, since there may be some disabled functionality that you need. There is also a note reminding you that no tool can replace the need for timely installation of service packs and patches.

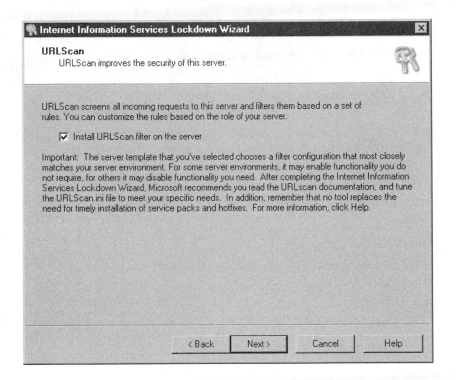

Tightening Security by Shutting Down

Immediately after you complete the installation of IIS, if you do not plan to use the server as a mail or newsgroup server, it's best to shut down these services, because without adequate security measures they can make your server vulnerable to attacks. To shut down these services, access Services in the MMC through the Administrative Tools folder. Search for Network News Transfer Protocol (NNTP) and Simple Mail Transfer Protocol (SMTP), highlight and right-click each, change Automatic in the Startup Type drop-down menu to Manual, and then click the Stop button. The IIS Lockdown utility is a download from Microsoft's web site that tightens the security of your web server and includes these steps.

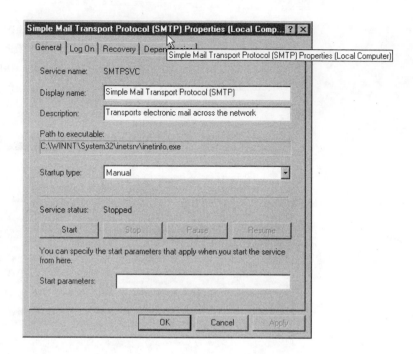

Watch the window closely and you will see each step of the process. Figure 13-3 depicts the IIS Lockdown utility disabling the SMTP mail service and removes your IISAdmin web site, which gives you the ability to manage your web server remotely, through a browser. However, you will not need the IIS administrative web site, as you'll have Terminal Service installed for remote administration of the entire server, so IISAdmin is just an extra component that becomes a liability.

Master Web Site Properties

You will be able to manage IIS through the Internet Services Manager option in the Administrative Tools folder, or as part of the Computer Management console. When you first open the Internet Services Manager, you have the option of global settings through the Master Properties dialog box, which you can access by right-clicking on the computer name in the left pane window and choosing Properties. Any changes you make here will affect all the related web sites.

The dialog box shown in Figure 13-4 appears, giving you the option of configuring the Computer MIME (Multipurpose Internet Mail Extensions) Map. This will register specific file types to file extensions (for example, a text file has an extension of .txt). The default settings for all the sites under IIS typically contain all the required file types. This option is for any new file type that you may need to register in the future.

Figure 13-3
The IIS Lockdown utility turns off functionality you don't need, for better security.

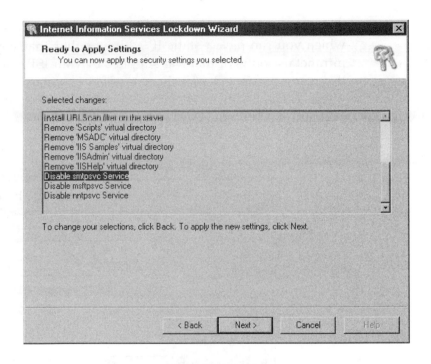

IIS Web Site Menu   To change the name of the web site, right-click the Default Web Site icon in the left pane of the Internet Services Manager window and

Figure 13-4
The Computer MIME Map links file types to their extensions.

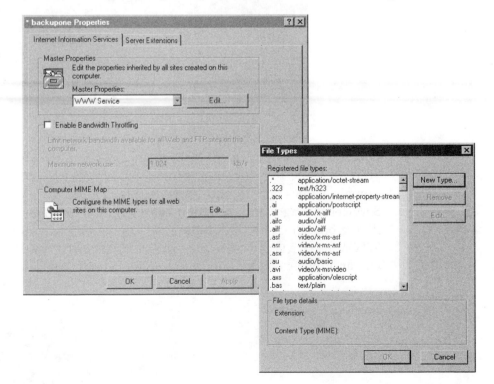

choose Properties. Then, in the Properties dialog box, select the Web Site tab, in which you can pick a static IP address either that you assigned (for internal intranet use only) or that was supplied by your ISP (for the Internet). Changing this name does not change the name of your web site as it would appear on the Internet. This is simply to manage it within IIS. The name of your web site is the URL resolved by the DNS server.

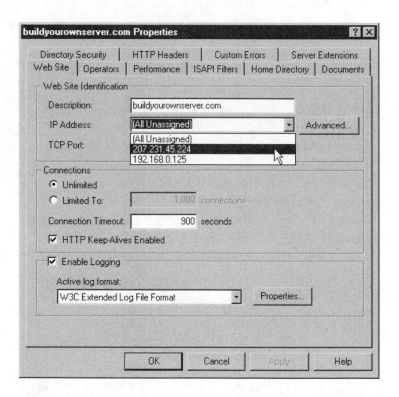

Directory Security   Directory Security gives you the ability to limit access to your web site by switching off any anonymous access, and restrict specific domain names and IP addresses. Right-click the computer name in Internet Services Manager, and then choose Properties. You'll open the Master Properties dialog box. Press the Edit button next to the drop-down menu (ensuring that WWW Service is chosen in the drop-down menu). Press the Directory Security tab, and then click the Edit button in the Anonymous Access section.

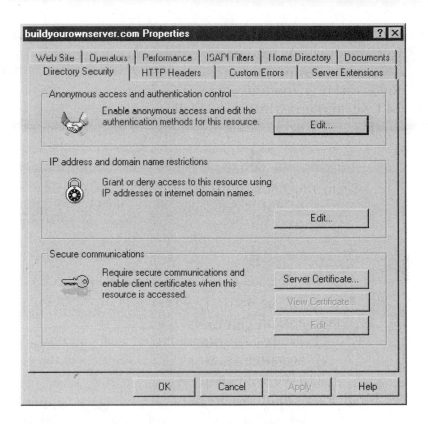

This opens the Anonymous User Account window, displaying IUSR_ *<servername>*, which is the account in Windows that allows anyone to access IIS (your web site) from the Internet. You can also add restricted IP addresses or domain names, and set up a certificate server for public and private key encryption (see Chapter 14).

Home Directory   Choose the Home Directory tab to see the local path of the directory in which the HTML resides. Here I kept the default setting of \inetpub\wwwroot for the directory from which the server will pull pages. The following list describes the other settings in this dialog box:

❏ **Script Source Access**   Choose this option if you've implemented special scripts (such as ASP) for forms, e-commerce, and databases. This is only available when Read or Write is enabled.

❏ **Read**   This is your default setting for a web site. You want your visitors to be able to read the content, but never modify it.

❏ **Write**   You also have the option of giving anonymous users write privileges (although I don't recommend it). We'll discuss how to properly configure this for administrative purposes in Chapter 14.

❏ **Directory Browsing**   When this option is selected, if no default HTML page is assigned and the visitor doesn't specify a specific web page, IIS will present an HTML version of the entire directory, files, subfolders, and scripts. This should be left disabled except for special circumstances. For example, people who are not Internet-savvy may have a difficult time grasping the concept of an FTP site and how to download and use an FTP client; this option will turn a designated virtual directory into an instant FTP-like environment, through HTTP. They need nothing but the URL to that directory and this option enabled for that specific virtual directory.

❏ **Log Visits**   While enabled, this gives you a record of when and who visits the web site. Logs are stored and defined in the Master Web Site Properties dialog box.

❏ **Index This Resource**   By enabling this option, Microsoft Indexing Service will index all the contents of the web site to provide faster search capabilities.

❏ **Application Name**   If you have an application that will execute from this web site, then you would enter the name here. For example, you may have a collaborative software application that initiates once the users are authenticated.

❏ **Execute Permissions**   This drop-down menu gives you the option of allowing anonymous visitors to execute applications on this web site. For example, if you add a database to this web site to accumulate data, visitor information, or deliver dynamic content, the database is an executable—an application that writes a file to the hard drive when executed, so it will not function without allowing execute permissions on the web site.

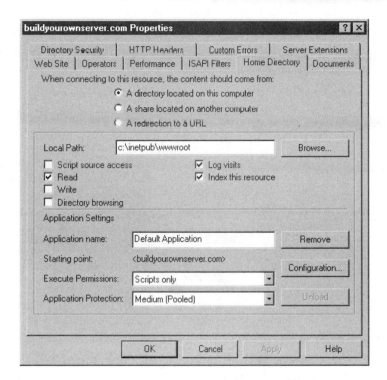

Documents   You can access the Documents tab by right-clicking the targeted web site in the left pane (or the Master Properties) and choosing Properties. Choose the Document tab from the collection at the top. This feature gives you the opportunity to add a default "index.html," which traditionally has been the introduction page on any web site. If someone types a URL, by default the Internet user will see this page first. That page is typically "Default" or "Index," although there are others you can use, as long as they are defined correctly; otherwise, your visitor will only see an error page.

This tab also gives you the option of adding a default footer to every page, such as a copyright notice, contact information, or a disclaimer.

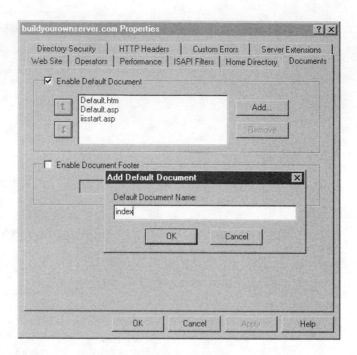

Custom Errors, Operators, and HTTP Headers   The Custom Errors tab displays the list of HTML documents that will appear, each covering a certain HTTP 1.1 error criteria, like the infamous 404 Error. This tab gives you the option of editing the files and changing default error pages.

The Operators tab lists the users and/or groups that have operator (administrator) privileges to the web site.

The HTTP Headers tab enables you to add customized headers to HTML documents, with specific expiration dates. This is primarily for date-sensitive content. For example, if a user frequents your web site often, the web browser will use the "cached" version of the site the next time the user visits (unless the user clicks the Refresh button). If you want the user to be up to date on what your web site has to offer, then you can set a time limit (see Figure 13-5) on how long a user may view a selected web page. Traditionally, web browsers will cache the content from frequently visited web sites so that instead of relying on your Internet connection, the page will draw from your own hard drive. The problem with this is that the content provider may not wish for you to see last week's content, but instead keep you up to date. The timing controls force the user's web browser to draw new content after an allotted time period. You can also use the Content Rating feature to warn visitors of content rating and expirations.

Performance

The Performance tab gives you control over the amount of bandwidth the web site is allowed to use. If you don't expect more than 10,000 visits in the course of a

Figure 13-5
You can insist that a
user's browser grab
your new online page,
rather than have their
computer grab it from
their local cache.

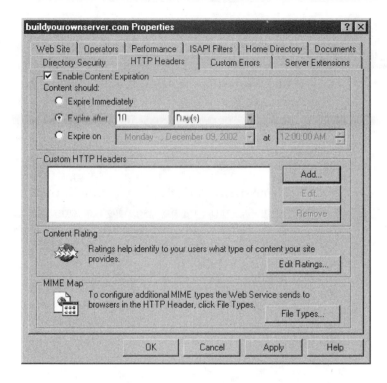

day, then setting the performance down to fewer than 10,000 will increase the
amount of bandwidth used by your internet LAN. You can also use the throttling
feature that limits the amount of bandwidth assigned to the web site.

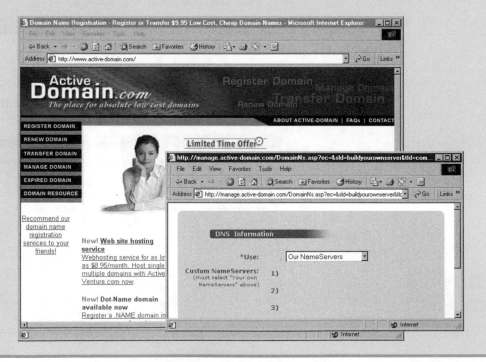

TIPS OF THE TRADE

Setting Up the Domain Name

If you need a domain name for your web site or would like to transfer an existing web address and host it on your new server, you will need a DNS server to resolve the web address. For example, www .buildyourownserver.com is assigned to a specific IP address, and the DNS servers are there to resolve any request for www .buildyourownserver.com to that specific IP address. However, if you don't like the idea of setting up a name server and DNS, you can dedicate your new server as the web server and assign the name resolution to someone else. You can transfer or register a new domain name for your web site at Active-Domain (www.active-domain.com) for about $10 per year. Active-Domain also provides you with a Control Panel function that allows you to plug in the target IP address of your web server, mail server, and FTP server (to name a few) using its own DNS servers. Active-Domain registers the domain name and resolves the URL to your web server's IP address, all for $10 per year.

File Transfer Protocol

FTP, much like its cousin the HTTP server, is cross-platform. Whatever client operating system you may be running, or FTP server, on whatever NOS—FTP works, as long as you're using TCP/IP. Its cross-platform nature is one of the reasons I like to use one at home for transferring large files. The download speed of most Internet connections is typically faster than the upload speed. For example, AT&T Broadband cable-modem service has a standard upstream speed of 256 Kbps, but a 1.5 Mbps maximum download speed. This means that a file that takes 15 minutes to download may take 90 minutes to upload. I find that when I'm working at home, using the high-speed Internet, it's next to impossible to upload any large files to the corporate FTP site, which would enable someone else to download a copy elsewhere. Recently, a colleague urgently needed a 150MB document we had worked on together. When I attempted to upload the file to the corporate FTP site, AT&T Broadband estimated that the amount of time required to upload the file would be about three hours (on top of which it would have taken another hour for my colleague to download the file). I could've driven to and from my colleague's house to hand-deliver a copy to her in under an hour!

Instead, I copied the file to my own FTP site at home. This was through my 100 Mbps network, so it took about seven minutes to upload it to my server, from which it took one hour for my colleague to download. Thus, we saved about three hours by avoiding the lengthy upload to the corporate FTP site.

In Windows, you don't even need any additional software to access an FTP site. You can either use the FTP utility built within MS-DOS or simply use Internet Explorer 5.0 or higher, which creates the appearance of being part of your LAN (see Figure 13-6).

Client-Side FTP

You can access any FTP site though Internet Explorer by typing **ftp.microsoft .com** in the address field and pressing ENTER. This makes the FTP site appear like just another computer on your network.

If you're attempting to access a secured FTP site, after you type the URL, press ENTER. You'll receive a message that you have no authorization to access the site. Select File | Login As. Enter your ID and Password and then click OK.

Changing or Disabling Ports for Safety

In an attempt to reduce the risk of inadvertently downloaded viruses, which can wreak havoc throughout the network system, many organizations will disable all ports, other than Port 80, for the Web, Port 25 for e-mail, and Port 443 for Secure Sockets Layer (SSL) encryption for authentication processes. FTP uses Port 21, thus negating the ability for anyone to use FTP sites outside the enterprise. Many companies will also change the port number. This helps to avoid the automated probes from hackers looking for FTP sites to use to store pirate software.

Figure 13-6
An FTP site is
cross-platform and all
you need is Internet
Explorer to access it.

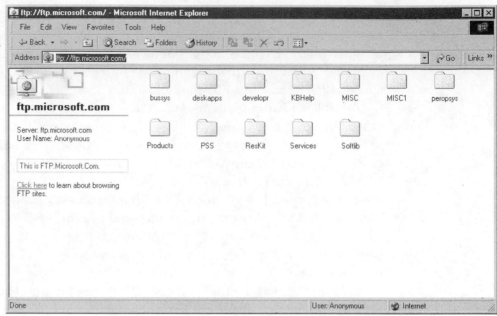

FTP Server Setup

Now that you have IIS on your server, you can provide your employees, partners, and customers with FTP access to data. You can set up two FTP sites. You can use one site to give you, as administrator, secure FTP access with full control (read/write permissions), and to give a select group of people read privileges (and no anonymous access). You can use the second site as an anonymous read-only FTP site for your company. Before setting up your web site, you should create an FTP-specific group in the Users & Group module in the Computer Management MMC (see Chapter 14 for details).

Next, open the Internet Services Manager in the Administrative Tools folder. There's already a Default FTP Site listed; you can either use that one or create a new one by right-clicking the server icon and choosing New | FTP Site. Right-click the FTP Site icon and choose Properties. The Properties dialog box for the FTP site appears, which includes the following tabs:

❑ **FTP Site** Use to set up the identification of the FTP site, by description (this has no bearing on the resolution of the name). The assigned IP address and port number are two important designations. The default port number for an FTP site is 21, and the name server (using DNS) or the router directs any FTP requests to this specific IP address. For example, the name server DNS record may look like the following:

Hostname	IP Address	Record Type
www	12.251.37.21	A (Address)
ftp	12.251.36.15	A (Address)

The A record type is a designated host address and must always be an IP address for the specific domain. Thereafter, in the preceding example, if the domain were buildyourownserver.com, then anyone with an HTTP request (www.buildyourownserver.com) would be directed to the server with the IP address 12.251.37.21. If someone had an FTP request (ftp.buildyourownserver.com), it would be directed to the server (or adapter; the same machine may have multiple adapters) with the IP address 12.251.36.15. Incidentally, you can access the same sites by bypassing the name server and DNS altogether by using the protocol request and IP address. For example, http:// 12.251.37.21 will take you to the same place as www.buildyourownserver.com.

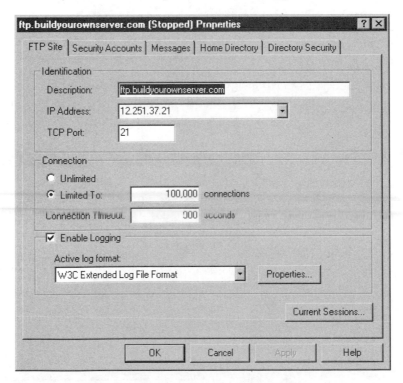

❏ **Security Account**   Lists options for anonymous login access and operators (administrators) for the FTP site. If you select Allow Only Anonymous Connections, no prompt will appear for an ID and password. The IUSR_*servername* is for anonymous access, just as with the public web site.

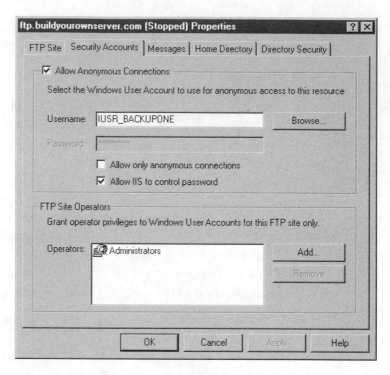

❑ **Messages**   Enables you to add a message to display to your visitors when they enter, and then exit. The Maximum Connections message is what they see if the number of users allowed access reaches its limit.

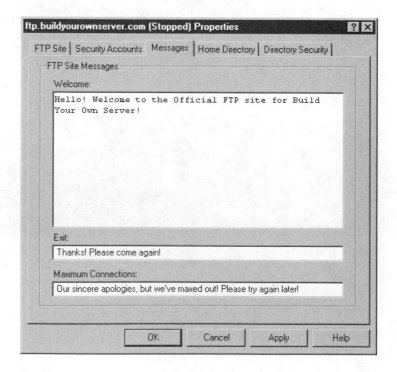

❏ **Home Directory**   Allows you to assign the directory to which the FTP users will be able to gain access. The default is \inetpub\ ftproot, but you can make it any directory on the local computer or one on another computer. In addition, this is where you assign the access rights for this directory through FTP. That includes Administrators. If you've given administrators full control to this directory, yet the Write box is not selected here, they will not be given write privilege to the directory through FTP.

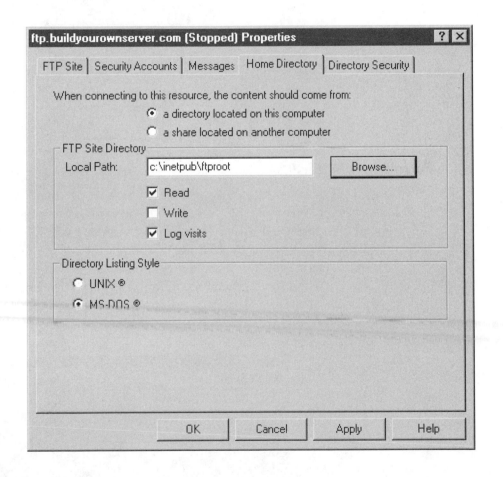

❏ **Directory Security**   Enables you to get very granular with the security of your FTP site. If you select the Grant Access radio button, anyone will gain access, with the exception of those you add to the list. To beef up security even more, you can select Denied Access and then just list the specific computers that can gain access through an IP address and subnet mask.

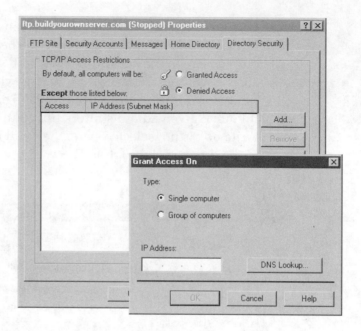

Permissions Wizard

The easiest way to secure your FTP site is to use the Permissions Wizard. To access the wizard, right-click the FTP site icon in the Internet Services Manager and then choose All Tasks. The wizard gives you two choices. If you select Inherit All Security Settings, the FTP site inherits all the computer security settings (and all the users and their assigned permissions). If you're planning to give only network users access, then this option will keep the permissions consistent with the network. Even if they access the FTP site from home, they will still be required to log in as they do at the office.

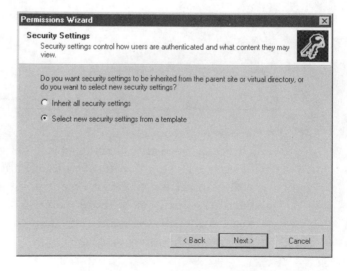

If you choose the second option, Select New Security Settings From A Template, everyone is given read privileges and only administrators are given full control. This is a typical setting for a public FTP site. If you do decide to use this method of assigning permissions to the FTP site, after you click Next, choose the recommended option Replace All Directory And File Permissions to avoid any confusion in permissions and access control.

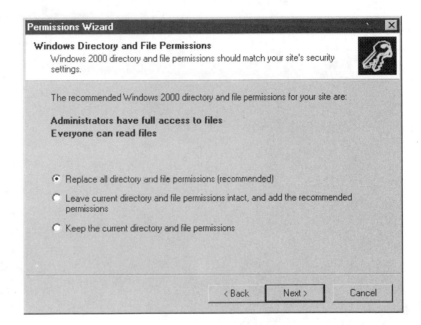

The following is a summary of the points of this chapter:

❏ The simplicity of the hyperlink within a browser environment makes it an intuitive tool for dissemination of information and training.

❏ When configuring IIS for Windows 2000 Server or Windows Server 2003, download and install the IIS Lockdown utility for added security. If you do not, you should manually turn off any service that you are not using.

❏ IIS not only is a simple HTTP web server but also can be configured as a sophisticated application server for dynamically generated web pages, forms, and database applications.

❑ When you use Internet Explorer 5.0 or above to access an FTP site, this will give the FTP site the appearance of being part of the Windows Explorer environment.

❑ When using the Permissions Wizard for both the web and FTP site configuration, it's best to choose a security template and replace existing permissions with that standard template.

Chapter 14

Permissions, Security, and Terminal Services

Tools of the Trade

Network operating system setup CD-ROM

Permissions and security constitute the cornerstone of the Windows 2000 Server and Windows Server 2003 architecture. Many people don't believe, or at least there was once a time when many people believed that Microsoft's NT Server was synonymous with intrusion. There are two misconceptions about digital security, and I'd like to clear them up right up front. This is something I learned first-hand during my almost three-year stint at an encryption technology startup in the mid-1990s called HyperLOCK Technologies. First, there is no such thing as 100 percent digital security, and if someone says there is, I'm sorry, but it just isn't so.

The second misconception is if you believe that your server is not a target of crackers who are really looking for sensitive intelligence data and not your Excel sheets of last month's receivables. It's not the data that many threats seek out, but the illegal and invisible use of the server itself. Your server can be used to spread a virus, to contribute to a denial-of-service attack, or to secretly store unwanted data.

Where There's a Will, There's a Way

HyperLOCK was acquired by a larger company in 2000. Its inventors created a method of extracting *random* bits out of an AVI movie file and using them as a key. This key also includes a header to reassemble the bits and play the movie or audio or show the image. There is no way to open the core file because bits are missing, making it even more secure than even a corrupt file or an "encrypted" file, which still has all its 1's and 0's. This method can increase security by extracting additional random bits.

With typical digital encryption, in anything from the serial number for a piece of software to Public Key Infrastructure (PKI), the method of encryption is to scramble the file and encapsulate it with a header file that knows how it was scrambled. When the unlocking mating procedure is successful, by way of a serial number or digital key, the header then unscrambles the file back to its original condition. HyperLOCK randomly extracts the bits, encapsulates those bits into a header, and places the encapsulated file in a remote location, accessed only through a web site, past strict authentication procedures. It impressed many companies who licensed the use of the method, from Warner Bros to BMG Music to Pokemon. The owner and inventor offered a $5,000 prize to anyone who could crack the highest level of security. No one could, but we continued to seek out someone who could, since that's how you find the vulnerabilities. This is one of the main reasons why Microsoft ships software that appears to be incomplete, using the world as a laboratory to find the vulnerabilities.

Eventually, two engineers cracked it. One, a scientist from Intel Corporation, reportedly cracked it in 15 minutes. The other is a lead software engineer at Rainbow Technologies. Of course, if you've encrypted a digital movie and are playing that movie on a monitor—once it's unencrypted—there's always videotaping the monitor, or intercepting the monitor's VGA signal, or using a screen capture application...my point is that there really isn't 100 percent security on anything distributed as perfect digital copies.

Cracking Encryption

The methods of cracking cryptographic algorithms include tracing specific "noise" or patterns based on ASCII characters within the file to regenerate the key. Windows 2000 Server and Windows Server 2003 also generate "noise," but with no discernible patterns. Another method of cracking encryption is by guessing the algorithm, but keys that are longer than 128 bits have 10^{38} possibilities.

The Danger of a Default Installation

About two years ago, I was writing an article about Windows 2000 Server and I decided to experiment with installing Windows 2000 Server on an older 166 MHz machine, just to see how it would perform (always multitasking). I was busy trying to meet a deadline, so this installation was an afterthought. In other words, I wasn't paying attention.

This machine, which was connected to the Internet through my cable modem, went through the installation process smoothly, but it took hours. I finally completed the installation that evening, but neglected to change the administrator name and add an administrator password. Leaving this password blank makes the computer vulnerable because any user can log on as the Administrator with the click of the mouse. I left the default settings, since I had much more to configure on it and I was running out of time.

It only took 90 minutes for my machine to buzz and shut down from system failure, infected by a worm called W32/Nimda@MM, which at the time was weaving its way through the Internet, specifically seeking out default installs of Windows 2000 Server running IIS. This worm spreads not only in the usual manner, via e-mail, but also via shared drives, folders, or files. It also scans the network for IIS servers to infect via the Microsoft Web Folder Transversal vulnerability (which has since been corrected in service pack 2). One of my fellow colleagues didn't believe that my machine, just sitting on its own, with a wide-open cable-modem connection to the Internet, became a target—that is, until his system went down at home shortly thereafter (he also uses the same broadband Internet service).

The lesson is that the amount of time and energy you contribute to setting up the system can quickly go down the drain if you don't focus on protecting the system from intrusion and infection.

Viruses, Worms, Trojan Horses, and DoS Attacks

If you've been working on a computer, you undoubtedly have seen a virus, worm, or Trojan horse in action. The chances are even greater once you are connected to the Internet, which provides a worldwide channel that enables these menaces to flourish. The entry point for most computer viruses or Trojan horses is through e-mail. Someone, somewhere, received or downloaded an executable or script and it embedded itself on the user's system either to violate the system and network immediately or to lie dormant for later destruction. The following are the different types of malicious code:

❏ **Virus** Disguised programming code that causes some unexpected and usually undesirable event.

❑ **Worm** A self-replicating virus that resides in active memory and duplicates itself, using invisible parts of the OS until the uncontrolled replication slows the system down to a crawl or causes it to crash.

❑ **Trojan horse** Programming code that is embedded within an apparently harmless program or data, but works in the background to secretly attack.

❑ **Denial of service attack (DoS)** When a worm or Trojan horse uses a computer to "attack" another computer until halted. A few years ago, PINGs from hundreds of computers that literally halted their company to a standstill bombarded both Yahoo.com and eBay.com. These were many different types of computers, many of which went unnoticed as a DoS instrument.

Antivirus Software

Antivirus software is an invaluable tool. Do not run any computer without first installing a full version of an antivirus program with automated update configured. The reason it's important to automate the update process is that antivirus software works by looking for specific pieces of code, or fingerprints, inside files that are downloaded or e-mailed. These fingerprints are encapsulated within virus definitions that are maintained by the antivirus software. If the antivirus software doesn't have updated virus definitions, it won't recognize threatening new viruses and may not block them.

I also recommend signing up for e-mail alerts to new threats. Ever since I lost everything on my hard drive from a malicious virus attack several years ago, I do not skimp on these applications.

Update Virus Protection Regularly

Always update your virus protection software regularly. Sign up for any virus alert e-mails, set up an automated update utility, and check the software company's web site for late-breaking news. I can't tell you enough how damaging a virus can be to your system. You could potentially lose all of your data, requiring you to start at the very beginning with a clean install.

Risk Management of Digital Assets

To protect your assets from malicious attacks, Robert Thibadeau, Ph.D., author of several programming languages, one of the founding directors and professor of the Robotics Institute in the School of Computer Science at Carnegie Mellon University, and consultant to the National Security Administration, promotes IPAAA, which stands for the following:

❏ **Integrity** Evaluate the integrity of the data.

❏ **Privacy** Hide the data and/or system from unauthorized people.

❏ **Authentication** Verify the data and/or system.

❏ **Authorization** Confirm proper acceptance.

❏ **Auditability** Maintain proof of system activities.

He also insists on establishing parameters for evaluating the risk of exposure to harmful intent because, depending on the type of business, data loss can be devastating. He recommends the following steps for a security analysis:

❏ Keep an inventory of information assets.

❏ Keep an inventory of information processing facilities.

❏ Identify potential threats.

❏ Calculate expected losses.

❏ Compare reduction in loss to cost of control.

Extra-Tight Security

The security architecture within Windows 2000 Server and Windows Server 2003 provides a multilevel method of securing your system from these types of attacks. However, the trick is configuring it properly. A password alone just won't cut it. Here are a few suggestions:

❏ *Use strong alphanumeric passwords.*

❏ *Purchase antivirus software.*

❏ *Update the NOS with all the recent service packs and critical patches.*

❏ *Educate your personnel on what types of e-mail messages to avoid downloading.*

Multilevel Deniability

Windows 2000 Server and Windows Server 2003 have a more object-oriented approach, rather than hierarchical, to descriptions and managing resources, permissions, and security. This is especially true if you choose to implement

Active Directory. Microsoft Windows NT (a Windows NOS predecessor) had two basic levels of securing files, which were file and share permissions. Windows 2000 Server and Windows Server 2003 have four levels: file, share, web permissions, and Encryption File System (EFS)—which locks files and folders for individual authenticated users. Those files and folders can also inherit those permissions on any related system. By shifting into an object-based thought process and keeping detailed documentation while assigning your security policy, you can avoid permission purgatory, which is easily possible in such multitiered security architecture.

File Permissions

File permissions are the only protection for objects accessed locally, while at the server's terminal. File permissions work only on the NTFS-formatted partitions and are not available on FAT or FAT32 partitions, leaving objects unsecured. There are six basic NTFS permissions: Read (R), Write (W), Execute (X), Delete (D), Change (P), and Take Ownership (O). You can access these permissions by right-clicking the specific file or folder (see Figure 14-1), and choosing Properties | Permissions | Advanced | View/Edit.

Figure 14-1
Right-click and choose Properties to access the folder attributes.

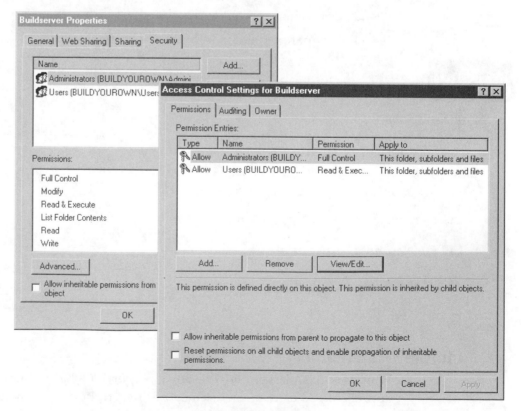

When configuring NTFS, it's important to understand that the least restrictive permission will dominate as any given user's authorization. For example, if a user is restricted to read-only access to a folder, but a designated group membership is assigned full control permission, that user will have full control of that resource. The following is an easy way to remember this:

Full Control + Read = Full Control

The exception is when no access combines with any other NTFS permission; the No Access restriction dominates:

Full Control + No Access = No Access

This happens to be one of the most common configuration problems I've come across when troubleshooting permissions. To begin assigning NTFS file permissions, right-click the folder (or file) you wish to secure and choose Properties, which presents the dialog box shown in Figure 14-2.

Figure 14-2
NTFS permissions can be accessed through the folder's Properties dialog box.

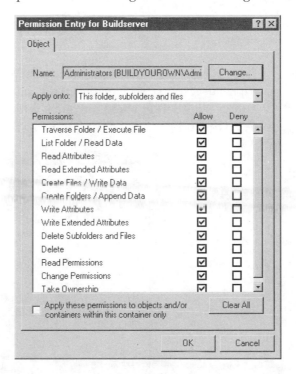

Choose the Security tab, the bottom of which is a list of the NTFS permissions (see Figure 14-3). Here you have the choice of adding or removing permissions for users and groups to access the resource. You also can assign detailed permissions by user and/or group.

Figure 14-3
The Windows 2000
Server security
permissions

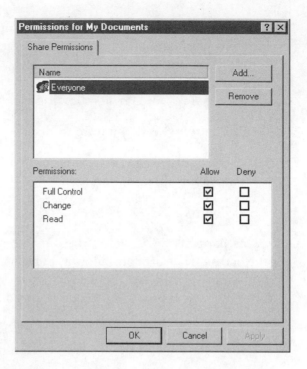

Note that the Everyone group does include everyone (including the anonymous group), so I recommend that you eliminate this group from any Windows 2000 Server share and stick with the Users or Domain Users (if using Active Directory) and Administrators (see Figure 14-4) to avoid conflicting

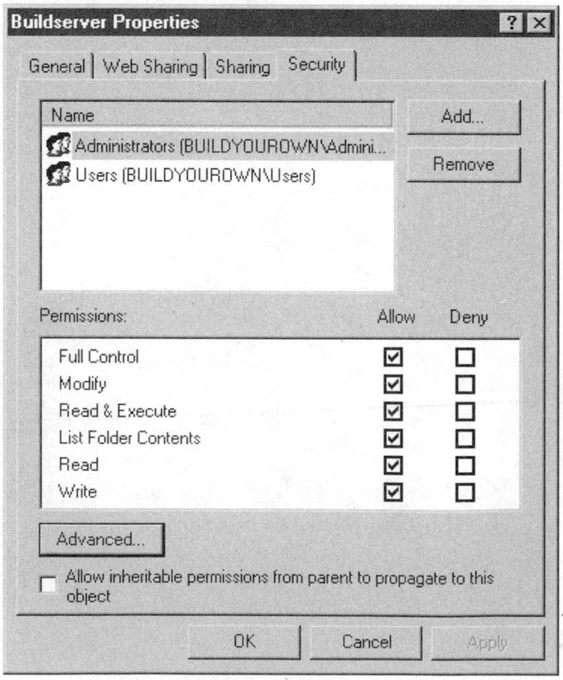

Figure 14-4
Simplified list of
permissible users

access policies and to promote maintainability. Windows Server 2003 has excluded the anonymous group from the Everyone group and thus cleared up this problem.

In the Properties dialog box, you also have the choice to set Advanced options. When you click Advanced, a new dialog box appears that provides more details on the groups with designated assigned access and permissions (see Figure 14-5). This is where you can make additional changes and determine whether those changes should affect subdirectories and objects or have the rights propagate from the parent folder.

Figure 14-5
Advanced NTFS
permissions options

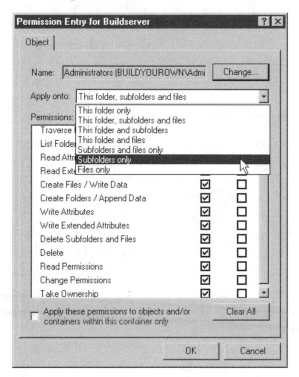

Back in the Properties dialog box, if you select the Allow Inheritable Permissions From Parent To Propagate To This Object check box at the bottom, the existing permissions that have been established for the "parent" folder are automatically assigned to the object. If you use the analogy of an office complex or campus protected by a security gate, the "parent" would be the front gate. If you choose to assign to your office building the same restrictions assigned to the front gate, then you've locked up everything within the building, including corporate and individual offices, to the designated users and groups. On the other hand, by choosing Reset Permissions On All Child Objects And Enable Propagation Of Inheritable Permissions, in the dialog box, you can funnel down permissions to the building and all its contents, detached from the front gate.

You can also have conflicts (actually, more confusion than conflict) if you assign new permissions to an object and its contents but then choose to also propagate permissions from the parent folder. Again, if the user has different permissions or is part of a group membership whose access is contrary to the individual's updated permissions, the least restrictive will apply (Full Control + Read = Full Control). However, if you've denied access to that group, this will evoke the Full Control + No Access = No Access formula.

When establishing NTFS security for Web access, give the Users group read access (RX) to allow all valid Windows 2000 Server or Windows Server 2003 Domain Users at least read access to your web sites. You can restrict access to specific resources by denying access, which will then override the read permissions.

If you move or copy a folder to another drive or folder with shared permissions, it will inherit the parent's share setting. The folder loses its original sharing permission, but it is free to inherit sharing from the new location.

Share Permissions

Providing access to shared folders across a local area network in Windows 2000 Server and Windows Server 2003 looks and works somewhat the same, with a few exceptions—one of which is that Windows Server 2003 has an interface much like Windows XP, in some ways very different than Windows 2000 Server. This provides an Explorer-like pane at the left of each opened folder that gives you the ability to share that object with a single click. Windows 2000 Server requires a bit more detail from the get go.

As shown in Figure 14-6, the Sharing tab offers the following options:

❑ **Share Name**   Choose a share name, which I recommend keeping the same as the folder's name to avoid confusion.

❑ **Comment**   Enter a comment in this field.

❑ **User Limit**   You can use this setting to ensure that you comply with software licenses.

❑ **Permissions**   Click this button to choose the users who can access your files and determine whether they have Full Control, Change, or Read permissions.

❑ **Caching**   Click this button to configure offline caching of a network folder locally, which will allow access to the content, even without a network connection. You have a choice of offering the file to automatically or manually cache to the user's local hard drive, providing better performance and reducing network congestion.

Figure 14-6
Setting up share
permissions

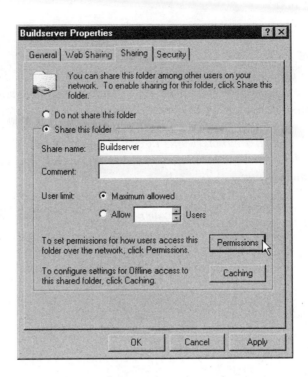

Securing Shared Resources   In Windows 2000 Server and Windows Server
2003, all drives on your computer are automatically shared using the name *drive*
letter$, such as C$ or D$. These drives do not have the hand icon that indicates
sharing in My Computer or Windows Explorer, and they're invisible when users
connect to your computer remotely (see Figure 14-7).

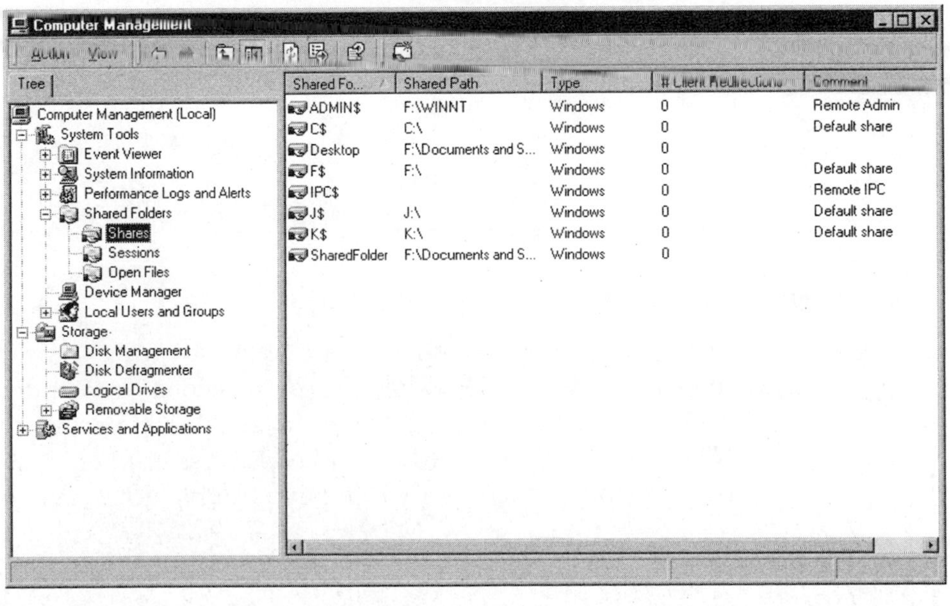

Figure 14-7
Managing share
permissions with
the Computer
Management MMC

Easy Access

Anybody can gain access to your computer over a network or the Internet if he or she knows your computer name, and the username and password of a user who is a member of the Administrators, Backup Operators, or Server Operators group. A user who gains access to your drive over the network or Internet can view all folders and files on that drive, even those that are protected using NTFS permissions, provided the NTFS permissions allow access to members of the Administrators, Backup Operators, or Server Operators group.

When sharing folders, and to keep your system secure, you should create a difficult password for the Administrator account. It is also a good idea to rename the Administrator account using the Local Users And Groups snap-in (see Figure 14-8) or the Active Directory Users And Computers snap-in if you're using AD.

Figure 14-8
The Local Users And Groups component of the Computer Management MMC

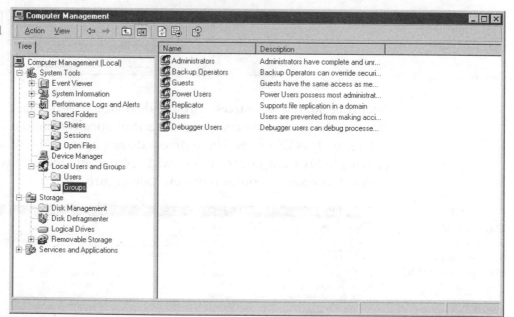

Web Permissions

Web permissions will allow share access by a web browser, typically for the Internet and extranet. The web permissions on Windows 2000 Server and Windows Server 2003 are subject to any NTFS permissions, so pick up your NTFS policy documentation and keep access privileges consistent or within the proper scope; otherwise, you'll have trouble accessing resources. In addition, any folder or file you assign web permissions to will appear in IIS as a virtual directory (see Figure 14-9).

To assign web permissions to an object, simply right-click the object and choose Properties. Select the Web Sharing tab, shown in Figure 14-9. Choose the appropriate web site you'd like to make available remotely, and select the Share This Folder radio button. Highlight the name that appears in the window, which makes an Edit Properties button appear. Press that button and a pop-up menu appears, giving you the following access permission options: Read gives everyone read only permissions; Write allows anyone assigned to write data to the folder, which is dangerous other than for Administrators. Script source access allows script-driven pages and code to function, and directory browsing for creating a web page with each object listed with a hyperlink. Executable applications (such as databases) also need specific permission of None, Scripts, or Execute (includes scripts).

Figure 14-9
Web sharing provides access through the Web without giving local users network access.

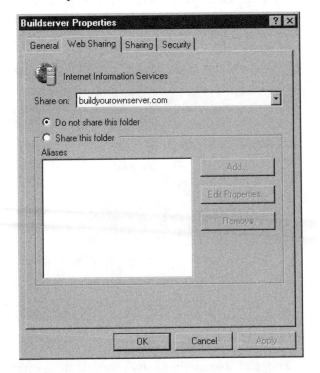

The most restrictive access—selecting Read from the access permissions list and None from the application permissions list—is not at all practical, since pages requiring script (such as ASP pages) and database interconnectivity and applications will require write and execute permissions. Once you make your choices, the name will be automatically added into the Aliases window, indicating that permissions have been granted. You should make sure that you've assigned these permissions to the desired web site, using the drop-down menu at the top of the dialog box.

After initiating a web share, if you're having trouble accessing the files and folders, check with your web server permissions first, before digging into the NTFS hierarchy.

Encryption

Windows 2000 Server and Server 2003 also provides the Encrypting File System (EFS) option on all folders and files. In the context menu, as shown in Figure 14-10, click the Advanced button in the attributes area of the General tab. You now have the option of encrypting the folder exclusively or all child objects within the folder as well. Once you encrypt the object, even if you move or copy the object to another related location or to another NTFS system, only you have the explicit permission to decrypt the object to view.

Figure 14-10
EFS provides
exclusive permissions,
even when the file
moves to another
related system.

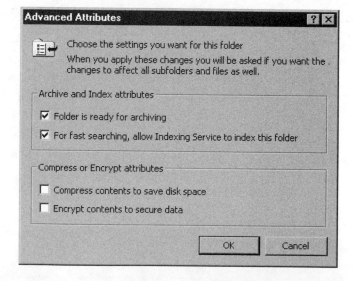

Windows 2000 Server and Windows Server 2003 have many layers of security. The multiple methods of authenticating internal and external users can provide security to a granular level, while the easy-to-use EFS encryption can protect access to specific files. EFS also provides an added invisible protection across the network through transparent encryption, and more flexibility than read, write, and execute.

Windows 2000 Server and Windows Server 2003 also provide the technology to use smart cards for access. Smart cards are usually durable plastic cards that contain a unique microprocessor. Embedded within the microprocessor is the encryption key, making it next to impossible to duplicate. In addition, in the event of a security breach, smart cards deactivate much like a credit card with a magnetic stripe; but with a microchip, rather than the magnetic stripe, smart cards have more room for more data and cryptography.

PKI and Certificates

In addition to the multilayer security architecture discussed previously in "Multilevel Deniability," Windows 2000 Server and Windows Server 2003 also include Public Key Infrastructure (PKI), with Secure Sockets Layer (SSL) for IIS, and IPSec.

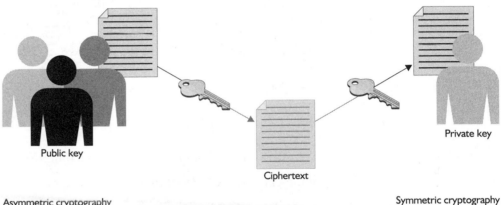

Public key

Ciphertext

Private key

Asymmetric cryptography   Symmetric cryptography

PKI is a method of protecting and authenticating data using a pair of keys. One key is published (called the *public key*), and the other is kept secret (called the *private key*). The encrypted data uses the public key to decrypt, but only the user with the private key knows how to unscramble that file. On the other hand, if a user encrypts a file using the private key, a public key can then validate the user's identity.

Windows 2000 Server and Windows Server 2003 include an IIS Certificate Wizard, which helps you configure the server to accept PKI for more secured transactions. You can access this wizard through the Directory Security tab in IIS by pressing the Server Certificate button in the Secure Communications windows of the Directory Security dialog box (see Figure 14-11).

Figure 14-11
Setting up your
server for PKI with
digital certificates
for authentication

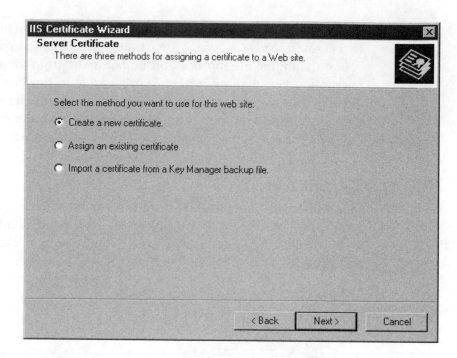

Windows 2000 Server and Windows Server 2003 also enable you to create your own certificates and set up your own certificate server. To install the Certificate Services component, follow these steps:

1. Access the Control Panel through the Start menu.

2. Double-click the Add/Remove Programs icon

3. Choose Add/Remove Windows Components in the left frame.

4. Highlight and mark the box for Certificate Services, and click Next.

You will need your setup CD unless you copied the i386 folder from the setup CD to your hard drive, in which case, when prompted to access the setup CD, you should click Browse and direct it to that specific folder.

In addition, if you've installed the latest service pack, you'll be prompted for the location of those files, too. Follow the installation wizard to create your own PKI certificate, and keep in mind that once you do this, you will not be able to change the name of the server or change the domain (if using Active Directory).

Terminal Services

Now that you have your server up and running, it's time to take off the monitor, keyboard, and mouse and turn on Terminal Services. Terminal Services enables you to log in remotely to a server and emulate the server's local desktop on your workstation. In essence, you can be administering several servers from a single laptop. I've found Terminal Services (built into both Windows 2000 Server and Windows Server 2003) to be an invaluable tool for server administration, and it's simple to install, configure, and use. Terminal Services on the server side basically installs itself. The client side requires a unique application that's made available by creating floppy installation disks on the Terminal Server.

Server-Side Installation

If you're the administrator for several servers, to be physically at all those separate locations, sitting at a terminal, is unrealistic—especially if you're great distances between servers. Realistically, you will need to be at your server minimally at best, as Windows 2000 Server and Windows Server 2003 are robust and can even be self-sufficient in maintenance issues.

Installing the server-side component is easy, if you haven't already done so during standard installation. Beginning at the Start menu, access the Control Panel and then double-click the Add/Remove Applications icon. Then, choose Add/Remove Windows Components in the left frame. Scroll down and select Terminal Services (see Figure 14-12) and click Next. If you are planning to use Terminal Services for administration, you do not need to install the Terminal Services Licensing component. This refers to client access licenses to use Terminal Services company-wide to share applications.

Figure 14-12

Begin the installation of Terminal Services

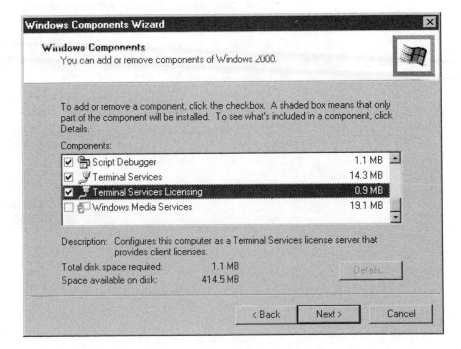

Windows Server 2003 has taken the concept of Terminal Services one step further with the Remote Desktop. Instead of an interface depicting the desktop of a single machine, the Remote Desktop provides multiple server desktops in a Windows Explorer environment. The list of Terminal Server connections in the left pane are listed very much like folders in the Windows Explorer environment, and the large display window on the right presents that particular server's desktop.

During the process of installation, you have to choose between Remote Administration Mode and Application Server Mode (see Figure 14-13). The Remote Administration Mode does not require any additional expense, giving you access privileges to your server for two administrators. This is all I need to use. However, the Application Server Mode is set up for running one or more applications remotely. For example, your bookkeeping department may want to share an accounting package with an accounting firm, or may want access to an Enterprise Resource Planning software package.

Figure 14-13
You have a choice of Remote Administration Mode or Application Server Mode with Terminal Services.

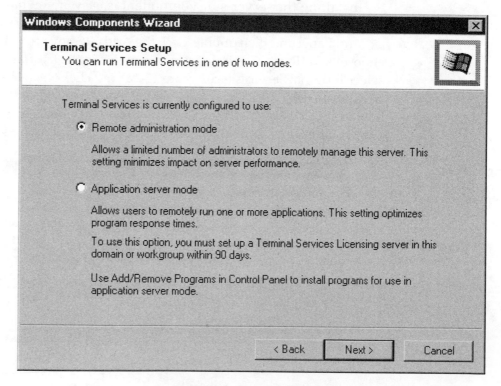

After you make your choice (either way, the administrative qualities of the two are the same), the rest of the installation process is straightforward and simple. After you successfully install Terminal Services, click the Terminal Services Configuration shortcut from the Start menu, and then choose Server Settings in the left pane (see Figure 14-14). In the right pane, you'll be given some information and configuration options, such as Permission Compatibility (the default is to use the active Windows permissions).

Figure 14-14
Option to change
the default Server
Settings for
Terminal Services

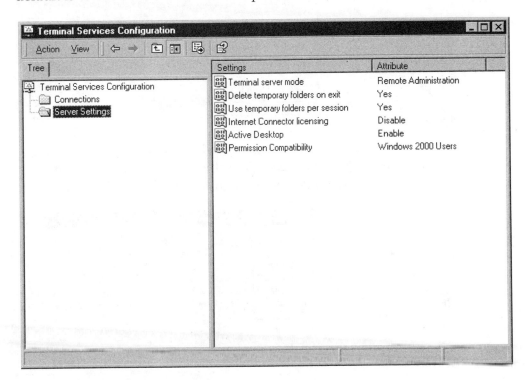

Client-Side Installation

Once you've completed the server-side installation, I recommend that you make the client software available to you and one other administrator. Typically, you're required to make installation disks; but you can access the client installation program directly, saving you the time it would take to create the floppy disks. The client software is in a folder called tsclient in the winnt system folder at winnt/system32/clients/tsclients/win32 (see Figure 14-15).

Figure 14-15
Temporarily sharing
the Terminal Services
client installation
directory on the
network

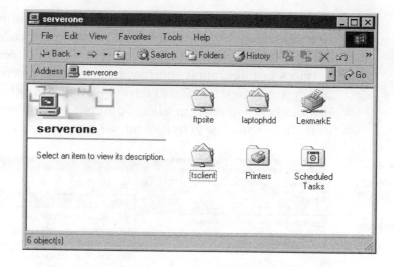

This will install a client application so that you can access your Terminal Server from anywhere. Upon launching the installation program, another wizard will appear to guide you through the installation process (see Figure 14-16).

Figure 14-16
The client-side
Terminal Services
Client Setup wizard

The installation of the Terminal Server client is more involved than the server-side applications—only because the default settings on the server side are adequate to get you started, whereas on the client side, you need to set up the connection to the Terminal Server. You will not be able to use Terminal Services without the client-side software.

From the Start menu, choose Programs, then the newly added Terminal Services Client, and then the Client Connection Manager. This will help you create a shortcut to access your Terminal Server. Select File | New Connection (or press

CTRL-N) to enter the Client Connection Manager Wizard (see Figure 14-17) and then click Next.

Figure 14-15
The Terminal Services Client Connection Manager Wizard

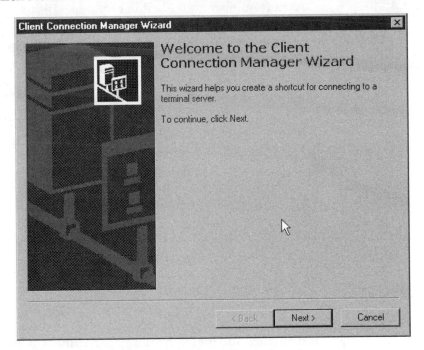

Windows then prompts you to create a connection, by choosing a name and then either the server name or IP address of the server. If you're reaching out to the Terminal Server through the Internet, you need to use either the static IP address or the domain name. For example, if your Terminal Server is also your web server, then you can access the server listing the domain name, or the IP address.

TIPS OF THE TRADE

A Broadband Network Connection

If you're planning to access Terminal Services over the Internet, you can do this on a broadband network connection (such as a LAN, Cable Modem, or DSL line) without any additional software. To make this work, you need to take two steps. First, make sure you use the IP address during the installation of the client-side software (using the Client Connection Manager Wizard). Second, if you have a router or firewall that manages the traffic in and out of your organization, you need to add permissions to use Port 3389.

TIPS OF THE TRADE

A port number is an identifier for a specific process. In TCP and UDP, a port number is a 16-bit integer in the header of a message that moves through the transport layers between a client and server. Incidentally, there are about 65,000 ports on a computer system, and it's unlikely, even as a server, that you'd use more than 1 percent. The most popular ports are within the range of 0 through 1023, with registered ports taking up 1024 through 49,191 and the remaining 49,192 through 65535 used as dynamic ports.

Other important port numbers to know:

Application	Default Port Number (Optional)
HTTP	80
FTP	21
SMTP	25
POP3	110
SSL	443

You can then add the login information in the Automatic Logon window, so you can skip the login step when connecting to the Terminal Server (see Figure 14-18).

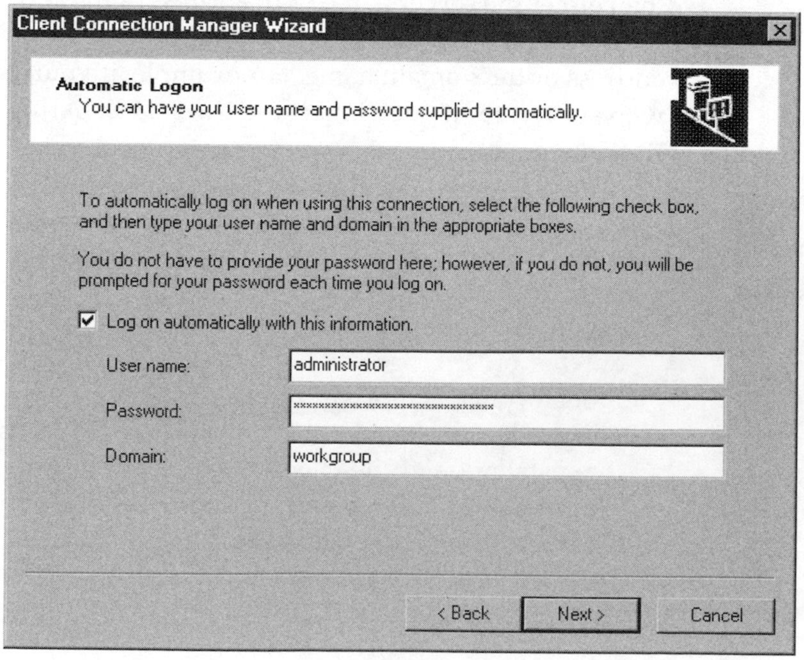

Figure 14-16
Automatic Logon option for Terminal Server

Once you've entered your login data, press next and you're prompted to choose a screen size the remote desktop will appear on your monitor. You can have the desktop window appear full screen—640×480, 800×600, or 1024×768.

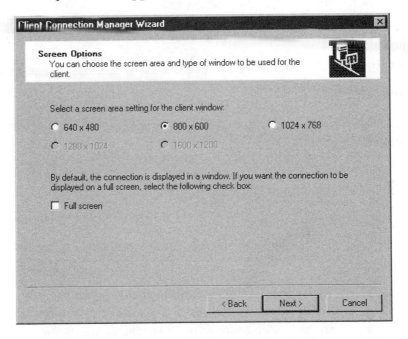

Once you've chosen your desired screen size, press Next; and on the Connection Properties page, you can select the Enable Data Compression and Cache Bitmaps check boxes to expedite the connection process.

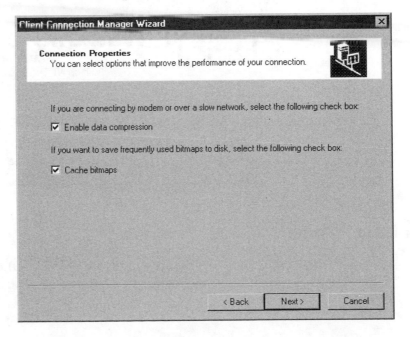

A Client Connection Manager window appears. This confirms that you've successfully installed the Terminal Server Client and you've completed the procedure to create a shortcut to your Terminal Server (see Figure 14-19).

Figure 14-17
Once you've completed the procedure to create a Terminal Server shortcut, just double-click the new icon that appears to open the remote desktop.

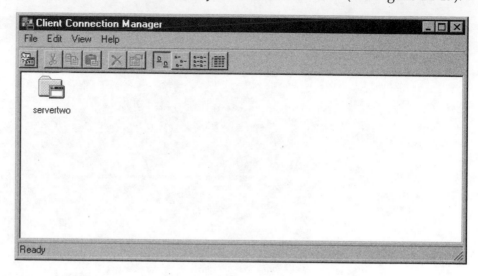

All that's left is to double-click the icon and log in to the server. How quickly the desktop appears will depend largely on the speed of your connection, but shouldn't be more than 60 seconds.

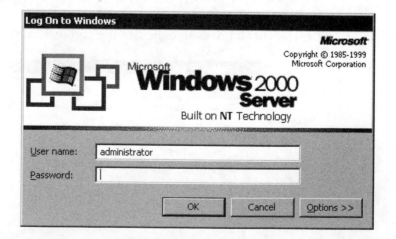

A Last Word

When evaluating the total cost of ownership (TCO) of a technology initiative, most organizations encompass two cost definitions: *direct costs*, which include the hardware, software, IT employees, and outsourced services, and *indirect costs*, which are somewhat more elusive, but sometimes even more important than direct costs. While direct costs are usually budgeted, indirect costs are invisible; thus accurately measuring the inefficiencies of a dynamically active system is difficult. These costs include down time and self-supporting end users, because of cultural self-reliance or lack of supporting infrastructure to come to their aid.

Many companies looking to cut IT costs will trim their direct costs without ever evaluating what the aftershock may involve. One way of decreasing indirect costs is by expanding the reach of your existing human resources. If you examine the new capabilities of the Windows 2000 Server and Windows Server 2003 security architecture, you'll see that there are many ways to assign permissions on a more granular level, to help reduce those indirect costs by spreading the workload throughout your company. For example, new printers sometimes require special print drivers that are not included in the Windows library (yet). You've disabled the ability for users to install them on-the-fly, but with Windows 2000 Server and Windows Server 2003, you can set up permissions to allow them to do so temporarily or assign a few people to lead the task in their own department. You can do the same with other situations that may arise, from e-mail to corrupted software to software updates.

It's all possible with your new server.

The following is a summary of some things to consider when evaluating security for your systems:

❏ Remove the Everyone group when creating shares in Windows 2000 Server to avoid conflicts (no need to do this in Windows Server 2003).

❏ For both the NTFS and sharing permissions, provide only the access level that the group requires, such as Full Control for the Administrators group, Read & Write for Users group, and so on.

❏ Stick with NTFS permissions to folders rather than individual files and make sure that all child objects (subfolders and files) inherit the permission from that parent folder.

❏ Create specific folders for each department or group, according to access requirements (Marketing folder for the marketing group, Sales folder for the sales group, and so on).

❏ Avoid the Deny option; it can create permission purgatory.

❏ Add the Internet Access Account (IUSR/*servername*) to the Log On Locally policy if you need to access the web site on the local server.

Index

References to figures and illustrations are in italics.

Y

INTERNATIONAL CONTACT INFORMATION

AUSTRALIA
McGraw-Hill Book Company Australia Pty. Ltd.
TEL +61-2-9900-1800
FAX +61-2-9878-8881
http://www.mcgraw-hill.com.au
books-it_sydney@mcgraw-hill.com

CANADA
McGraw-Hill Ryerson Ltd.
TEL +905-430-5000
FAX +905-430-5020
http://www.mcgraw-hill.ca

GREECE, MIDDLE EAST, & AFRICA
(Excluding South Africa)
McGraw-Hill Hellas
TEL +30-210-6560-990
TEL +30-210-6560-993
TEL +30-210-6560-994
FAX +30-210-6545-525

MEXICO (Also serving Latin America)
McGraw-Hill Interamericana Editores S.A. de C.V.
TEL +525-117-1583
FAX +525-117-1589
http://www.mcgraw-hill.com.mx
fernando_castellanos@mcgraw-hill.com

SINGAPORE (Serving Asia)
McGraw-Hill Book Company
TEL +65-863-1580
FAX +65-862-3354
http://www.mcgraw-hill.com.sg
mghasia@mcgraw-hill.com

SOUTH AFRICA
McGraw-Hill South Africa
TEL +27-11-622-7512
FAX +27-11-622-9045
robyn_swanepoel@mcgraw-hill.com

SPAIN
McGraw-Hill/Interamericana de España, S.A.U.
TEL +34-91-180-3000
FAX +34-91-372-8513
http://www.mcgraw-hill.es
professional@mcgraw-hill.es

UNITED KINGDOM, NORTHERN, EASTERN, & CENTRAL EUROPE
McGraw-Hill Education Europe
TEL +44-1-628-502500
FAX +44-1-628-770224
http://www.mcgraw-hill.co.uk
computing_neurope@mcgraw-hill.com

ALL OTHER INQUIRIES Contact:
Osborne/McGraw-Hill
TEL +1-510-549-6600
FAX +1-510-883-7600
http://www.osborne.com
omg_international@mcgraw-hill.com

Save money and do it yourself !

These highly visual, step-by-step, show-and-tell guides provide you with hands-on success!

over
200
photos